W9-CGO-346

The Oral Experience
of Literature

The Oral Experience of Literature

SENSE, STRUCTURE, AND SOUND

By

Jean DeSales Bertram

SAN FRANCISCO STATE COLLEGE

CHANDLER PUBLISHING COMPANY

An Intext Publisher · Scranton, Pennsylvania 18515

INTERNATIONAL STANDARD BOOK NO. 0–8102–0043–0

COPYRIGHT © 1967 BY CHANDLER PUBLISHING COMPANY

LIBRARY OF CONGRESS CATALOG CARD NO. 67-13375

PRINTED IN THE UNITED STATES OF AMERICA

Because of Ruth Cecelia Bertram
who first taught me to read aloud

Contents

Foreword

The oral experience of literature involves listening as well as reading aloud. Through listening, the ear can be so sensitized that the silent reader *hears* literature much as an actor *sees* a play on the printed page. Through training, the ear and the voice can be developed as aids to the perception and the projection of literature. The joint experience of listening and reading aloud can augment insight into the whole of literature.

Part One of this book presents some approaches to the appreciation and criticism of the written word. It is hoped that material in this portion will promote analysis and understanding of all forms of literature.

Part Two suggests how the ear and the voice may be disciplined and trained as contributing agents in the oral awareness of literature. The author gratefully acknowledges her debt to Dr. Virgil A. Anderson, Professor Emeritus of Speech Pathology and Audiology, Stanford University School of Medicine, for his review of and commentary on Chapters 5 to 8. The author, however, assumes full responsibility for the material. These three chapters have been prepared at the request of teachers and students who have expressed the need for a concise reference with vocal exercises and diction drills related to oral interpretation. One cannot communicate orally with any degree of success unless he can be heard and understood. A clear knowledge of how to articulate distinctly and how to use the voice efficiently benefits oral reader and listener alike. This knowledge should not, however, be reduced to a method or to a series of techniques and tricks, for the "golden voice" and stereotyped gestures of bygone elocution training cannot of themselves convey meaning with any degree of sincerity. No mere techniques can supersede the necessity for perceiving the emotional and intellectual content of the literature. The ear- and voice-training information presented in Part Two is admittedly general and basic. For that very reason it is hoped that all teachers, whether their major subject be mathematics, science, history, English or drama, will find in it some matter of value to their students and to themselves in their teaching. Its uses may be varied acccording to the course and the instructor. Those desiring detailed references are invited to use the annotated bibliography at the end of the section. Those seeking additional help with diction drills and voice-training exercises may utilize recordings available as a supplement to this book.

Part Three outlines suggested procedures for relaxation and platform poise. Part Four offers some ideas on planning a reading hour. Part Five presents six sample programs with some references to ways in which oral interpretation can be helpful in many phases of the curriculum.

Those who feel the need of a reading list to assist them in selecting literature for oral presentation are referred to the nineteenth edition of *Good Reading*, edited by J. Sherwood Weber and published in 1964 by Mentor Books of New York. This publication contains numerous book lists which are annotated and presented according to subject matter.

JEAN DESALES BERTRAM

The Oral Experience
of Literature

1. Introduction

———•—•———

A reader derives maximum benefits when he reads for a purpose. This truth about reading is also truth about listening: a person gets much more out of listening when he knows what to listen for and how to listen. By directed experiences in listening and in reading aloud, he may develop his critical appraisal of the written word. Discipline of the ear and establishment of good listening habits enable the silent reader to observe with the ear, to become aware of sound, sense, and structure in literature, and to communicate these values in oral reading. Through such awareness he may deepen his appreciation and extend his critical perception of prose, poetry, and drama. For a moment consider:

Sound: As you listen to a reading of Goethe's "Der Erlkönig," you may not know the meaning of a single German word, yet find the sound of the words suggesting certain feelings and ideas. When sensitive to the unique qualities of vowel sounds and to the interruption of their smooth flow by consonant sounds, the ear serves the reader by making him aware of the meaning of sounds as well as the meaning or sense of the written word.

Sense: He whose ear is trained to catch changes in quality, inflection, and pitch will be increasingly alert to the unfoldment of ideas and feelings on the printed page. This listener can alert his ear and mind if he knows what to listen for in literature. For example, if the material is exposition he listens for explanation and clarification, sometimes even for information. If argumentation, he listens for reasons and logic, anticipating an appeal to his intellect. If narration, he listens for the story line. From description he expects images—visual, auditory, tactile, gustatory, olfactory images which prompt thermal, organic, kinetic, or kinaesthetic reactions. From a mood piece he expects to derive primarily an emotional perception of experience.

Structure: Awareness of structure of words and ideas is perhaps the last perception which the ear achieves. For example, one of the major difficulties for the modern theatre patron attending a Shakespeare play comes in attuning his ear to the structure and flow of the speech. One does not hear blank verse every day, and the listener must orient his ear to this mode of expression. Consciousness of structure can enhance the perception of character development. For example, in *Pygmalion* or its musical version *My Fair Lady,* compare Eliza's speech in the opening scene with her speech in the last scene. There is a difference between her *OOoowww* and *AAaahhh* (sound) and between the level of her fears: *how-can-I-sell-my-flowers* as opposed to *how-can-I-return-to-my-old-ways* (sense). What is more significant in contrasting Eliza's lines, however, is the change in the total *structure,* the way in which she phrases what she says.

PRINCIPLES OF ORAL INTERPRETATION

The communication of intellectual and emotional values through the sound, sense, and structure of literature is the purpose of oral interpretation. The oral reader is charged with the responsibility of bringing out the meaning and emotion expressed through the written word and of transmitting the author's concepts from the page to the audience. The major focus for the interpreter must, therefore, be upon the author's intent and purpose, for in proportion to his understanding of the author's purpose the interpreter will find a basis for communicating with his listeners. The audience should expect communication. The interpreter in turn may expect reaction. Neither can function without the other.

That you develop insights into literature is important in your development as an oral reader. You may come to this study with little or no background in literature, or you may count among your old friends such entertaining storytellers as Aesop, the medieval minstrels and troubadours, Shakespeare, Molière, and Goethe. The more widely and the more thoughtfully you read, the more prepared you will be to make judgments about what would be suitable for your audience and what would be appropriate for a given situation. Read, read, read—as much as you possibly can; try to read more than you can.

Whatever your interests, literature provides information and imaginative treatment of them, for literature is the biography of man from the moment man began to word his ideas and feelings. Consider, for example, the folk and fairy tales. Woven into every line are the hopes and fears, needs and desires, dreams and aspirations of men who lived and dealt with the mysteries and challenges of ancient days. How often one finds in these old tales vivid descriptions of delicious feasts served beside warm fires and in the midst of congenial people. So many feasts recorded for posterity should not surprise us. Our forebears did not often experience the glowing satisfaction of full bellies, nor know the constant warmth derived from well-regulated heating systems, nor even have the opportunity of frequently sharing ideas and feelings with others.

Consider also the Greek myths. Do you remember those heartfelt yearnings of man to create great engines for his use? Do you remember Daedalus, and Icarus who flew so near the sun that its heat melted the wax which attached his wings? Or Bellerophon, who bridled the great winged horse Pegasus? What prompted these stories but the aspiration of men avid to fly in the air like eagles? Indeed, such aspirations were voiced in oral literature thousands of years before inventive men flew airplanes or soared in balloons.

In the Panchatantra from ancient India we learn the homely little morals which stories can take from insects and animals. In the tall tales of Tom Hickathrift in England or of Paul Bunyan in America, we have the hearty humor of the invincible hero who grows bigger and better with every telling —not unlike the tales your neighborhood fisherman tells. The fairies and witches and spirits who cast spells of enchantment all through Shakespeare and Washington Irving are but expressions of man's intense desire to control his environment. In an atomic age, they illuminate the horrendous prospect of what can happen if we misuse the control we have achieved. For all the enchantment and mysticism of Spenser, Maeterlinck, Yeats, and Claudel, there is a morality in these expressions of man's desire to control, a morality which does not preach but which shows by example the effects of great power rightly used, perhaps no more nobly used anywhere than by Prospero in Shakespeare's *The Tempest*. The literature of Homer is the literature of man today for, like Odysseus, man yet wanders through life meeting monsters like Scylla and Charybdis—only these demons now take the form of mental pressures rather than that of physical fiends.

A theme popular with Italian audiences of the year 200 B.C. was that of the young man or maiden forced to marry the mate of his parent's choice. This same theme was given a fresh treatment by Molière in the seventeenth century and more recently by C. Y. Lee in *The Flower Drum Song*.

Ever since Adam and Eve were driven forth from the garden of Eden, man has been trying to find paradise. Milton glorified the search in the seventeenth century. The site of paradise is vividly described by Bloody Mary as she points to Bali Hai in *South Pacific*.

Literature is the biography of man, and man is the polychrome delineated variously by such writers as Chaucer who chuckled over the foibles of men embarking to Canterbury on a pilgrimage, by Dante who observed others and himself through others in his *inferno* and *purgatorio* and *paradiso*, by Carl Sandburg who perceives man in *The People, Yes* as a many-sided prism reflecting the entire spectrum of light.

You can grow in your own perception of man, men, and yourself by pondering, imagining, and re-creating all the vivid details in the books you read. You will grow as you listen to the diverse selections which you share with one another and as you engage in the vital experience of preparing a reading. You will find great fun and deeply moving moments in proportion to your own investment in reading.

Your primary physical tool for this work is your voice. Your voice is the most individual and distinctive aspect of your personality. Had you ever stopped to think how many times your judgment of a person is actually a judgment of that individual's voice? Suppose, for example, you telephone the bus station and ask for the departure and arrival times for a visit home. A dull monotone voice answers: "One moment, please." Then returning to the wire, the voice reads the schedule with such an air of indifference and with such rapidity that you must ask to have it repeated. Or a high-pitched, strident voice snaps, "May I help you?" Help? You? That voice *never* could.   A pleasing voice quality is highly desirable if you want to convince or persuade rather than alienate an audience. But a pleasing voice quality is not enough. A student gifted with a "golden voice"—a melodious and beautiful speaking voice enhanced by clear enunciation and articulation—is not necessarily gifted as an oral interpreter. Beautiful sounds cannot make up for lack of intellectual and emotional insights into a piece of literature. The oral reader must not only have control over his vocal instrument but he must also have a keen mind fortified with an energetic desire to communicate those ideas and feelings found in his silent reading.

JUDGING THE LITERATURE

The selection of literature is the very basis of reading aloud. If the interpreter finds that the material challenges him constantly to do his best and provides him with something to say to his audience, then the three-part relationship among author-reader-listener will undoubtedly be dynamic, stimulating fresh thoughts and new ideas. On the other hand, if the work does not inspire interest throughout rehearsal and performance, if there are only a few intellectual and emotional values to be projected, then the oral reader cannot hope to communicate anything beyond tedium, boredom, and a general sense of wasting everyone's time.

"But," you may well ask, "how can I know what will appeal to my audience?" Above all, you must find a work which you yourself enjoy. If the reader isn't interested in the selection he can't hope to make it interesting to the listeners. It is easy to put aside what bores him at the outset. But perhaps he finds a piece which he likes the first time he reads it, then loses interest as he works with it. The reader is well advised to read a work aloud but in private several times before making a commitment to it. The work must bear living with and repeating. Each return should unfold new depths and vistas for interpretation.

The work will probably hold the reader's interest through repeated readings if the author has had something to say, if he has been animated by purpose, theme, or both. Such a requirement need not restrict the choice to high-flown and lofty writing, for certainly the work which entertains and charms fulfills a valid purpose. (*The New Yorker* offers many works of this kind.) Whatever is said must be said in a distinctive manner which sets the author's writing apart from other works dealing with the same purpose or theme. Your taste will guide you away from reading such cliches as "the sun sank in the west," "busier than a hound dog scratching fleas," or "slow but sure." A theme may be an old one, may even be overworked, but if the style of writing is fresh and original a book or story can achieve distinction.

The writing should stimulate the imagination: that is, inspire the reader to react by supplying details and arguments not explicitly stated. (*The Wind in the Willows* exemplifies writing that prompts one to perceive more than is said.)

The piece must be a sincere, honest expression of thought and feeling. These qualities do not demand virtuous dullness; satire can evince a special honesty. (See Ring Lardner *On Conversation*.)

The organization of thought and feeling must be architecturally sound in structure. (Read *The Declaration of Independence*.) The writing should be clear, well-organized, and believable within its context, as is the bitter forecast in *1984* and as are the dream-sequence tales of *Alice's Adventures in Wonderland*.

PREPARING FOR THE ORAL READING

The oral reader is a person through whom the author is interpreted to the audience. He uses both his mental and physical faculties to let the intellectual and emotional qualities of the piece be played through his mind and his voice to the audience. In the total process of communication between author and audience via the oral reader, the reader is responsible for six steps in his preparation.

First, the reader should determine the author's purpose and define values inherent in the selection. He must think through the selection sufficiently to present the matter with some force and conviction. Turn for a few minutes to page 24 and read the excerpt from *The Pickwick Papers*. After reading the selection to yourself, try to decide what is the author's focal point. Is it:

To give a picture of nineteenth-century life in England?

To present various characters?

To show what winter travel and Christmas activities were like in Dicken's time?

To convey the difficulties of life itself—its hardships, inconveniences, and petty personal annoyances; and also to express the inevitable triumph of some characters' optimism over such difficulties?

(See page 9 for one student's answers to these questions as indicated by his introduction to the selection.) Can you suggest some other possible focal points? Justify your answer.

How can a choice of focal point affect your presentation? Try formulating the focal point into a major question which your audience should be able to answer at the conclusion of your reading. Students of composition know that they must have a plan before they begin writing and they often find that the plan is more easily developed if an outline of remarks is first developed and then a statement of the major premise written out in detail. The oral reader must have direction and purpose to his artistic endeavor. The formulation of the major question may have the same salutary effect upon the reader that the outline has for the writer.

Second, the oral reader must look up words he does not know. He must both master the correct pronunciation and understand the precise meaning of each reference.

Third, the reader must grasp the idea and emotion of the selection. Such technical details of reading aloud as pitch, inflection, timing, facial expression, gestures, bodily attitude and alertness can be dictated only by idea and emotion. *The Fall of the House of Usher,* for example, demands a serious facial expression, a body attitude and muscle tone that suggest tension and alertness motivated by fear and circumspection; not so *The Secret Life of Walter Mitty,* wherein tensions are introduced in an atmosphere of amusing frustration and good humor.

Fourth, in rehearsing his reading aloud, the reader will benefit by experimenting, by trying his selection aloud in several different ways, hearing the differences. As the study goes onward, let each rehearsal be a period of discovery. By his particular sound patterns the author reveals much. The sound patterns often open thought to aspects of sense and structure which are overlooked when the reader makes decisions too quickly without listening to the material as it is rendered in various ways. To assume an approach or to take an attitude toward the material on the second or even the fifth reading is to limit inspiration and unfoldment.

The reader should use the rehearsal time to train his ear as well as his mind. If he has no tape recorder for the sessions, he can stand in a corner, book in one hand, perhaps cupping one ear with the other hand, and let the walls serve as a sounding board to tell him how the reading sounds. Increasing his sensitivity to the sound will sharpen his mental ear so that the more he rehearses aloud in this manner the easier it will be for him to hear a story which he must read silently much as a musician scanning a score will mentally hear it before he begins to play.

Fifth, the oral reader must determine the right speed for the reading. Many good students will carefully follow the above suggestions, have the material well in hand, and then read it so rapidly that the audience cannot comprehend or appreciate what the author is saying. The ear does not take in messages as quickly as the eye; allowance must be made accordingly for the listener. Rate for oral reading is governed first by the literary work itself. However exciting the subject-matter may be, the reading should never be so fast that the audience cannot understand or savor the selection. The oral reader needs also to understand the value of a pause before and after his oral presentation. He must not begin until the audience has given him undivided attention. He must let the ideas and emotions expressed in the work stand alone quietly for a moment before he closes the book.

Sixth, the reader should prepare and use an introduction. When an interpreter has failed to do so, the critique afterwards invariably includes the observation from some members of the student audience: "It was a good reading after he got into it, but it took me a long time to get with it." Or, "I wasn't sure where we were going or what the reading was trying to do. I lost a lot by not knowing the direction before the reader started." An audience needs at least a short warm up to start it listening, much as an orchestra needs a down beat to start it playing. In fact, people scarcely care whether they listen unless the reader makes them want to listen. An introduction that piques the interest of the listener, that tells him something but leaves him wanting to know more, that indicates where the reading is headed but stops short of telling all, is the introduction that will draw the listener right into the reading. Even good listeners who honestly try to attend to the material have obstacles to surmount. The wise interpreter accepts the fact that the members of any audience come to the performance with many other things on their minds—a bill or a term paper due tomorrow, a family crisis, a job problem, a health difficulty, a date, a mid-term exam scheduled for next hour. These problems entice listeners to be mentally absent from a lecture or reading. The reader, therefore, needs to take the audience by the ears and then lead them through the introduction to the right concourse and the right gate so that all will want to step aboard with him and take this journey, for every experience in literature is a journey of one sort or another. Here are some sample introductions prepared by students:

"Mr. Pickwick's Christmas," an excerpt from Chapter XXVIII of the *Pickwick Papers,* is a bright and sparkling piece full of the good humor we customarily associate with the Yule season. However gay it seems, though, there is throughout the selection a broad undercurrent of stark realism. The difficulties and inconveniences of travel by stage coach, the hard and bitter cold of the England winter, the sharp clashes and irritating conflicts between personalities contrast vividly with the effervescence and cheerfulness of the Pickwickians. The characters dominate the scene. Their optimism triumphs over environment. Pickwick and his friends emerge in all their joy.

In *The Wind in the Willows,* Kenneth Grahame uses animals instead of people as characters. Each animal, however, is distinctly a symbol of some character-type quite familiar to each of us in everyday experience. The sequence you will hear today tells of timid Mole and his adventures alone in the Wild Wood.

How many times each of us has been required to make a choice—a choice between colleges, a choice between studying or skiing, a choice between pursuing a career in law or one in dentistry. Robert Frost makes us aware of the seriousness of decisions both big and small in his poem "The Road Not Taken."

Can genuine understanding exist between two people whose motivations and attitudes are utterly divergent the one from the other? Or even if there is understanding, is it possible for one character to change, to adapt himself to the other? We find a mother and daughter facing such questions in Act One, Scene Two, of *The Glass Menagerie* by Tennessee Williams.

Read selections beginning on pages 24, 31, and 33. How would you introduce each selection? How many different approaches are possible for each introduction?

RESPONDING AS A LISTENER

Though the oral reader needs to help the audience by offering some simple and brief introduction, the audience cannot expect the reader to do everything in the communication process. As a listener, each member of the audience must cooperate with the oral reader. He must, for example, discipline his own thought so that he does not lapse into fake listening, assuming the pose of an interested listener while ruminating over his own affairs. Nor must he be content with partial listening, alternately tuning into the reading and into his own mental meanderings on bypaths unrelated to the selection. Nor must he permit himself biased listening, withholding his mind from active participation until he hears a concept with which he is in full accord and then attending only to those portions which corroborate his own views.

Even if uninterested in the subject, the listener should think about what he is hearing and keep thinking. The result in nearly every instance will be that the listener becomes engrossed in the topic. If the reader is rapid, dull, or guilty of manifesting other negative qualities, the listener can let his thought dwell on the ideas, feelings, and images of the material rather than on a condemnation of the reader. Such discipline will enable the listener to establish (at least) some positive relationship with the author if not with the reader.

The listener does well to ask himself relevant mental questions and to seek the answers while listening. His curiosity and anticipation will serve as signposts to mark the important points along the way through the reading. The listener who is willing to discover something new is much more likely to be challenged and stimulated than the one who seeks only to fortify his already established attitudes. When the material is new and unfamiliar the listener helps himself by making every effort to relate the material to his own background of the subject. However meager his knowledge, this effort at making a relationship with his existing knowledge will help him to find the concrete within the abstract and to bring organization out of confusion in his thinking.

Each listener should continue to invent ways of staying alert to the reading. What works for one may not work for another. The important point is keep trying to listen actively during the entire reading.

SUMMARY

By observing the subtleties of sound, sense, and structure, the reader can develop his taste in literature. His awareness of the relationship between the written and spoken word should extend his taste to include appreciation and criticism of the author as creator and of the oral interpreter as re-creator. By knowing what to listen for, the listener may expand his perceptions and insights into literature.

In this course, each student will assume three different roles from time to time, each with a distinct function.

1. His function as an interpreter is to communicate.
2. His function as an audience is to react.
3. His function as a student of this subject is to:
   a. Augment his literary background by reading as much as he can— at first perhaps for volume, later certainly with discrimination.
   b. Observe the subtleties of sound, sense, and structure in literature.
   c. Develop awareness of the relationship between the written word and the spoken word.
   d. Know what to listen for in literature.
   e. Practice daily and faithfully a few simple exercises for the development of his vocal instrument.

Some guides follow for judging the literature, for preparing as a reader, and for contributing as a listener.

THREE SETS OF GUIDES
For Judging the Literature

1. The author must have something to say. He must be animated by purpose or theme or both.

2. The author must say what he has to say in a distinctive manner.

3. The writing should stimulate imagination.

4. The piece must be a sincere, honest expression of thought and feeling.

5. The organization of thought and emotion must be architecturally sound in structure.

6. The work must bear living with and repeating.

For Preparing as a Reader

1. The reader should determine the author's purpose and define values inherent in the selection.

2. The reader must check the meaning and pronunciation of all words he does not know.

3. The reader must let the idea and emotion of the selection dictate the techniques for reading.

4. The reader must rehearse his reading aloud and experiment in rehearsal.

5. The reader must control his rate of reading and understand the value of a pause.

6. The reader should help the listener by preparing an introduction.

For Contributing as a Listener

1. Even if uninterested in the subject, the listener must think about what he is hearing.

2. Despite any reading faults manifested by the interpreter, the listener must focus his thoughts on the literature rather than on censure of the reader.

3. The listener must ask mental questions and seek answers while listening.

4. The listener should be willing to discover something new.

5. The listener should relate the material to his background of the subject.

6. The listener should continue to invent ways of staying alert to the reading.

Part One

WHAT TO LISTEN FOR
IN LITERATURE

———◆●◆———

PREVIEW

Interpreter and listener alike may orient themselves to the literature being read by recognizing its form.

Form	What to Listen For
PROSE:	
Exposition	Information: who, what, when, where, how, why.
Argumentation	Logic: Does the author's appeal to emotion negate his appeal to reason?
Narration	Story quality, action or plot line, character development, sometimes mood and atmosphere.
Description	Details of setting, sensory images, mood and atmosphere.
POETRY:	
Nonsense	Relief from reason
Haiku	Images
Lyric	Personal reactions and use of images.
Ballads and narratives	Action or plot line; relationship of characters; mood or atmosphere.
DRAMA:	
Comedy, tragedy, drama.	Idea and character development as you try to visualize setting, characters, movement.

The interpreter of prose is likely to succeed in communication if:

1. He focuses on the mutual relationships among sound, sense, and structure.
2. He visualizes the material as he reads aloud.
3. He selects details for emphasis in the oral presentation.
4. He is sensitive to the movement within the selection.
5. He makes clear the point of view from which the work was written.

The interpreter of poetry may usefully follow a five-point program in preparation for his reading:

1. Select for reading a poem that he himself enjoys and that will suit the tastes and experiences of his audience.
2. Read the poem silently once or twice to become familiar with words, idea, mood.
3. Anticipate the difficulties.
4. Read the poem aloud many different ways in rehearsal.
5. Prepare an introduction.

The interpreter of drama must:

1. Help the listener visualize setting, characters, and movement.
2. Let his face and voice reflect differences among characters.
3. Decide where and how he will place the characters during the reading.
4. Use gestures to support, clarify, and illumine the literary work. Gestures that call attention away from the selection are not acceptable.
5. Explain only those stage directions which are necessary.

2. Prose

The oral interpreter and the listener may well view themselves as a team whose united purpose is to perceive the sound, the sense, and the structure of the literary work. Communication is enhanced in proportion to the effort each puts forth to assume an active role in the perception process.

As the listener attends to the sound of the selection, for example, let him give himself up to the sensory impact of the sound of the words. Does the sound seem to trip quickly, crisply onward: ". . . people [were] fixed there for an instant in incomparably rich and vivid little pictures of their life and destiny."—Thomas Wolfe. Or does the sound suggest a gliding, easy-flowing sense: "There was no lingering of the daylight; but, after the snuffing out of the sun, darkness and the bright appearing of stars."—Elizabeth Yates. Or a measured, slow quality? "Before long we came to an open path or glade where the darkness was not profound."—W. H. Hudson. The sound of words may have much the same effect as the sound of music: they may make you want to march instantly or they may make you want to stretch slowly. The sound of the words contributes immeasurably to the dominant feeling or mood of a piece heard. At the first level of listening to the sound of the words, the listener lets himself be bathed in the physical sensation of the sound. At the second level, he perceives the correlation between the sound and the sense of the words.

The oral reader, as part of his preparation, will have progressed through both levels of listening and will know precisely the contribution that the sounds make to the sense of the words. He will already have related the values of these sounds and the sense of the work to the author's intent and purpose. The oral interpreter is responsible for bringing into focus the mutual relationships among sound, sense, and structure.

Interpreter and listener alike may orient themselves to the sense of the selection by recognizing the form of the literary work. What elements, for example, distinguish exposition from other forms of prose? What is the purpose of exposition and how does knowledge of this purpose help an audience to listen effectively? What corresponding questions and answers bear on argumentation, persuasion, narration, description, and other forms?

EXPOSITION

The object of exposition being to impart information, the listener seeks specific answers to specific questions: *who? what? when? where? how? why?* Exposition may be closely interwoven with mood, as in *The Fall of the House of Usher* and as in *Moby Dick,* but even so exposition conveys a distinct oneness in focus not found in other forms of prose. The listener's role then is clearly to obtain as much information as possible, and for this reason he must attend to exposition with perhaps more singleness of purpose than to other forms of prose. Consider, for example, the exposition in the first three paragraphs of *The Fall of the House of Usher.*

THE FALL OF THE HOUSE OF USHER /
Edgar Allan Poe

During the whole of a dull, dark, and soundless day in the autumn of the year, when the clouds hung oppressively low in the heavens, I had been passing alone, on horseback, through a singularly dreary tract of country, and at length found myself, as the shades of evening drew on, within view of the melancholy House of Usher. I know not how it was, but, with the first glimpse of the building, a sense of insufferable gloom pervaded my spirit. I say insufferable; for the feeling was unrelieved by any of that half-pleasurable, because poetic, sentiment with which the mind usually receives even the sternest natural images of the desolate or terrible. I looked upon the scene before me—upon the mere house, and the simple landscape features of the domain, upon the bleak walls, upon the vacant eye-like windows, upon a few rank sedges, and upon a few white trunks of decayed trees, with an utter depression of soul which I can compare to no earthly sensation more properly than to the after-dream of the reveller upon opium, the bitter lapse into everyday life, the hideous dropping off of the veil. There was an iciness, a sinking, a sickening of the heart, an unredeemed dreariness of thought which no goading of the imagination could torture into aught of the sublime. What was it, I paused to think, what was it that so unnerved me in the contemplation of the House of Usher? It was a mystery all insoluble; nor could I grapple with the shadowy fancies that crowded upon me as I pondered. I was forced to fall back upon the unsatisfactory conclusion that while beyond doubt there are combinations of very simple natural objects which have the power of thus affecting us, still the analysis of this power lies among considerations beyond our depth. It was possible, I reflected, that a mere different arrangement of the particulars of the scene, of the details of the picture, would be sufficient to modify, or perhaps to annihilate, its capacity for sorrowful impression; and, acting upon this idea, I reined my horse to the precipitous brink of a black and lurid tarn that lay in unruffled lustre by the dwelling, and gazed down, but with a shudder even more thrilling than before, upon the remodelled and inverted images of the gray sedge, and the ghastly tree-stems, and the vacant and eye-like windows.

Nevertheless, in this mansion of gloom I now proposed to myself a sojourn of some weeks. Its proprietor, Roderick Usher, had been one of my boon companions in boyhood; but many years had elapsed since our last meeting. A letter, however, had lately reached me in a distant part of the country, a letter from him, which, in its wildly importunate nature, had admitted of no other than a personal reply. The MS. gave evidence of nervous agitation. The writer spoke of acute bodily illness, of a mental disorder which oppressed him, and of an earnest desire to see me, as his best and indeed his only personal friend, with a view of attempting, by the cheerfulness of my society, some alleviation of his malady. It was the manner in which all this, and much more, was said, it was the apparent heart that went with his request, which allowed me no room for hesitation; and I accordingly obeyed forthwith what I still considered a very singular summons.

Although as boys we had been even intimate associates, yet I really knew little of my friend. His reserve had been always excessive and habitual. I was aware, however, that his very ancient family had been noted, time out of mind, for a peculiar sensibility of temperament, displaying itself, through long ages, in many works of exalted art, and manifested, of late, in repeated deeds of munificent yet unobtrusive charity, as well as in a passionate devotion to the intricacies, perhaps even more than to the orthodox and easily recognizable beauties, of musical science. I had learned, too, the very remarkable fact that the stem of the Usher race, all time-honored as it was, had put forth, at no period, any enduring branch; in other words, that the entire family lay in the direct line of descent, and had always, with very trifling and very temporary variation, so lain. It was this deficiency, I considered, while running over in thought the perfect keeping of the character of the premises with the accredited character of the people, and while speculating upon the possible influence which the one, in the long lapse of centuries, might have exercised upon the other—it was this deficiency, perhaps, of collateral issue, and the consequent undeviating transmission, from sire to son, of the patrimony with the name, which had, at length, so identified the two as to merge the original title of the estate in the quaint and equivocal appellation of the "House of Usher," an appellation which seemed to include, in the minds of the peasantry who used it, both the family and the family mansion.

Below are some observations on the sound, sense, and structure of these opening paragraphs.

Sound: In the opening paragraph of *The Fall of the House of Usher* we find a predominance of the [ɪ], [ɛ], [i], [ʌ], [ə], sounds in that order of frequency. These sounds are all relatively short, three of them formed in front position with high or moderate tension. The choice of words bearing such sounds contributes to the sense of nervousness and tension pervading the narrator's view of the house. The sound of the words themselves conveys a formality of tone and style.

Sense: In the first paragraph the narrator (one *who*) tells *where* he is, and through the development of mood answers to some extent *how*. The second paragraph elaborates on *who* by including Roderick Usher, gives details *why* the narrator and Usher are to be together and hints at *what* is the narrator's purpose. The third paragraph is a more objective account than the preceding two paragraphs, and information as to Usher's family background is necessary to the reader's understanding later *how* some things could be possible.

Structure: Poe starts on a large canvas, painting his background material at first broadly and in bold dark colors. Gradually he turns his attention to little details. The consistent point of view in these opening paragraphs lends unity to the material the listener and the reader see through the narrator's eyes, hear through his ears, and assess all things through his mind. The length of the sentences is appropriate to the narrator's thoughts: in the main they are long, qualified, and complex.

ARGUMENTATION AND PERSUASION

Argumentation and persuasion appeal in turn to reason and emotion. The listener must be on guard to determine the extent to which the reasoning is logical and orderly and to determine whether the appeal to emotions negates the appeal to the mind. In the *Fourth Oration against Catiline,* Cicero has one purpose in mind: to persuade the Senate to execute the followers of Catiline who have been captured. He builds his arguments carefully to achieve his purpose. He opens his discourse on a note of appreciation for the concern which he says individual senators have expressed for him as consul of the Roman republic. His careful phrasing is designed to nullify any arguments which may be voiced against him personally. He constantly directs the thought of his listeners to themselves, their homes, their country. Finding numerous ways to reiterate his bases for demanding the life of the conspirators, Cicero persuades through sound, sense, and structure.

THE FOURTH ORATION AGAINST CATILINE /
Marcus Tullius Cicero [1]

You have a consul preserved out of many dangers and plots, and from death itself, not for his own life, but for your safety. All ranks agree for the preservation of the republic with heart and will, with zeal, with virtue, with their voice. Your common country, besieged by the hands and weapons of an impious conspiracy, stretches forth her hands to you as a suppliant; to you she recommends herself, to you she recommends the lives of all the citizens, and the citadel, and the Capitol, and the altars of the household gods, and the eternal unextinguishable fire of Vesta, and all the temples of all the gods, and the altars and the walls and the

---

[1]"Orations of Marcus Tullius Cicero." Translated by Charles Duke Yonge with introduction by Charles Hermann Ohly. Pp. 63-64 in *The World's Great Classics,* revised edition. New York: Colonial Press, 1900.

houses of the city. Moreover, your own lives, those of your wives and children, the fortunes of all men, your homes, your hearths, are this day interested in your decision.

You have a leader mindful of you, forgetful of himself—an opportunity which is not always given to men; you have all ranks, all individuals, the whole Roman people (a thing which in civil transactions we see this day for the first time), full of one and the same feeling. Think with what great labor this our dominion was founded, by what virtue this our liberty was established, by what kind favor of the gods our fortunes were aggrandized and ennobled, and how nearly one night destroyed them all. That this may never hereafter be able not only to be done, but not even to be thought of, you must this day take care. And I have spoken thus, not in order to stir you up who almost outrun me myself, but that my voice, which ought to be the chief voice in the republic, may appear to have fulfilled the duty which belongs to me as consul.

Observe how Cicero structures his ideas in these two paragraphs taken from the final seven in the Oration. He uses the first paragraph here to set forth his three-part theme and in the second paragraph plays a variation on each of the three parts. An outline of his remarks might run something like this:

I. Paragraph One:
   A. Kind of leadership.
   B. Agreement on one point: preservation of the Roman republic.
   C. Emphasis on responsibility of Senate in making decisions which affect:
      1. Country.
      2. Family.
      3. Self.

II. Paragraph Two:
   A. Kind of leadership, again, plus supplementary observation.
   B. Agreement for all; reiterated.
   C. Emphasis further on responsibility for this decision and importance of:
      1. Country.
      2. Personal duty.

The structure of these two paragraphs is that of a carefully complete mosaic within the larger design of the entire Oration. The thoughts and the sentences are clearly balanced and in their balance distinctly move forward, ever forward to a definite peak. Some of the key words in these balances are *with* ("*with* heart and will, *with* zeal, *with* virtue, *with* their voice"), *to you* ("stretches forth her hands *to you* as a suppliant; *to you* she recommends herself, *to you* she recommends the lives"), *by* ("*by* what virtue this our liberty was established, *by* what kind favor of the gods our fortunes were aggrandized and ennobled.")

He constantly reminds his audience of the one point on which all are agreed and throws them utterly off guard by disavowing intent to incite them. Listeners today, however, recognize an obvious appeal to emotions in Cicero's references to country, home, self—all made during a period of intense national consciousness of Roman achievements and glories.

For a modern piece of argumentation, study the excerpt that follows.

EXCELLENCE: CAN WE BE EQUAL AND EXCELLENT TOO? / John W. Gardner[2]

[1] Our society cannot achieve greatness unless individuals at many levels of ability accept the need for high standards of performance and strive to achieve those standards within the limits possible for them. We want the highest conceivable excellence, of course, in the activities crucial to our effectiveness and creativity as a society; but that isn't enough. If the man in the street says, "Those fellows at the top have to be good, but I'm just a slob and can act like one"—then our days of greatness are behind us. We must foster a conception of excellence which may be applied to every degree of ability and to every socially acceptable activity. A missile may blow up on its launching pad because the designer was incompetent or because the mechanic who adjusted the last valve was incompetent. The same is true of everything else in our society. We need excellent physicists and excellent mechanics. We need excellent cabinet members and excellent first-grade teachers. The tone and fiber of our society depend upon a pervasive and almost universal striving for good performance.

[2] And we are not going to get that kind of striving, that kind of alert and proud attention to performance, unless we can instruct the whole society in a conception of excellence that leaves room for everybody who is willing to strive—a conception of excellence which means that whoever I am or whatever I am doing, provided that I am engaged in a socially acceptable activity, some kind of excellence is within my reach. As James B. Conant put it, "Each honest calling, each walk of life, has its own elite, its own aristocracy based upon excellence of performance."

[3] We cannot meet the challenge facing our free society unless we can achieve and maintain a high level of morale and drive throughout the society. One might argue that in any society which has spread prosperity as widely as ours has, morale will be universally high. But prosperity and morale are not inseparable. It is possible to be prosperous and apathetic. It is possible to be fat and demoralized. Men must have goals which, in their eyes, merit effort and commitment; and they must believe that their efforts will win them self-respect and the respect of others.

[4] This is the condition of society we must work toward. Then, unhampered by popular attitudes disparaging excellence, we can dedicate ourselves to the cultiva-

[2]Pages 131-134 from *Excellence,* by John W. Gardner. Copyright © 1961 by John W. Gardner. Reprinted by permission of Harper & Row, Publishers. The bracketed paragraph numbering is added for convenience of reference in this book.

tion of distinction and a sense of quality. We can demand the best of our most gifted, most talented, most spirited youngsters. And we can render appropriate honor to that striving for excellence which has produced so many of mankind's greatest achievements.

[5] It is important to bear in mind that we are now talking about an approach to excellence and a conception of excellence that will bring a whole society to the peak of performance. The gifted individual absorbed in his own problems of creativity and workmanship may wish to set himself much narrower and very much more severe standards of excellence. The critic concerned with a particular development in art, let us say, may wish to impose a far narrower and more specialized criterion of excellence. This is understandable. But we are concerned with the broader objective of toning up a whole society.

[6] This broader objective is critically important, even for those who have set themselves far loftier (and narrower) personal standards of excellence. We cannot have islands of excellence in a sea of slovenly indifference to standards. In an era when the masses of people were mute and powerless it may have been possible for a tiny minority to maintain high standards regardless of their surroundings. But today the masses of people are neither mute nor powerless. As consumers, as voters, as the source of Public Opinion, they heavily influence levels of taste and performance. They can create a climate supremely inimical to standards of any sort.

[7] I am not saying that we can expect every man to be excellent. It would please me if this were possible: I am not one of those who believe that a goal is somehow unworthy if everyone can achieve it. But those who achieve excellence will be few at best. All too many lack the qualities of mind or spirit which would allow them to conceive excellence as a goal, or to achieve it if they conceived it.

[8] But many more can achieve it than now do. Many, many more can *try* to achieve it than now do. *And the society is bettered not only by those who achieve it but by those who are trying.*

[9] The broad conception of excellence we have outlined must be built on two foundation stones—and both of them exist in our society.

1. *A pluralistic approach to values.* American society has always leaned toward such pluralism. We need only be true to our deepest inclinations to honor the many facets and depths and dimensions of human experience and to seek the many kinds of excellence of which the human spirit is capable.

2. *A universally honored philosophy of individual fulfillment.* We have such a philosophy, deeply embedded in our tradition. Whether we have given it the prominence it deserves is the question which we must now explore.

Gardner uses persuasion, but his appeal is essentially to reason rather than to emotions. Like most authors who write argumentation, he too recognizes structure as the very basis for sense in argument. Notice his plan of organization:

I. Statement of the Problem

   A. Paragraph [1]

   B. Paragraph [2]

II. Suggestion for Solution
    A. Paragraph [3]
    B. Paragraph [4]

III. Importance of an Objective in Achieving Solution
    A. Paragraph [5]
    B. Paragraph [6]

IV. Appraisal of Possible Results of Proposed Solution
    A. Paragraph [7]
    B. Paragraph [8]

V. Summary: Paragraph [9]

In analyzing the above structure, it is interesting to observe that within these nine paragraphs Gardner used the word *unless* three times and *but* seven times. In other words, there are a total of ten words of condition— more than one per paragraph. Why are these words of condition pertinent? Study the author's organization and structure. Is it consistent? Does the organization advance the author's idea sentence by sentence? Is his thesis clear? Is his approach direct?

NARRATION AND DESCRIPTION

Two other important forms of prose are narration and description. You may know the selection is narration if you find elements of story quality, action or plot line, character development. As you listen you may grasp the sense of the narration by letting yourself experience the story vicariously, by visualizing setting and action in your thought, by empathizing with the characters.

If the selection is description, you will note details of setting, images appealing to the senses, color words adding depth and dimension to the images. As you listen for the sense of the description, you may help yourself by recalling a similar scene or experience of your own, by constructing vivid images in your mind—images which you can mentally see, hear, smell, taste, and touch. Such mental pictures are said to be visual, auditory, olfactory, gustatory, and tactile images. You may be aware of a sense of movement outside yourself (kinetic), or of your own muscular involvement (kinaesthetic), or an inner reaction (organic).

To perceive the structure of narration or description, the listener tries to note the flow of ideas and feelings expressed through the words, the organization of details, the length of sentences and the appropriateness of their length to the idea and feeling. The listener learns to appraise the structure by attending to the author's choice of words and the extent to which these words are peculiarly distinctive for the author's intent and purpose. He assesses the degree of suggestion: Does the author give so much concrete detail that little or nothing is left to the imagination? Or is the detail carefully selected to inspire one's imagination to fill in many details? The listener tries to decide whether the work is a good, honest piece of writing. He is particularly alert to whether the selection elicits a response.

The interpreter, having appraised the structure well in advance of his oral reading, must translate his perception into communication. He must impart the ideas and feelings of the work as an artistic whole. One of the best ways in which the reader can help his listeners to receive what he has to communicate is to visualize as he reads aloud.

Visualization demands that the oral reader create mental pictures as he reads. If the selection refers to a tree on the landscape, he visualizes a particular tree. He makes himself see that tree in detail—the height and width of it, the color of its trunk, the type of illumination whether natural or artificial, the number and type of leaves, the varying shades or colors of the leaves, the rhythm of the tree. If the piece is relating a story in which a man is running, the reader makes himself see a particular man running. He notices how the man runs. (There can be almost as much difference in the ways three different people run as there is in the ways those same three people laugh or speak.) The reader empathizes with the runner's physical reaction to the pavement or road, with the runner's emotional reaction to the situation. One word of caution: the reader must discipline his own visualization process so that he develops mental pictures only for the material he is reading aloud as he says it. He must not look ahead and visualize ahead. If he does, the impact of the presentation will be weakened and he may not even convey any clear mental pictures at all to his listeners. The listener's mind is very like a blank screen. When the oral reader begins to visualize he brings objects into view on the listener's mental screen, and it is possible for these objects to emerge in vivid detail as clearly as the viewer might see them on a color television set.

The interpreter must decide what is to be emphasized in oral reading. He must admit that he cannot give equal weight to every word and every image. Just as a painter chooses from among a multitude of details in order to direct the attention of the viewer, so the interpreter chooses to emphasize those details which will focus his listener's attention as the author would have it focused. Before he begins to read aloud, the interpreter will have worked out for himself a definite sense of proportion within the work and the relationship which each detail bears to the whole.

The interpreter must be sensitive to movement within the literary work. He must be aware of the slightest shift in idea, feeling, mood. He must be prepared to suggest that shift or change by altering his reading rate, by pausing at appropriate places, and by control of timing which reflects accurately the intention of the author. The shifts may be expressed through a rising inflection or a downward inflection. However carefully the oral reader may have calculated the movement, he will, if he is artistic, not reveal his response in any mechanical way but will let the shifts and changes appear to have emerged spontaneously.

Awareness of the point of view of the narration or description is often helpful to both reader and listener. Is the story being told or is the scene being described from the point of view of one who is outside the story, outside the scene? If so, the writer has used an omniscient point of view. Is the story being told by one character? Does this character report the facts as he witnesses them? Or does he reveal a personal and emotional reaction to what he relates? In the first instance, the approach is objective; in the second, subjective. Does the scene come to us from the mind of one character? If so, the writer has used a stream-of-consciousness technique. Try to think of as many ways as you possibly can for the oral reader to reveal the point of view. Will his tone and attitude be the same for all points of view? Explain.

To clarify some of the points discussed you may wish now to study excerpts from *The Pickwick Papers, The Wind in the Willows,* and *The Old Man and the Sea.* At the conclusion of each you will find questions designed to help you arrive at the understanding necessary for adequate visualization, emphasis, sensitivity, and clarity in presentation.

In the passages from *The Pickwick Papers* you will find description and narration from the omniscient point of view.

THE PICKWICK PAPERS / Charles Dickens[3]

. . . The coachman mounts to the box, Mr. Weller jumps up behind, the Pickwickians pull their coats round their legs, and their shawls over their noses; the helpers pull the horse-cloths off, the coachman shouts out a cheery "All right," and away they go.

They have rumbled through the streets, and jolted over the stones, and at length reach the wide and open country. The wheels skim over the hard and frosty ground; and the horses bursting into a canter at a smart crack of the whip, step along the road, as if the load behind them: coach, passengers, cod-fish, oyster barrels, and all: were but a feather at their heels. They have descended a gentle slope, and enter upon a level, as compact and dry as a solid block of marble, two miles long. Another crack of the whip, and on they speed, at a smart gallop; the horses tossing their heads and rattling the harness, as if in exhilaration at the rapidity of the motion; while the coachman, holding whip and reins in one hand takes off his hat with the other, and resting it on his knees, pulls out his handkerchief, and wipes his forehead: partly because he has a habit of doing it, and partly

---

[3]Chapter XXVIII, with excisions.

because it's as well to show the passengers how cool he is, and what an easy thing it is to drive four-in-hand, when you have had as much practice as he has. Having done this very leisurely (otherwise the effect would be materially impaired), he replaces his handkerchief, pulls on his hat, adjusts his gloves, squares his elbows, cracks the whip again, and on they speed, more merrily than before.

. . . Mr. Winkle, who sits at the extreme edge, with one leg dangling in the air, is nearly precipitated into the street, as the coach twists round the sharp corner by the cheese-monger's shop, and turns into the market-place; and before Mr. Snodgrass, who sits next to him, has recovered from his alarm, they pull up at the inn yard, where the fresh horses, with cloths on, are already waiting. The coachman throws down the reins and gets down himself, and the other outside passengers drop down also: except those who have no great confidence in their ability to get up again: and they remain where they are, and stamp their feet against the coach to warm them—looking, with longing eyes and red noses, at the bright fire in the inn bar, and the sprigs of holly with red berries which ornament the window. . . .

Such was the progress of Mr. Pickwick and his friends by the Muggleton Telegraph, on their way to Dingley Dell; and at three o'clock that afternoon, they all stood, high and dry, safe and sound, hale and hearty, upon the steps of the Blue Lion: having taken on the road quite enough of ale and brandy, to enable them to bid defiance to the frost that was binding up the earth in its iron fetters, and weaving its beautiful net-work upon the trees and hedges. Mr. Pickwick was busily engaged in counting the barrels of oysters, and superintending the disinterment of the codfish, when he felt himself gently pulled by the skirts of the coat. Looking round, he discovered that the individual who resorted to this mode of catching his attention, was no other than Mr. Wardle's favourite page: better known to the readers of this unvarnished history by the distinguishing appellation of the fat boy.

"Aha!" said Mr. Pickwick.

"Aha!" said the fat boy. . . .

"Well, you look rosy enough, my young friend!" said Mr. Pickwick.

"I've been asleep, right in front of the tap-room fire," replied the fat boy, who had heated himself to the colour of a new chimney-pot, in the course of an hour's nap. "Master sent me over with the shay-cart, to carry your luggage up to the house. He'd ha' sent some saddle-horses, but he thought you'd rather walk: being a cold day."

"Yes, yes," said Mr. Pickwick, hastily, for he remembered how they had travelled over nearly the same ground on a previous occasion. "Yes, we would rather walk. Here, Sam!"

"Sir," said Mr. Weller.

"Help Mr. Wardle's servant to put the packages into the cart, and then ride on with him. We will walk forward at once."

Having given this direction, and settled with the coachman, Mr. Pickwick and his three friends struck into the footpath across the fields, and walked briskly away: leaving Mr. Weller and the fat boy, confronted together for the first time. Sam looked at the fat boy with great astonishment, but without saying a word, and began to stow the luggage rapidly away in the cart, while the fat boy stood quietly by, and seemed to think it a very interesting sort of thing to see Mr. Weller working by himself.

"There," said Sam, throwing in the last carpet-bag, "There they are!"

"Yes," said the fat boy, in a very satisfied tone, "there they are."

"Vell, young twenty stun," said Sam, "you're a nice specimen of a prize boy, you are!"

"Thank'ee," said the fat boy.

"You ain't got nothin' on your mind, as makes you fret yourself, have you?" inquired Sam.

"Not as I knows on," replied the boy.

"I should rayther ha' thought, to look at you, that you was a labourin' under an unrequited attachment to some young 'ooman," said Sam.

The fat boy shook his head.

"Vell," said Sam, "I'm glad to hear it. Do you ever drink anythin'?"

"I likes eating better," replied the boy.

"Ah," said Sam, "I should ha' s'posed that; but what I mean is, should you like a drop of anythin' as'd warm you? but I s'pose you never was cold, with all them elastic fixtures, was you?"

"Sometimes," replied the boy; "and I likes a drop of something, when it's good."

"Oh, you do, do you?" said Sam, "come this way, then!"

The Blue Lion tap was soon gained, and the fat boy swallowed a glass of liquor without so much as winking; a feat which considerably advanced him in Mr. Weller's good opinion. Mr. Weller having transacted a similar piece of business on his own account, they got into the cart.

"Can you drive?" said the fat boy.

"I should rayther think so," replied Sam.

"There, then," said the fat boy, putting the reins in his hand, and pointing up a lane. "It's as straight as you can go; you can't miss it."

With these words, the fat boy laid himself affectionately down by the side of the cod-fish; and placing an oyster-barrel under his head for a pillow, fell asleep instantaneously.

"Well," said Sam, "of all the cool boys ever I set my eyes on, this here young gen'lm'n is the coolest. Come, wake up, young dropsy!"

But as young dropsy evinced no symptoms of returning animation, Sam Weller sat himself down in front of the cart, and starting the old horse with a jerk of the rein, jogged steadily on, towards Manor Farm.

Meanwhile, Mr. Pickwick and his friends having walked their blood into active circulation, proceeded cheerfully on. The paths were hard; the grass was crisp and frosty; the air had a fine, dry, bracing coldness; and the rapid approach of the grey twilight (slate-coloured is a better term in frosty weather) made them look forward with pleasant anticipation to the comforts which awaited them at their hospitable entertainer's. It was the sort of afternoon that might induce a couple of elderly gentlemen, in a lonely field, to take off their great-coats and play at leap-frog in pure lightness of heart and gaiety; and we firmly believe that had Mr. Tupman at that moment proffered "a back," Mr. Pickwick would have accepted his offer with the utmost avidity.

However, Mr. Tupman did not volunteer any such accommodation, and the friends walked on, conversing merrily. As they turned into a lane they had to cross, the sound of many voices burst upon their ears; and before they had even had time to form a guess as to whom they belonged, they walked into the very centre of the party who were expecting their arrival—a fact which was first notified to the Pickwickians, by the loud "Hurrah," which burst from old Wardle's lips, when they appeared in sight. . . .

But if they were social and happy outside the house, what was the warmth and cordiality of their reception when they reached the farm! The very servants grinned with pleasure at sight of Mr. Pickwick; and Emma bestowed a half-demure, half-impudent, and all pretty look of recognition, on Mr. Tupman, which was enough to make the statue of Bonaparte in the passage unfold his arms, and clasp her within them.

The old lady was seated in customary state in the front parlour, but she was rather cross, and, by consequence, most particularly deaf. She never went out her-self, and like a great many other old ladies of the same stamp, she was apt to consider it an act of domestic treason, if anybody else took the liberty of doing what she couldn't. So, bless her old soul, she sat as upright as she could, in her great chair, and looked as fierce as might be—and that was benevolent after all.

"Mother," said Wardle, "Mr. Pickwick. You recollect him."

"Never mind," replied the old lady with great dignity. "Don't trouble Mr. Pickwick about an old creetur like me. Nobody cares about me now, and it's very nat'ral they shouldn't." Here the old lady tossed her head, and smoothed down her lavender-coloured silk dress, with trembling hands.

"Come, come, ma'am," said Mr. Pickwick, "I can't let you cut an old friend in this way. I have come down expressly to have a long talk, and another rubber with you; and we'll show these boys and girls how to dance a minuet, before they're eight-and-forty hours older."

The old lady was rapidly giving way, but she did not like to do it all at once; so she only said, "Ah! I can't hear him."

"Nonsense, mother," said Wardle. "Come, come, don't be cross, there's a good soul. Recollect Bella; come, you must keep her spirits up, poor girl."

The good old lady heard this, for her lip quivered as her son said it. But age has its little infirmities of temper, and she was not quite brought round yet. So she smoothed down the lavender-coloured dress again, and turning to Mr. Pick-wick, said, "Ah, Mr. Pickwick, young people was very different, when I was a girl."

"No doubt of that, ma'am," said Mr. Pickwick, "and that's the reason why I should make much of the few that have any traces of the old stock,"—and saying this, Mr. Pickwick gently pulled Bella towards him, and bestowing a kiss upon her forehead, bade her sit down on the little stool at her grandmother's feet. Whether the expression of her countenance, as it was raised towards the old lady's face, called up a thought of old times, or whether the old lady was touched by Mr. Pickwick's affectionate good-nature, or whatever was the cause, she was fairly melted; so she threw herself on her granddaughter's neck, and all the little ill-humour evaporated in a gust of silent tears.

A happy party they were, that night. Sedate and solemn were the score of rubbers in which Mr. Pickwick and the old lady played together; and uproarious was the mirth of the round table. . . .

Mr. Pickwick was awakened, early in the morning, by a hum of voices and a pattering of feet, sufficient to rouse even the fat boy from his heavy slumbers. He sat up in bed, and listened. The female servants and female visitors were running constantly to and fro; and there were such multitudinous demands for warm water, such repeated outcries for needles and thread, and so many half-suppressed entreaties of "Oh, do come and tie me, there's a dear!" that Mr. Pickwick in his innocence began to imagine that something dreadful must have occurred: when he grew more awake, and remembered the wedding. The occasion being an important one, he dressed himself with peculiar care, and descended to the breakfast room. . . .

Let us briefly say, then, that the ceremony was performed by the old clergyman, in the parish church of Dingley Dell, and that Mr. Pickwick's name is attached to the register, still preserved in the vestry thereof; that the young lady with the black eyes signed her name in a very unsteady and tremulous manner; and that Emily's signature, as the other bridesmaid, is nearly illegible; that it all went off in very admirable style; that the young ladies generally, thought it far less shocking than they had expected; and that although the owner of the black eyes and the arch smile informed Mr. Winkle that she was sure she could never submit to anything so dreadful, we have the very best reasons for thinking she was mistaken. To all this, we may add, that Mr. Pickwick was the first who saluted the bride: and that in so doing, he threw over her neck, a rich gold watch and chain, which no mortal eyes but the jeweller's had ever beheld before. Then the old church bell rang as gaily as it could, and they all returned to breakfast. . . .

At dinner they met again, after a five-and-twenty mile walk, undertaken by the males at Wardle's recommendation, to get rid of the effects of the wine at breakfast. . . .

The dinner was as hearty an affair as the breakfast, and was quite as noisy, without the tears. Then came the dessert, and some more toasts. Then came the tea and coffee; and then, the ball.

The best sitting room at Manor Farm was a good, long, dark-panelled room with a high chimney-piece, and a capacious chimney, up which you could have driven one of the new patent cabs, wheels and all. At the upper end of the room, seated in a shady bower of holly and evergreens, were the two best fiddlers, and the only harp, in all Muggleton. In all sorts of recesses, and on all kinds of brackets, stood massive old silver candlesticks with four branches each. The carpet was up, the candles burnt bright, the fire blazed and crackled on the hearth; and merry voices and light hearted laughter rang through the room. If any of the old English yeomen had turned into fairies when they died, it was just the place in which they would have held their revels.

If anything could have added to the interest of this agreeable scene, it would have been the remarkable fact of Mr. Pickwick's appearing without his gaiters, for the first time within the memory of his oldest friends.

"You mean to dance?" said Wardle.

"Of course I do," replied Mr. Pickwick. "Don't you see I am dressed for the purpose?" Mr. Pickwick called attention to his speckled silk stockings, and smartly tied pumps.

"*You* in silk stockings!" exclaimed Mr. Tupman jocosely.

"And why not, sir—why not?" said Mr. Pickwick, turning warmly upon him.

"Oh, of course there is no reason why you shouldn't wear them," responded Mr. Tupman.

"I imagine not, sir—I imagine not," said Mr. Pickwick in a very peremptory tone.

Mr. Tupman had contemplated a laugh, but he found it was a serious matter; so he looked grave and said they were a very pretty pattern.

"I hope they are," said Mr. Pickwick, fixing his eyes upon his friend. "You see nothing extraordinary in these stockings, *as* stockings, I trust, sir?"

"Certainly not—oh, certainly not," replied Mr. Tupman. He walked away; and Mr. Pickwick's countenance resumed its customary benign expression.

"We are all ready, I believe," said Mr. Pickwick, who was stationed with the old lady at the top of the dance, and had already made four false starts, in his excessive anxiety to commence.

"Then begin at once," said Wardle. "Now!"

Up struck the two fiddles and the one harp, and off went Mr. Pickwick into hands across, when there was a general clapping of hands, and a cry of "Stop, stop!"

"What's the matter?" said Mr. Pickwick, who was only brought to by the fiddles and harp desisting, and could have been stopped by no other earthly power, if the house had been on fire.

"Where's Arabella Allen?" cried a dozen voices.

"And Winkle?" added Mr. Tupman.

"Here we are!" exclaimed that gentleman, emerging with his pretty companion from the corner; as he did so, it would have been hard to tell which was the redder in the face, he or the young lady with the black eyes.

"What an extraordinary thing it is, Winkle," said Mr. Pickwick, rather pettishly, "that you couldn't have taken your place before."

"Not at all extraordinary," said Mr. Winkle.

"Well," said Mr. Pickwick, with a very expressive smile, as his eyes rested on Arabella: "well, I don't know that it *was* extraordinary, either, after all."

However, there was no time to think more about the matter, for the fiddles and harp began in real earnest. Away went Mr. Pickwick—hands across—down the middle to the very end of the room, and half way up the chimney, back again to the door—poussette everywhere—loud stamp on the ground—ready for the next couple—off again—all the figure over once more—another stamp to beat out the time—next couple, and the next, and the next again—never was such going! At last, after they had reached the bottom of the dance, and full fourteen couple after the old lady had retired in an exhausted state, and the clergyman's wife had been substituted in her stead, did that gentleman, when there was no demand whatever on his exertions, keep perpetually dancing in his place, to keep time to the music: smiling on his partner all the while with a blandness of demeanour which baffles all description.

. . . Mr. Pickwick . . . was standing under the mistletoe, looking with a very pleased countenance on all that was passing around him, when the young lady with the black eyes, after a little whispering with the other young ladies, made a sudden dart forward, and putting her arm around Mr. Pickwick's neck, saluted him affectionately on the left cheek; and before Mr. Pickwick distinctly knew what was the matter, he was surrounded by the whole body, and kissed by every one of them.

It was a pleasant thing to see Mr. Pickwick in the centre of the group, now pulled this way, and then that, and first kissed on the chin, and then on the nose, and then on the spectacles: and to hear the peals of laughter, which were raised on every side; but it was a still more pleasant thing to see Mr. Pickwick, blinded shortly afterwards with a silk handkerchief, falling up against the wall, and scrambling into corners, and going through all the mysteries of blindman's buff, with the utmost relish for the game, until at last he caught one of the poor relations, and then had to evade the blindman himself, which he did with a nimbleness and agility that elicited the admiration and applause of all beholders. The poor relations caught the people who they thought would like it; and when the game flagged, got caught themselves. When they were all tired of blindman's buff, there was a great game at snapdragon, and when fingers enough were burned with that, and all the raisins were gone, they sat down by the huge fire of blazing logs, to a substantial supper, and a mighty bowl of wassail, something smaller than an ordinary washhouse copper, in which the hot apples were hissing and bubbling with a rich look, and a jolly sound, that were perfectly irresistible.

"This, said Mr. Pickwick, looking around him, "this is, indeed, comfort."

"Our invariable custom," replied Mr. Wardle. "Everybody sits down with us on Christmas-eve, as you see them now—servants and all; and here we wait, until the clock strikes twelve, to usher Christmas in, and beguile the time with forfeits and old stories. Trundle, my boy, rake up the fire."

Up flew the bright sparks in myriads as the logs were stirred. The deep red blaze sent forth a rich glow, that penetrated into the farthest corner of the room, and cast its cheerful tint on every face.

"Come," said Wardle, "a song—a Christmas song! I'll give you one, in default of a better."

"Bravo!" said Mr. Pickwick.

"Fill up," cried Wardle. "It will be two hours, good, before you see the bottom of the bowl through the deep rich colour of the wassail; fill up all round, and now for the song."

QUESTIONS

1. What is the author's focal point?

2. Into how many sections may this particular selection be divided with respect to

    a. Setting?

    b. Characterization of Pickwick though encounter with various characters?

    c. Action?

3. What is the effect when the dance is started, stopped, and resumed?
4. How does the author build momentum in the last paragraph?
5. What is the dominate mood of the selection? What variations in feeling are there?

On the following pages you will find description and narration from a subjective point of view.

THE WIND IN THE WILLOWS / Kenneth Grahame[4]

[1] It was a cold still afternoon with a hard steely sky overhead, when he slipped out of the warm parlour into the open air. The country lay bare and entirely leafless around him, and he thought that he had never seen so far and so intimately into the insides of things as on that winter day when Nature was deep in her annual slumber and seemed to have kicked the clothes off. Copses, dells, quarries and all hidden places, which had been mysterious mines for exploration in leafy summer, now exposed themselves and their secrets pathetically, and seemed to ask him to overlook their shabby poverty for a while, till they could riot in rich masquerade as before, and trick and entice him with the old deceptions. It was pitiful in a way, and yet cheering—even exhilarating. He was glad that he liked the country undecorated, hard, and stripped of its finery. He had got down to the bare bones of it, and they were fine and strong and simple. He did not want the warm clover and the play of seeding grasses; the screens of quickset, the billowy drapery of beech and elm seemed best away; and with great cheerfulness of spirit he pushed on towards the Wild Wood, which lay before him low and threatening, like a black reef in some still southern sea.

[2] There was nothing to alarm him at first entry. Twigs crackled under his feet, logs tripped him, funguses on stumps resembled caricatures, and startled him for the moment by their likeness to something familiar and far away; but that was all fun, and exciting. It led him on, and he penetrated to where the light was less, and trees crouched nearer and nearer, and holes made ugly mouths at him on either side.

[3] Everything was very still now. The dusk advanced on him steadily, rapidly, gathering in behind and before; and the light seemed to be draining away like flood-water.

[4] Then the faces began.

[5] It was over his shoulder, and indistinctly, that he first thought he saw a face: a little evil wedge-shaped face, looking out at him from a hole. When he turned and confronted it, the thing had vanished.

[6] He quickened his pace, telling himself cheerfully not to begin imagining things, or there would be simply no end to it. He passed another hole, and another, and another; and then—yes!—no!—yes! certainly a little narrow face, with hard

[4]Reprinted with the permission of Charles Scribner's Sons from *The Wind in the Willows,* pages 46-50, by Kenneth Grahame. Copyright, 1908, 1933, 1953, 1954 by Charles Scribner's Sons. The bracketed paragraph numbering is added for convenience of reference in this book.

eyes, had flashed up for an instant from a hole, and was gone. He hesitated—braced himself up for an effort and strode on. Then suddenly, as if it had been so all the time, every hole, far and near, and there were hundreds of them, seemed to possess its face, coming and going rapidly, all fixing on him glances of malice and hatred: all hard-eyed and evil and sharp.

[7] If he could only get away from the holes in the banks, he thought, there would be no more faces. He swung off the path and plunged into the untrodden places of the wood.

[8] Then the whistling began.

[9] Very faint and shrill it was, and far behind him, when first he heard it; but somehow it made him hurry forward. Then, still very faint and shrill, it sounded far ahead of him, and made him hesitate and want to go back. As he halted in indecision it broke out on either side, and seemed to be caught up and passed on throughout the whole length of the wood to its farthest limit. They were up and alert and ready, evidently, whoever they were! And he—he was alone, and unarmed, and far from any help; and the night was closing in.

[10] Then the pattering began.

[11] He thought it was only falling leaves at first, so slight and delicate was the sound of it. Then as it grew it took a regular rhythm, and he knew it for nothing else but the pat-pat-pat of little feet, still a very long way off. Was it in front or behind? It seemed to be first one, then the other, then both. It grew and it multiplied, till from every quarter as he listened anxiously, leaning this way and that, it seemed to be closing in on him. As he stood still to hearken, a rabbit came running hard towards him through the trees. He waited, expecting it to slacken pace, or to swerve from him into a different course. Instead, the animal almost brushed him as it dashed past, his face set and hard, his eyes staring. 'Get out of this, you fool, get out!' the Mole heard him mutter as he swung round a stump and disappeared down a friendly burrow.

[12] The pattering increased till it sounded like sudden hail on the dry-leaf carpet spread around him. The whole wood seemed running now, running hard, hunting, chasing, closing in round something or—somebody? In panic, he began to run too, aimlessly, he knew not whither. He ran up against things, he fell over things and into things, he darted under things and dodged round things. At last he took refuge in the deep dark hollow of an old beech tree, which offered shelter, concealment—perhaps even safety, but who could tell? Anyhow, he was too tired to run any further and could only snuggle down into the dry leaves which had drifted into the hollow and hope he was safe for the time. And as he lay there panting and trembling, and listened to the whistlings and the patterings outside, he knew it at last, in all its fullness, that dread thing which other little dwellers in field and hedgerow had encountered here, and known as their darkest moment —that thing which the Rat had vainly tried to shield him from—the Terror of the Wild Wood!

QUESTIONS AND COMMENTS

1. What is the author's focal point: Emotion? Characterization? Setting? Story?

2. What is the effect of paragraph [1]?

3. To what extent does the author give you explicit details and to what extent does he appeal to your imagination?

4. Notice in paragraph [2] that the author becomes more specific in nouns *(twigs, logs, funguses)* and verbs *(crackled, tripped, crouched)*.

5. What is the significance of references to light in paragraphs [2] and [3]?

6. Paragraphs [4], [8], and [10] are short—one line. Why?

7. In paragraph [5], notice the subjective words (for example, "evil wedge-shaped face") that convey Mole's thought and attitude.

8. In paragraph [6] the author increases his use of subjective words *(malice, hatred, evil, sharp)*.

9. Contrast pace and mood within paragraph [6].

10. What is the effect of the action in paragraph [12].

11. Contrast this selection with the excerpt from *The Pickwick Papers*.

    a. Did you visualize more in one than in another?

    b. Did you visualize more vividly in one than in another?

    c. Which provided the greater opportunity to construct details on the basis of your own experience?

On the following pages you will find narration through stream of consciousness.

THE OLD MAN AND THE SEA / Ernest Hemingway [5]

On the next turn, he nearly had him. But again the fish righted himself and swam slowly away.

You are killing me, fish, the old man thought. But you have a right to. Never have I seen a greater, or more beautiful, or a calmer or more noble thing than you, brother. Come on and kill me. I do not care who kills who.

Now you are getting confused in the head, he thought. You must keep your head clear. Keep your head clear and know how to suffer like a man. Or a fish, he thought.

"Clear up, head," he said in a voice he could hardly hear. "Clear up."

Twice more it was the same on the turns.

I do not know, the old man thought. He had been on the point of feeling himself go each time. I do not know. But I will try it once more.

He tried it once more and he felt himself going when he turned the fish. The fish righted himself and swam off again slowly with the great tail weaving in the air.

[5]Reprinted with the permission of Charles Scribner's Sons from *The Old Man and the Sea,* pages 100-105, by Ernest Hemingway. Copyright 1952 by Ernest Hemingway.

I'll try it again, the old man promised, although his hands were mushy now and he could only see well in flashes.

He tried it again and it was the same. So, he thought, and he felt himself going before he started; I will try it once again.

He took all his pain and what was left of his strength and his long gone pride and he put it against the fish's agony and the fish came over onto his side and swam gently on his side, his bill almost touching the planking of the skiff and started to pass the boat, long, deep, wide, silver and barred with purple and interminable in the water.

The old man dropped the line and put his foot on it and lifted the harpoon as high as he could and drove it down with all his strength, and more strength he had just summoned, into the fish's side just behind the great chest fin that rose high in the air to the altitude of the man's chest. He felt the iron go in and he leaned on it and drove it further and then pushed all his weight after it.

Then the fish came alive, with his death in him, and rose high out of the water showing all his great length and width and all his power and his beauty. He seemed to hang in the air above the old man in the skiff. Then he fell into the water with a crash that sent spray over the old man and over all of the skiff.

The old man felt faint and sick and he could not see well. But he cleared the harpoon line and let it run slowly through his raw hands and, when he could see, he saw the fish was on his back with his silver belly up. The shaft of the harpoon was projecting at an angle from the fish's shoulder and the sea was discolouring with the red of the blood from his heart. First it was dark as a shoal in the blue water that was more than a mile deep. Then it spread like a cloud. The fish was silvery and still and floated with the waves.

The old man looked carefully in the glimpse of vision that he had. Then he took two turns of the harpoon line around the bitt in the bow and laid his head on his hands.

"Keep my head clear," he said against the wood of the bow. "I am a tired old man. But I have killed this fish which is my brother and now I must do the slave work."

QUESTIONS

1. In both the second and last paragraph of this selection Hemingway used the word *brother*. What is the significance of this word?

2. What is the author's focal point? The fight between the old man and the fish? Or the relation between the two? Or the concept of brotherhood? Or something else? To make your decision you would do well to read the entire story. The Old Man begins his personal reaction to the fish by noting the fish's "nobility." Later he refers to the fish as "friend" and ultimately as "brother.".

3. The full import of the word *brother* may be more clear to your listeners if you not only set the scene for the final struggle between the two but also note the Old Man's developing awareness of the fish's qualities.

3. Poetry

———•◦•———

Poetry was meant to be read aloud. As in music, so in poetry the symbols on the printed page must be translated into sound before the composition can be fully appreciated. A musician does not read a score silently for an hour or more. He may glance over the score before he begins to play, but he wants as quickly as possible to translate the printed notes into sound and so he sings or hums or plays his instrument. The oral reader of poetry, too, may study the work silently for a short time, but he needs also to bring life and meaning to the printed word as quickly as possible through his voice. The voice is an instrument—unique and individual. Use your voice. Let the sounds be played through it so the poem may emerge in a full revelation of its sense and structure.

How do you prepare a poem for reading? Here is a five-step guide that will usually help:

1. *Select the poem to read.* Consider the tastes and experiences of your audience. Not all poems can be meaningful to everyone. The poem should, above all, be one that appeals to you.

2. *Read the poem silently only once or twice to familiarize yourself with words, idea, mood.* Go to a good dictionary to check the meaning and pronunciation of any words which you do not know or of which you may be even the least bit uncertain. Some poems may state precisely what is meant, but more than likely the author reveals meaning through his use of symbols, images, tone, structure, or a combination of these elements.

3. *Anticipate the difficulties.* If an allusion is not clear to you or if you think it may not be clear to your listeners, develop a simple and accurate explanation. If the flow and structure of the language is one that poses some sort of articulatory problem in projecting the images and the sense, reread those parts until you have mastered them. Some readers find passages in Swinburne's poetry quite tongue-twisting because of the alliteration; others find Whitman difficult to read aloud because of his long lines

and sentences. Work and rework on the portions that present any kind of difficulty.

4. *Read the poem aloud—not once but many times.* Become accustomed to your voice, to the structure and flow of the poem. Especially try to read for thought phrases and for complete ideas. Until they gather experience reading poetry aloud, many readers tend to pause at the end of each line as if the line carried a stop sign. But poetic sentences often run on for several lines before the idea is completed. Read first for idea. Then seek to capture the cadence and distinctive rhythm of the work. The poet uses cadence, rhythm, and meter to serve his idea and feeling. The oral reader uses these techniques to serve him in projecting the intellectual and emotional content. The poem must be read aloud many times before the oral performance is perfected. A concert artist would not think of playing in public a sonata which he had rehearsed at his private keyboard only once. So through his voice the oral interpreter must play and sound the words in order to learn more and more of the inward values in the poem. And there is no value in simply repeating the words in exactly the same intonation pattern each time. During every reading, let yourself be willing to discover something new about the work. Explore. Experiment. Does the thought and feeling suggest to you that your rate be increased at one point? Would an elongation of vowels in one passage communicate values more precisely? You should look within the work itself to find justification for everything you do. You should be alert to the slightest shift, change, or expansion in meaning, and let those shifts be portrayed clearly through your reading. Delay adopting an attitude toward the work. Ask questions and seek answers as you read aloud. Work until you are certain of the full meaning of the poem. Let your interpretation unfold throughout the rehearsal sessions.

5. *Prepare an introduction.* The intensity and economy of poetry make it imperative that the oral reader do all within his power to prepare the listener. Your introduction may take different turns. You may share with your audience an individual experience of which the poem reminds you. You may refer to some current or past event. You may note the relationship of other subject matter to the general subject of the poem. The prime value of the introduction is that it helps the listener leave his own problems and attend to the poem.

Afer having read the poem aloud as effectively as you can, pause for a slow count of five. Letting the poem BE in a silence that follows the completed reading can make this silence the most active moment of the presentation for the listeners. These quiet seconds may be the very ones needed to let the poem be experienced, and when it is experienced it becomes meaningful.

Many believe that poetry is more difficult to read aloud than prose or drama. But is that belief warranted? Poetry is a natural language. Children live in it and speak in it. Listen to any child or group of children. The rhythm and cadence of their speech, the flow of their language as they play, have much of poetry. This natural poetry becomes self-conscious prose as children are molded by convention, sophistication, and requirements to conform. The oral reader who surrenders to the sweep of language, to the intensity of the emotion, to the vividness of the images, and who learns to discipline his mind and voice and body in the oral presentation of the poem will find poetry as much fun as other forms of literature, if not more.

But the oral reader may well acknowledge that a poetry reading calls for the best kind of listening. The intensity of the poet's expression, the economy of statement, the very design of the structure—all demand that the listener attend to poetry with far closer concentration and more careful focus than he might be required to give to most prose and drama. These demands on the listener put corresponding demands on the oral reader. Thus you may find poetry challenging, but you should not look upon reading it as more difficult than any other assignment in oral literature.

NONSENSE VERSE

A poem may delight the listener on many levels for many reasons.

> Once upon a time
> The goose drank wine,
> The monkey chewed tobacco
> On the streetcar line.
> Now the car line broke,
> The monkey choked,
> And they all went to heaven
> In a little green boat.[1]

This nonsense poem may elicit a smile because the words sound absurd. It may seem amusing to you because the whole idea of a goose drinking wine and of a monkey chewing tobacco is ridiculous. The picture of these two floating to heaven in a boat—specifically a green boat—provides a surprise element which is equally ridiculous. The structure of the poem with its differing cadences, irregular metrical feet, and break in rhyme scheme afforded by lines three and seven keep the ear and mind alert by reason of its variety. There is repetition of pattern and change of pattern. This combination of repetition and change is also part of the appeal and

---

[1] I have never seen these lines in print. The words come by way of my grandmother, who reported them as she had heard and learned them.

delight. The poem is sheer nonsense, and it is not important to analyze the reasons for its appeal beyond the recognition that each of us now and then needs nonsense as a relief and a change from reason.

THE BALLAD

Some poems delight the hearer because of their story element. Economy of words marks the narrative in verse form. The story line is more simple and more direct in poetry than in prose. Only the barest details are sketched, for example, in the old ballad "Get Up and Bar the Door." In this story poem a husband and wife argue over who will get up and close a door blown open by the wind. They arrive at a basis for settling their argument but neither takes any action until they are set upon by two strangers.

GET UP AND BAR THE DOOR[2]

It fell about the Martinmas time,
    And a gay time it was then,
When our goodwife got puddings to make,
    And she's boild them in the pan.

The wind sae cauld blew south and north,
    And blew into the floor;
Quoth our goodman to our goodwife,
    "Gae out and bar the door."

"My hand is in my hussyfskap,
    Goodman, as ye may see;
An it should nae be barrd this hundred year,
    It's no be barrd for me."

They made a paction tween them twa,
    They made it firm and sure,
That the first word whaeer shoud speak,
    Shoud rise and bar the door.

Then by there came two gentlemen,
    At twelve o clock at night,
And they could neither see house nor hall,
    Nor coal nor candle-light.

"Now whether is this a rich man's house,
    Or whether is it a poor?"
But neer a word wad ane o them speak,
    For barring of the door.

---

[2]From *English and Scottish Popular Ballads,* ed. Helen Child Sargent and George Lyman Kittredge, 1904.

And first they ate the white puddings,
  And then they ate the black;
Tho muckle thought the goodwife to hersel,
  Yet neer a word she spake.

Then said the one unto the other,
  "Here, man, tak ye my knife;
Do ye tak aff the auld man's beard,
  And I'll kiss the goodwife."

"But there's nae water in the house,
  And what shall we do then?"
"What ails ye at the puddin-broo,
  That boils into the pan?"

O up then started our goodman,
  An angry man was he:
"Will ye kiss my wife before my een,
  And scad me wi pudding-bree?"

Then up and started our goodwife,
  Gied three skips on the floor:
"Goodman, you've spoken the foremost word,
  Get up and bar the door."

Traditional ballads were often rendered with a refrain, sometimes delivered by the speaker alone but usually said as a communal response by the listeners. There are no rules about the use of the refrain. How would you use the refrain in this next ballad?

THE CRUEL MOTHER[3]

There was a duke's daughter lived in York,
So secretly she loved her father's clark.

She loved him long and many a day,
Till big with child she went away.

She went into the wide wilderness;
Pitied she be for her heaviness.

She leaned her back unto a thorn,
And there she has her twa babes born.

"Smile na sae sweet, my bonie babes,
An ye smile sae sweet, ye'll smile me dead."

She's howket a grave by the light o' the moon,
And there she's buried her sweet babes in.

---

[3]Adapted for this book from various versions, including that in Sargent and Kittredge, cited above, and others in *The English and Scottish Popular Ballads,* ed. Francis James Child, editions of 1886 and 1898.

As she was going to the church,
She saw twa pretty babes in the porch.

"O sweet babes, an thou were mine,
I wad cleed thee in silk so fine."

"O mother dear, when we were thine,
Ye did na prove to us sae kind.

"But out ye took a wee pen-knife:
Ye parted us and our sweet life.

"The coldest earth it was our bed,
The green grass was our coverlid.

"But now we're in the heavens hie,
And ye've the pains o' hell to drie."

The refrain reads:

Fine flowers in the valley,
And the green leaves they grow rarely.

The phrase "fine flowers" would seem to symbolize the duke's daughter, perhaps herself a veritable flower of loveliness. The line "The green leaves they grow rarely" presents an image which embodies a major event in the ballad: the newborn babes are not allowed to grow. Try using the refrain one line at a time between the lines of the ballad proper. Try the two lines together at the end of each stanza. Experiment with other ways. Which seems most effective? What is your justification for your decision?

JAPANESE POETRY: HAIKU

The Western world is becoming increasingly aware of Far Eastern poetry. The poetry known in Japan as *haiku* or *hokku* is descriptive and full of imagery. Feeling is merely suggested. The verse must appear in strict form—three lines, seventeen syllables, with five syllables each in the first and third line and seven syllables in the second line. (Translations in English sometimes deviate by a syllable.) Usually some key word refers directly or by inference to a season of the year. An abrupt switch to a different viewpoint in the course of the poem requires a voice cue from the reader; in these printed English versions it is placed by three dots. Here are a few haiku of poets whose writings span nearly two centuries.

BASHO (1644-1694)[4]

Now that eyes of hawks
Are darkened . . . in dusky night
The quails are chirping.

---

[4]From *Japanese Haiku*, Mount Vernon, N.Y.: The Peter Pauper Press, 1955. Copyright 1955 The Peter Pauper Press.

No oil to read by
And so I'm off to bed . . . ah!
My moonlit pillow.

Dewdrops, let me cleanse
In your brief sweet waters
These dark hands of life.

Ah me! I am one
Who spends his little breakfast
Morning-glory gazing.

Ivy creeps over
Ancient wooden door-sill
Under a waning moon.

Here, where a thousand
Captains swore grand conquest . . .
Grass their monument.

BUSON (1716-1783)[5]

White chrysanthemum . . .
Before that perfect flower
Scissors hesitate.

Deep in the forest,
Hear the woodcutter's dull axe . . .
And the woodpecker.

The pebbles are clear,
Clear are the fish swimming there . . .
Deep autumn water.

ISSA (1763-1827)[6]

Hi! Kids mimicking
Cormorants . . . You are more like
Real cormorants than they!

Giddy grasshopper
Take care . . . do not leap and crush
These pearls of dewdrop.

Dim the grey cow comes
Mooing mooing and mooing
Out of the morning mist.

Nice: wild persimmons . . .
And notice how the mother
Eats the bitter parts.

---

[5]From *Japanese Haiku,* as above.
[6]From *Japanese Haiku,* as above.

On the death of his child:

> Dew evaporates
> And all our world is dew . . . so dear,
> So fresh, so fleeting.

The orphan speaks:

> The year-end party . . .
> I am even envious
> Of scolded children.

THE LYRIC POEM

A form of poetry combining sensory images with intensity of emotion is known as the lyric. The lyric is not concerned with a story but with a personal experience—what the poet feels, or hears, or thinks, or sees. The lyric is usually short and often has a singing quality. To perceive the lyric as a sensory experience, consider Shakespeare's "Winter," from *Love's Labor's Lost* (Act V, Scene 2).

First, read this poem through:

WINTER / William Shakespeare

> When icicles hang by the wall,
>   And Dick the shepherd blows his nail,
> And Tom bears logs into the hall,
>   And milk comes frozen home in pail,
> When blood is nipp'd, and ways be foul,
>   Then nightly sings the staring owl,
>   To-who,
> Tu-whit, to-who, a merry note,
> While greasy Joan doth keel the pot.
>
> When all aloud the wind doth blow,
>   And coughing drowns the parson's saw,
> And birds sit brooding in the snow,
>   And Marian's nose looks red and raw;
> When roasted crabs hiss in the bowl,
>   Then nightly sings the staring owl,
>   To-who,
> Tu-whit, to-who, a merry note,
> While greasy Joan doth keel the pot.

Next, take note of the meaning of several words that you may have had difficulty locating in dictionaries. *Nail* means *horn*; *to keel* means *to stir*; a *saw* is a *saying*; the hissing *crabs* are *crabapples*.

Now make yourself aware of some of the images and reactions and sensory appeals—elements that make the poem a lyric:

When icicles hang by the wall,
> [*visual image; thermal reaction to cold*
And Dick the shepherd blows his nail,
> [*auditory image*
And Tom bears logs into the hall,
> [*tactile image; kinaesthetic reaction*
And milk comes frozen home in pail,
> [*gustatory appeal; thermal reaction*
When blood is nipp'd and ways be foul,
> [*tactile sense; visual image of roads (ways)*
Then nightly sings the staring owl,
> [*auditory and visual images*
To-who, / Tu-whit, to-who, a merry note,
> [*auditory images*
While greasy Joan doth keel the pot.
> [*visual, tactile, gustatory images; thermal reaction*
When all aloud the wind doth blow,
> [*auditory and tactile images; thermal reaction*
And coughing drowns the parson's saw,
> [*auditory and visual images of a congregation*
> *coughing while a minister tries to preach*
And birds sit brooding in the snow,
> [*visual images—white snow, perhaps dark feathers*
And Marian's nose looks red and raw;
> [*visual and tactile images*
When roasted crabs hiss in the bowl,
> [*auditory images with olfactory and gustatory appeal*
Then nightly sings the staring owl,
To-who, / Tu-whit, to-who, a merry note,
While greasy Joan doth keel the pot.

You may have begun to prepare yourself for offering an oral interpretation of this short and famous lyric poem—or perhaps you have prepared yourself to listen to it as some other person reads it.

The oral interpreter needs to identify and to think through the sensory images, the movement patterns, and the inner reactions expressed in the literature. The greater his attention to these details the more effectively he will visualize during his oral reading. Such thoughtful analysis promotes awareness, the key to creativity and artistry in reading aloud. Those who read aloud too rapidly usually do so because they do not allow sufficient time to visualize or because they do not visualize in sufficient detail. Preparation time is always well invested when spent on images, movement, and reactions within the literature. The dividends from the investment: communication from author to interpreter, interpreter to listener.

Lyrics are especially adaptable to an interesting experiment in the relationship between sound and sense. Those of you who can speak a foreign tongue might read aloud a lyric in that language and on the basis of the oral reading alone, let the class decide what was the predominant mood of the poem. Try it. Goethe's poems, any of Dante's sonnets, and Villon's ballads are fun to use. Learn to listen for patterns of sound in poetry. Those patterns have been planned as carefully as the structure of the poem.

A particularly interesting use of sound patterns to reinforce meaning may be found in Carl Sandburg's "Jazz Fantasia," written at a time when jazz was still a recent development. Sandburg had something to say to jazzmen about their medium. He recognized jazz as an art form which could interpret quiet as well as noisy moments in our modern times.

JAZZ FANTASIA / Carl Sandburg [7]

Drum on your drums, batter on your banjos,
sob on the long cool winding saxophones.
Go to it, O jazzmen.

Sling your knuckles on the bottoms of the happy
tin pans, let your trombones ooze, and go husha-
husha-hush with the slippery sand-paper.

Moan like an autumn wind high in the lonesome tree-
tops, moan soft like you wanted somebody terrible,
cry like a racing car slipping away from a motorcycle
cop, bang-bang! you jazzmen, bang altogether drums,
traps, banjos, horns, tin cans—make two people fight
on the top of a stairway and scratch each other's eyes
in a clinch tumbling down the stairs.

Can the rough stuff . . . now a Mississippi steamboat
pushes up the night river with a hoo-hoo-hoo-oo . . .
and the green lanterns calling to the high soft stars
. . . a red moon rides on the humps of the low river
hills . . . go to it, O jazzmen.

Sound patterns and images in contemporary poetry express in some measure each artist's interpretation of his times. Much of Robert Frost's poetry has conversational rhythms, as if the poet were talking to a friend, sharing an experience within the poem. Frost's images frequently employ objects in nature, recognizable in day-to-day outdoor living. E. E. Cummings deftly adapts sound patterns and rhythms to his subject matter. The rhythm of children at play—running, pirating, hop-scotching—pervades the sound patterns of "Chanson Innocent" and the images are vivid, almost

---

[7]From *Smoke and Steel* by Carl Sandburg, copyright, 1920, by Harcourt, Brace & World, Inc.; renewed 1948, by Carl Sandburg. Reprinted by permission of the publishers.

piercingly bright in the way that children so often report their own awareness and sensory delight. But in "Poem, or Beauty Hurts Mr. Vinal,"
Cummings sounds very much like a barker at the circus or a television
commercial—sound patterns, rhythms, and images are highly appropriate
to his subject. Dylan Thomas's poetry surfeits the listener's ear with a lush-
ness of sound in an auditory labyrinth where poetic sound patterns swing
and loop and dangle and twine from line to line. Read such poems as "The
Force that through the Green Fuse Drives the Flower," "Our Eunuch
Dreams," "In the Beginning," "All, All and All the Dry Worlds Lever,"
"In Memory of Ann Jones," and "Poem on His Birthday." The period, the
end of a Thomas poem, is somehow not the end of its sound in the mental
ear. Thomas's ever-moving sounds, together with rhythms and images,
combine to create a spontaneous force, contagiously vigorous, which like a
time capsule seems almost to explode on into space for here time, there
time, now time, then time.

A poem is in part a measure of the poet's own mind and spirit, for a
writer cannot put on paper what he himself has not already perceived. A
vivid example of this point may be found in a group of three poems by
T. S. Eliot. These poems reflect a marked change in the author's outlook
over a period of five years. Taken together they reveal his growth from
doubt to religious faith. "The Hollow Men," written in 1925, illustrates
his despair and frustration. "Journey of the Magi," written in 1927, is
Eliot's own journey in search of a faith which he does not quite find. "Ash
Wednesday," written three years later, in 1930, marks Eliot's reconcilia-
tion of his doubts and acceptance of a religious faith. The rhythms of the
church service are found throughout this last piece. Many of the references
will be clear if the reader remembers Eliot's debt to Dante. The first two of
these poems are printed here, with some suggestions of analysis for oral
interpretation.

Throughout "The Hollow Men," be aware of the sound patterns. Note
the relationship between the sound and the sense of the piece.

THE HOLLOW MEN / T. S. Eliot[8]

Mistah Kurtz—he dead.
        A penny for the Old Guy.

I

        We are the hollow men
        We are the stuffed men

Leaning together
Headpiece filled with straw. Alas!
Our dried voices, when
We whisper together
Are quiet and meaningless
As wind in dry grass
Or rats' feet over broken glass
In our dry cellar

Shape without form, shade without color,
Paralyzed force, gesture without motion;

Those who have crossed
With direct eyes, to death's other Kingdom
Remember us—if at all—not as lost
Violent souls, but only
As the hollow men
The stuffed men.

II

Eyes I dare not meet in dreams
In death's dream kingdom
These do not appear:
There, the eyes are
Sunlight on a broken column
There, is a tree swinging
And voices are
In the wind's singing
More distant and more solemn
Than a fading star.

Let me be no nearer
In death's dream kingdom
Let me also wear
Such deliberate disguises
Rat's coat, crowskin, crossed staves
In a field
Behaving as the wind behaves
No nearer—

Not that final meeting
In the twilight kingdom

III

This is the dead land
This is cactus land
Here the stone images
Are raised, here they receive

The supplication of a dead man's hand
Under the twinkle of a fading star.

Is it like this
In death's other kingdom
Waking alone
At the hour when we are
Trembling with tenderness
Lips that would kiss
Form prayers to broken stone.

IV

The eyes are not here
There are no eyes here
In this valley of dying stars
In this hollow valley
This broken jaw of our lost kingdoms

In this last of meeting places
We grope together
And avoid speech
Gathered on this beach of the tumid river

Sightless, unless
The eyes reappear
As the perpetual star
Multifoliate rose
Of death's twilight kingdom
The hope only
Of empty men.

V

Here we go round the prickly pear
Prickly pear prickly pear
Here we go round the prickly pear
At five o'clock in the morning.

Between the idea
And the reality
Between the motion
And the act
Falls the Shadow
                    For Thine is the Kingdom

Between the conception
And the creation
Between the emotion
And the response
Falls the Shadow
                    Life is very long

Between the desire
And the spasm
Between the potency
And the existence
Between the essence
And the descent
Falls the Shadow

For Thine is the Kingdom

For Thine is
Life is
For Thine is the

This is the way the world ends
This is the way the world ends
This is the way the world ends
Not with a bang but a whimper.

In section I of the poem, what is the effect of the [a], [æ], [o] and [ɔ] sounds?

In section II, the poet shifts to predominantly [ɪ], [i], [ɛ], and [aɪ] sounds. What is the effect? How does the tenor of section II contrast with that of section I?

In section III, what shifts do you notice? How do these changes contribute to the total effect of the poem?

In section IV, the poet returns to a consideration of eyes. Why? What symbolism is implied by "Sightless"?

Section V begins with nursery-rhyme fragments and repeats fragments from the Lord's Prayer. In what way do these fragments represent good choices for the author's purpose?

Now read "Journey of the Magi" and the detailed analysis that follows it.

JOURNEY OF THE MAGI / T. S. Eliot[9]

"A cold coming we had of it,
Just the worst time of the year
For a journey, and such a long journey:
The ways deep and the weather sharp,
The very dead of winter."
And the camels galled, sore-footed, refractory,
Lying down in the melting snow.

---

[9]From *Collected Poems 1909-1962* by T. S. Eliot, copyright, 1936, by Harcourt, Brace & World, Inc.; copyright, ©, 1963, 1964, by T. S. Eliot. Reprinted by permission of the publishers.

There were times we regretted
The summer palaces on slopes, the terraces,
And the silken girls bringing sherbet.
Then the camel men cursing and grumbling
And running away, and wanting their liquor and women,
And the night-fires going out, and the lack of shelters,
And the cities hostile and the towns unfriendly
And the villages dirty and charging high prices:
A hard time we had of it.
At the end we preferred to travel all night,
Sleeping in snatches,
With the voices singing in our ears, saying
That this was all folly.

Then at dawn we came down to a temperate valley,
Wet, below the snow line, smelling of vegetation;
With a running stream and a water-mill beating the darkness,
And three trees on the low sky,
And an old white horse galloped away in the meadow.
Then we came to a tavern with vine-leaves over the lintel,
Six hands at an open door dicing for pieces of silver,
And feet kicking the empty wine-skins.
But there was no information, and so we continued
And arrived at evening, not a moment too soon
Finding the place; it was (you may say) satisfactory.

All this was a long time ago, I remember,
And I would do it again, but set down
This set down
This: were we led all that way for
Birth or Death? There was a Birth, certainly,
We had evidence and no doubt. I had seen birth and death,
But had thought they were different; this Birth was
Hard and bitter agony for us, like Death, our death.
We returned to our places, these Kingdoms,
But no longer at ease here, in the old dispensation,
With an alien people clutching their gods.
I should be glad of another death.

"Journey of the Magi" might be termed Eliot's journey—or any man's journey—between attitudes presented in "The Hollow Men" expressing "shape without form, shade without color, / paralyzed force, gesture without motion" and in "Ash Wednesday" wherein he asks, "Teach us to sit still" and "Let my cry come unto Thee." In "Journey of the Magi" he is still moving, journeying out of the despair expressed in "The Hollow Men" into the peaceful resignation of "Ash Wednesday." Perhaps the journey has meaning and significance for the reader or listener who is himself making a similar effort to pass from doubt to faith.

This journey of Eliot's carried him into the Christian faith, and the oral interpreter of "Journey of the Magi" needs to take this fact into account. The interpretation can, however, have meaning for listeners journeying toward any other faith or between two poles of belief. In whichever event, is the interpretation to speed their journey? To turn them? To halt them? The reader is challenged to find ways of respecting the expectations and outlooks of his listeners while proceeding with his personal interpretation, an interpretation that inescapably must have a viewpoint.

The analysis that follows proceeds from my viewpoint. Your analysis, if it is truly yours, must proceed from your own viewpoint. If you and I are each as faithful as possible to the author's intention, the two analyses should meet on some common ground, though they need not coincide in all details. And no analysis is the end; so long and so often as we reflect upon a poem, we find new meanings, perceive symbols not recognized before, test and revise our interpretations in the light of ever-growing experience. No living person gives the same oral interpretation a second time—exact repetition is the function of the phonograph, not of an interpreter.

Consider a moment the title. Why a journey of the *Magi*? Why not journey of the *wise men*? Poet's prerogative, you say? Perhaps, but Eliot is too much the master of precision, too much the thinker, to exercise a prerogative carelessly. The Bible refers to "wise men" (Matthew II, i). Are Eliot's Magi not wise? In historic record, the Magi were a priestly order of ancient Media and Persia. Their religion included belief in the advent of a saviour and in the principles of good and of evil as deities, both of whom they worshiped. In his very title, then, Eliot signifies that he is not taking a journey with faith in good alone: he sees both the good and the evil. Certainly this concept is consistent with his belief that the poet should "be able to see beneath both beauty and ugliness; to see the boredom, and the horror, and the glory."

> "A cold coming we had of it,

Note the quotation mark; the first five lines of the poem are a remark or speech that the remainder of the poem affirms and enlarges. These first five lines appear to be a direct reminiscence by one of the Magi, long after the immensely significant event. He speaks to another of the Magi, as the continuation reveals— to the poet, to Eliot. Or these five lines may be a spoken thought of the poet, the rest of the poem his further meditation. In either case, the reminiscence reaches deeper than the surface. A coming? The Magi came literally to Christ at the Nativity; the poet came to Christ in the Christian Church. And the coming was cold—through and out of extreme doubt, extreme intellectual loneliness. To a reader or listener knowing that Eliot felt poetry must not only "be found through suffering, but can find its material only in suffering," this passage would seem to indicate that he has experienced all the bitterness and loneliness and sense of isolation which accompanies doubt.

> Just the worst time of the year
> For a journey, ...

Eliot takes this journey at the "worst time of the year"—at the time in his years when doubt completely overwhelms him.

> ... and such a long journey:

It is a long journey in consciousness from doubt into the realm of faith.

> The ways deep ...

It is not an easy road to walk. One must delve deep within his own thinking, within the scriptures, within the lives of the prophets, to understand and to arrive at a faith.

> ... and the weather sharp,

The way from doubt to faith is not comfortable, but sharp, like cold weather or a two-edged sword.

> The very dead of winter."

The dead of winter in the reminiscence, the dead of winter in the poet's thinking: he has gone all the way down to the depths of doubt. Perhaps in the dead of this winter he would hug the tatters of his old belief about him, hoping they will keep him warm. But does he? In the second stanza he reveals that he does not. Meanwhile, he enlarges on what has been said by the first speaker:

> And the camels galled, sore-footed, refractory,
> Lying down in the melting snow.

The travelers had accepted the journey and its discomfort; not so those around them. And why *melting* snow? It hints that the cold will pass—the wintry doubt with its attendant sense of isolation will give way to warmth, to a sense of companionship, of becoming a part of civilization. Even so,

> There were times we regretted
> The summer palaces on slopes, the terraces,
> And the silken girls bringing sherbet.

The life of earthly pleasures and ease is not easily given up, however im-

perative the literal or symbolic journey to which the travelers are com-
mitted.

> Then the camel men cursing and grumbling
> And running away, and wanting their liquor and women,

Reluctant companions—camels and camel men—hamper the travelers;
men with no sense of goal hold back those who seek it. But one cannot
separate himself from such men—he needs them and must progress in their
presence, or his journey halts.

> And the night-fires going out, . . .

The warmth and the light—purpose, hope, understanding—are hard to
sustain

> . . . and the lack of shelters,

Between the East and Bethlehem, between doubt and faith, resting places
are lacking.

> And the cities hostile and the towns unfriendly
> And the villages dirty and charging high prices:

Cities and towns and villages, each in their degree, are places where people
hold themselves secure and keep aloof from travelers who pass through
them toward great goals. The settled, the provincial, the petty and slothful
and greedy, all in their own nature hamper those who seek for something
distant and greater.

Such were some of the handicaps faced by the Magi and by the poet.
"A cold coming" is not denied, but the cold was not all.

> A hard time we had of it.

This line echoes the first line and ends the catalogue of troubles.

> At the end we preferred to travel all night,
> Sleeping in snatches,

The travelers press on. Whoever comes to his goal—as we know the Magi
and the poet came to theirs—must push on and work free from the hin-
drances. The great journeys are not made wholly in the sunlight, nor are
travelers permitted adequate rest.

> With the voices singing in our ears, saying
> That this was all folly.

Even resolution cannot end misgiving. The will, however firm, cannot bring
certainty.

Here, with the first stanza ended, the poem turns to new matters.

> Then at dawn we came down to a temperate valley,

The hardships eventually become tempered. One finds some serenity as the goal is neared.

> Wet, below the snow line, smelling of vegetation;

There is remission of the arid coldness, a sense of life and growth.

> With a running stream and a water-mill beating the darkness,

The darkness that persists at dawn, before full light comes, is beaten back by the energy of life, the running stream that overcomes doubt and stagnation.

> And three trees on the low sky,

But there is a foreboding—three trees now, in the dawn of the Nativity; three crosses yet to rise, on Calvary at the Crucifixion. These are Christian symbols of hope and redemption and sacrifice. The poet in his journey is coming near to important events.

> And an old white horse galloped away in the meadow.

The horse, the white horse, the bearer of ancient heroes in ancient triumphs, is old. The triumphs are outworn. At this time of their journey, triumph is not for the Magi, nor for the poet; the old horse gallops away, the old supports are withdrawn.

> Then we came to a tavern with vine-leaves over the lintel,
> Six hands at an open door dicing for pieces of silver,
> And feet kicking the empty wine-skins.

Even in the temperate valley, even as the travelers near their goal, even as the poet approaches what he seeks to achieve, there is no escape from the greed and scoffing and contempt. These must be passed. The lines suggest these figurative meanings, though the poet alludes to events and incidents in the gospels.

> But there was no information, and so we continued

Where one meets greed and scoffing and contempt, one seldom finds guidance; it is necessary to keep on in the direction of one's best expectations. Having come so far in this direction, one must follow it further.

> And arrived at evening, . . .

—an evening of fulfillment, after the dawn of hope in the temperate valley.

> . . . not a moment too soon
> Finding the place; . . .

Such places and such fulfillments are never found too soon.

> ... it was (you may say) satisfactory.

Satisfactory. One can say nothing more; certainly what had preceded was less than satisfactory.

The stanza ends. The account of the journey has been reviewed. Yet questions remain.

> All this was a long time ago, I remember,
> And I would do it again, ...

Long and hard as the journey was, he would nevertheless take it again.

> ... but set down
> This set down
> This: were we led all that way for
> Birth or Death? ...

Now we come to the end result of this journey. Was it Birth? That is, was it spiritual awakening? Or was it Death? That is, was there greater emphasis on the seeker's loss rather than on his gain?

> ... There was a Birth, certainly,
> We had evidence and no doubt. ...

He did experience a spiritual awakening.

> ... I had seen birth and death,
> But had thought they were different; ...

He speaks of the coming and going in the world where he thought birth was joyous and death was sad, but in Birth and Death he found a reversal; for

> ... this Birth was
> Hard and bitter agony for us, like Death, our death.

This spiritual awakening required effort, struggle against all the earthly forces of lethargy and ignorance. Therein lay its "hard and bitter agony."

> We returned to our places, these Kingdoms,

We returned to our normal mode of living on this earth, in the sense that we resumed once more our regular routine of life. Why a capital *K* for *Kingdoms*? Perhaps to recognize that "the kingdom of God is within you," and that it is within man's power to lay hold on this faith which he has found on his journey.

> But no longer at ease here, in the old dispensation,

He is no longer satisfied with the completely earthly pleasures and ways of doing things.

> With an alien people clutching their gods.

The people he once knew and understood and liked now seem alien to him, for like Virgil's Aeneas they clutch their household gods; but these are gods of lethargy, indifference, and ignorance.

> I should be glad of another death.

He is no longer willing to follow the old ways, but he still finds it difficult at times to take a stand alone among this alien people. He would be glad of another death, of another transition in his thinking to an even greater faith. And from here the next step is into "Ash Wednesday."

Having had some questions to guide you through "The Hollow Men" and an analysis to accompany you through "Journey of the Magi," you may develop your own approach to the two Eliot poems just presented, and to "Ash Wednesday," which is not printed here.

A SAMPLE ANALYSIS OF A POEM

The value of making a systematic analysis of a poem before proceeding with an oral interpretation should by now be evident. An example of this kind of study is given in the next several pages, the poem being Walt Whitman's "Out of the Cradle Endlessly Rocking." Some may choose not to make such a detailed investigation. In any event, the material is here for those who are interested. A thorough analysis involves a statement of the poet's theme and of his attitude toward that theme; an exploration of the characters, symbols, or motifs; awareness of the occasion which prompted the composition of the piece; a discussion of the significance of the work in the author's life and of the relationship of this particular selection to other significant works by the author. Analysis of content should include study of the way in which the poet develops his idea, examination of his sensory images, recognition of tone quality and sound effects within the poetic form. Cognizance of the artistic center of the piece gives focus to the oral presentation. The analysis should include observations as to why the work is appealing.

Now read the poem. The sense-stimulation notes are printed for convenience at the bottom of each page, so that you may read the work through silently once to familiarize yourself with it. Because it is a long poem, try also on your first quiet reading to become aware of the sensory images. Then as you reread the poem, consult the notes, developing your awareness in detail. Think through the poem, perceive with all your senses the unfolding scenes, then proceed to the analysis which follows.

OUT OF THE CRADLE ENDLESSLY ROCKING /
Walt Whitman

I

Out of the cradle endlessly rocking,
Out of the mocking-bird's throat, the musical shuttle,
Out of the Ninth-month midnight,
Over the sterile sands, and the fields beyond, where the child, leaving his bed,
        wander'd alone, bare-headed, barefoot,
Down from the shower'd halo,   5
Up from the mystic play of shadows, twining and twisting as if they were alive,
Out from the patches of briers and blackberries,
From the memories of the bird that chanted to me,
From your memories, sad brother—from the fitful risings and fallings I heard,
From under that yellow half-moon, late-risen, and swollen as if with tears,   10
From those beginning notes of sickness and love, there in the transparent mist,
From the thousand responses of my heart, never to cease,
From the myriad thence-arous'd words,
From the word stronger and more delicious than any,
From such, as now they start, the scene revisiting,   15
As a flock, twittering, rising, or overhead passing,
Borne hither—ere all eludes me, hurriedly,
A man—yet by these tears a little boy again,
Throwing myself on the sand, confronting the waves,
I, chanter of pains and joys, uniter of here and hereafter,   20
Taking all hints to use them—but swiftly leaping beyond them,
A reminiscence sing.

Lines	Sense Stimulations and Images
1	motion—kinetic
2	auditory image; motion—kinetic
3	motion—kinetic
4-5	visual image; muscular activity—kinaesthetic
6-7	visual image; motion—kinetic
8-9	auditory image; deep inner nostalgia—organic
10	visual image
11	auditory and visual images
12	deep inner reaction—organic
13-14	auditory image
15	visual image; motion—kinetic
16-17	auditory image; motion—kinetic
18	tactile image; inner pain—organic
19-22	muscular activity—kinaesthetic; inner questioning—organic

2

Once, Paumanok,
When the snows had melted—when the lilac-scent was in the air, and the Fifth-
     month grass was growing,
Up this sea-shore, in some briers,   25
Two guests from Alabama—two together,
And their nest, and four light-green eggs, spotted with brown,
And every day the he-bird, to and fro, near at hand,
And every day the she-bird, crouch'd on her nest, silent, with bright eyes,
And every day I, a curious boy, never too close, never disturbing them,   30
Cautiously peering, absorbing, translating.

3

Shine! shine! shine!
Pour down your warmth, great Sun!
While we bask—we two together.

Two together!   35
Winds blow South, or winds blow North,
Day come white, or night come black,
Home, or rivers and mountains from home,
Singing all time, minding no time,
While we two keep together.   40

4

Till of a sudden,
May-be kill'd, unknown to her mate,
One forenoon the she-bird crouch'd not on the nest,
Nor return'd that afternoon, nor the next,
Nor ever appear'd again.   45

And thenceforward, all summer, in the sound of the sea,
And at night, under the full of the moon, in calmer weather,

Lines	Sense Stimulations and Images
23	visual image; response to direct address
24	olfactory and visual images
25-29	visual images
30-31	muscular activity and tension—kinaesthetic
32-34	visual and tactile images; motion—kinetic; inner joy—organic
35-38	visual images; motion—kinetic
39-40	auditory image; inner joy—organic
41-45	deep inner fear and shock—organic
46	auditory image
47	visual image

Over the hoarse surging of the sea,
Or flitting from brier to brier by day,
I saw, I heard at intervals, the remaining one, the he-bird,   50
The solitary guest from Alabama.

5

Blow! blow! blow!
Blow up, sea winds, along Paumanok's shore!
I wait and I wait, till you blow my mate to me.

6

Yes, when the stars glisten'd,   55
All night long, on the prong of a moss-scallop'd stake,
Down, almost amid the slapping waves,
Sat the lone singer, wonderful, causing tears.

He call'd on his mate;
He pour'd forth the meanings which I, of all men, know.   60

Yes, my brother, I know;
The rest might not—but I have treasur'd every note;
For once, and more than once, dimly, down the beach gliding,
Silent, avoiding the moonbeams, blending myself with the shadows,
Recalling now the obscure shapes, the echoes, the sounds and sights after
    their sorts,   65
The white arms out in the breakers tirelessly tossing,
I, with bare feet, a child, the wind wafting my hair,
Listen'd long and long.

Lines	Sense Stimulations and Images
48	auditory image
49	visual image; motion—kinetic
50-51	visual and auditory images; inner frustration—organic
52-53	tactile image; motion—kinetic
54	inner frustration—organic
55-56	visual image; sense of motion in the universe—kinetic
57-58	auditory images; inner pain—organic
59-60	auditory image; inner pain—organic
61	inner compassion—organic
62	auditory image
63-64	visual image; muscular activity—kinaesthetic
65-66	visual and auditory images; motion—kinetic
67	visual and tactile images
68	auditory image

Listen'd, to keep, to sing—now translating the notes,
Following you, my brother. 70

7

Soothe! soothe! soothe!
Close on its wave soothes the wave behind,
And again another behind, embracing and lapping, every one close,
But my love soothes not me, not me.
Low hangs the moon—it rose late; 75

O it is lagging—O I think it is heavy with love, with love.

O madly the sea pushes, pushes upon the land,
With love—with love.

O night! do I not see my love fluttering out there among the breakers?
What is that little black thing I see there in the white? 80

Loud! loud! loud!
Loud I call to you, my love!
High and clear I shoot my voice over the waves;
Surely you must know who is here, is here;
You must know who I am, my love. 85

Low-hanging moon!
What is that dusky spot in your brown yellow?
O it is the shape, the shape of my mate!
O moon, do not keep her from me any longer.

Land! land! O land! 90
Whichever way I turn, O I think you could give me my mate back again, if you
*   only would;*
For I am almost sure I see her dimly whichever way I look.

O rising stars!
Perhaps the one I want so much will rise, will rise with some of you.

Lines	Sense Stimulations and Images
69-73	auditory image; inner frustration—organic, accentuated by visual and auditory contrasts
74-78	inner sadness intensified by visual appeal of moon and sea—organic; motion—kinetic
79-80	frustration—organic, intensified through visual contrasts
81-85	auditory image; frustration and anguish reach one of the minor climaxes—organic
86-89	anguish—organic, intensified through visual images
90-92	visual images; muscular activity and tension—kinaesthetic; mounting frustration—organic
93-94	visual image; motion—kinetic; hope—organic; muscular tension—kinaesthetic

O throat! O trembling throat!   95
Sound clearer through the atmosphere!
Pierce the woods, the earth;
Somewhere listening to catch you, must be the one I want.

Shake out, carols!
Solitary here—the night's carols!   100
Carols of lonesome love! Death's carols!
Carols under that lagging, yellow, waning moon!
O, under that moon, where she droops almost down into the sea!
O reckless, despairing carols.

But soft! sink low;   105
Soft! let me just murmur;
And do you wait a moment; you husky-noised sea;
For somewhere I believe I heard my mate responding to me,
So faint—I must be still, be still to listen;
But not altogether still, for then she might not come immediately to me.   110

Hither, my love!
Here I am! Here!
With this just-sustain'd note I announce myself to you;
This gentle call is for you, my love, for you.

Do not be decoy'd elsewhere!   115
That is the whistle of the wind—it is not my voice;
That is the fluttering, the fluttering of the spray;
Those are the shadows of leaves.

O darkness! O in vain!
O I am very sick and sorrowful.   120

O brown halo in the sky, near the moon, drooping upon the sea!
O troubled reflection in the sea!
O throat! O throbbing heart!
O all—and I sing uselessly, uselessly all the night.

Lines	Sense Stimulations and Images
95-98	hope—organic, intensified by auditory and visual images
99-102	frustration and despair—organic, accented by auditory and visual images
103	visual image; motion—kinetic
104	despair—organic
105-109	frantic hopefulness—organic, intensified by auditory images
110	developing muscular tension—kinaesthetic
111-114	muscular activity and mounting tension—kinaesthetic; auditory images
115-118	fear—organic, intensified by auditory and visual images; motion—kinetic
119-120	utter despair and frustration—organic
121-124	motion—kinetic; despair and frustration—organic, intensified by visual and auditory images

Yet I murmur, murmur on!   125
O murmurs—you yourselves make me continue to sing, I know not why.

O past! O life! O songs of joy!
In the air—in the woods—over fields;
Loved! loved! loved! loved! loved!
But my love no more, no more with me!   130
We two together no more.

8

The aria sinking;
All else continuing—the stars shining,
The winds blowing—the notes of the bird continuous echoing,
With angry moans the fierce old mother incessantly moaning,   135
On the sands of Paumanok's shore, gray and rustling;
The yellow halfmoon enlarged, sagging down, drooping, the face of the sea almost
    touching;
The boy extatic—with his bare feet the waves, with his hair the atmosphere
    dallying,
The love in the heart long pent, now loose, now at last tumultuously bursting,
The aria's meaning, the ears, the Soul, swiftly depositing,   140
The strange tears down the cheeks coursing,
The colloquy there—the trio—each uttering,
The undertone—the savage old mother, incessantly crying,
To the boy's Soul's questions sullenly timing—some drown'd secret hissing,
To the outsetting bard of love.   145

9

Demon or bird! (said the boy's soul,)
Is it indeed toward your mate you sing? or is it mostly to me?
For I, that was a child, my tongue's use sleeping,
Now I have heard you,
Now in a moment I know what I am for—I awake,   150
And already a thousand singers—a thousand songs, clearer, louder and more sor-
    rowful than yours,
A thousand warbling echoes have started to life within me,
Never to die.

Lines	Sense Stimulations and Images
125	auditory image
126	auditory image; sense of renewal—organic
127-131	utter dejection and inner pain of loss—organic, intensified by auditory and visual images
132-137	motion—kinetic; auditory, visual, and tactile images
138-140	rapture—organic; muscular activity and tension—kinaesthetic; visual and tactile images
141-145	tactile, auditory, and visual images; inner tension—organic
146-153	self-awareness aroused; despair and frustration seeking the resolution—organic, intensified by auditory images

O you singer, solitary, singing by yourself—projecting me;
O solitary me, listening—nevermore shall I cease perpetuating you;   155
Never more shall I escape, never more the reverberations,
Never more the cries of unsatisfied love be absent from me,
Never again leave me to be the peaceful child I was before what there, in the night,
By the sea, under the yellow and sagging moon,
The messenger there arous'd—the fire, the sweet hell within,   160
The unknown want, the destiny of me.

O give me the clew! (it lurks in the night here somewhere;)
O if I am to have so much, let me have more!
O a word! O what is my destination? (I fear it is henceforth chaos;)
O how joys, dreads, convolutions, human shapes, and all shapes, spring as from
        graves around me!   165
O phantoms! you cover all the land and all the sea!
O I cannot see in the dimness whether you smile or frown upon me;
O vapor, a look, a word! O well-beloved!
O you dear women's and men's phantoms!

A word then, (for I will conquer it,)   170
The word final, superior to all,
Subtle, sent up—what is it?—I listen;
Are you whispering it, and have been all the time, you sea-waves?
Is that it from your liquid rims and wet sands?

                                    10

Whereto answering, the sea,   175
Delaying not, hurrying not,
Whisper'd me through the night, and very plainly before daybreak,
Lisp'd to me the low and delicious word DEATH;
And again Death—ever Death, Death, Death,
Hissing melodious, neither like the bird, nor like my arous'd child's heart,   180
But edging near, as privately for me, rustling at my feet,
Creeping thence steadily up to my ears, and laving me softly all over,
Death, Death, Death, Death, Death.

Lines	Sense Stimulations and Images
154-161	self-awareness and mounting exaltation—organic, intensified by auditory and visual images
162-163	inner tension—organic; suggestion of muscular tension—kinaesthetic
164-169	inner tension—organic; doubts and fears intensified by indistinguishable visual images
170-172	inner tensions—organic
173-174	auditory and visual images
175-183	inner realization—organic, intensified by auditory image

Which I do not forget,
But fuse the song of my dusky demon and brother,   185
That he sang to me in the moonlight on Paumanok's gray beach,
With the thousand responsive songs, at random,
My own songs, awaked from that hour;
And with them the key, the word up from the waves.
The word of the sweetest song, and all songs,   190
That strong and delicious word which, creeping to my feet,
The sea whisper'd me.

Whitman's theme, or subject, is the mystery of love and of death. This theme is developed in 192 lines of free verse divided into ten numbered sections. Whitman recalls that in his boyhood he watched two birds who were joyous in their togetherness until the she-bird disappeared never to return. The birds become the symbol, or motif, of love and raise a question in the boy's mind: To whom and of what is the bird singing? The boy, or poet, finds his answer in the sea.

The attitude which the poet takes is one of questioning. Quite clearly he experiences deep seasons of questions in his consciousness, in his very spirit. Here is an almost reverential kind of questioning, and the solution is persistently sought. Whitman refers to the total experience as "a reminiscence" (line 22) and characterizes himself as "uniter of here and hereafter" (line 20). This comment, combined with the omniscient point of view in the poem, emphasizes the philosophical implications of *reminiscence*.

The dominant spirit is one of a mystic struggle. By the use of symbols, the poet handles the mood with striking simplicity. Through the broad tides of mysticism runs a strong undercurrent of frustration which bursts into a spirit of exaltation as the poet is released from frustration when he finds the answer in an understanding of death. Frustration is strongest in lines 119-124 but is felt throughout in his development of contrasts. The contrasts begin with lines 44-51, where the staccato suddenness and the surge of sorrow contrast with lines 32-40, in which the complete joy of being together has been celebrated. Then in lines 71-98 the contrasts are amplified. References to objects in nature undulate, rise and fall, like a bird in flight from the waves up to the moon, down low to the sea, out to the night around and beyond, down to the waves, up to the moon, down again to land, up to stars. In their normal visual appeal the images would take our view from the

Lines	Sense Stimulations and Images
184-188	inner resolution and acceptance—organic, intensified by auditory and visual images
189-190	motion—kinetic; auditory and visual images
191	motion—kinetic
192	inner sublimity—organic, in response to auditory appeal

depths to the heights, but the poet sets all these in close relationship: the moon and stars just rising and close over the water, the water lapping the land. After the risings and fallings in lines 71-98 give way to the consistently structured climb up to the strongest point of frustration in lines 119-124, there is a gentle leveling in lines 127-131 and an artistic glide downward in lines 132-137 to another plateau, where we meet the boy again and build consistently upward to another climax in lines 161-163, where the poet's frustration, though apart from the bird, is like the bird's. In contrast to the emotional burst expressed by the bird is the consistent building up to the answer which the poet finds in lines 178-179 in the word *death*. From this peak the poet leads us to a cradled and hushed level in his two closing lines.

The characters or symbols present are the boy, the bird, and the sea. Whitman uses these motifs to express the mystic struggle raging within himself. The boy symbolizes the poet, the self-awareness of the creator; the bird, the lover, specifically love; the sea becomes the answerer whose answer is the revelation of the mystery of death.

An actual experience in his boyhood prompted the composition of "Out of the Cradle." Written in 1859 when Whitman was forty years old, the poem was originally composed four years after the first edition of *Leaves of Grass*. Whitman made revisions as much as seventeen to eighteen years after its initial draft. The poem fits into the Whitman concern with "being himself." Certainly the mystery of love and of death had always occupied his thoughts. It is not surprising that he should reflect upon this theme in his maturity. He was to continue reflecting upon it until the end of his days. The poem is an arch example of Whitman's belief in the democracy of death.

"When Lilacs Last in the Dooryard Bloomed" (1865-1866) is another significant composition to which we might compare the theme and spirit of "Out of the Cradle," for in that poem he elaborates upon the universality of death and greets death as a transition from life to life, even as a further adventure in life. Whitman was concerned with death in many other poems. Some in which he expressed his thoughts most beautifully were "To Think of Time" (1855)—"life goes on, we pass;" "Night on the Prairies" (1860) —"O I see now that life cannot exhibit all to me, as the day cannot, / I see that I am to wait for what will be exhibited by death;" "Whispers of Heavenly Death" (1868)—"death is well provided for;" "As I Watched the Ploughman Ploughing" (1871)—"death is the harvest;" and "On the Beach at Night" (1871)—"something there is more immortal even than the stars."

Analysis of the Thought

Lines 1-22—The poet tells us that he is reminiscing about his boyhood.

Lines 23-31—The he-bird and she-bird are introduced. The boy is presented "cautiously peering, absorbing, translating" but "never too close, never disturbing them." Note the maturity of the poet being projected into the figure of the boy. The child might peer and absorb but only the mature being can translate.

Lines 32-34—The sun serves to symbolize the warmth of the love and joy which the birds experience in their being together.

Lines 35-40—Here Whitman amplifies the togetherness which the birds enjoy.

Lines 41-45—The she-bird disappears. Note the contrast in both rhythm and feeling to the rhythm and feeling of lines 32-34.

Lines 46-51—The sea is introduced. The he-bird is sorrowing for his mate. Note the beauty of that sorrowing against the figure of the sea. Catch the prophetic note here. The sea is to whisper the answer in line 168.

Lines 52-54—The wind is used as a fitting element for amplifying the storminess (the frustration) which the he-bird experiences in his anguish of hopeful waiting for the she-bird.

Lines 55-58—The stars compare with the tears which the lone singer, the sad singer, the bird, brings to the boy's eyes.

Lines 59-60—Here the bird and the boy are brought together with the poet (as the boy) understanding the meaning of the bird. Up to this point we feel the boy has kept himself in the background "cautiously peering, absorbing, translating" (line 31). Now they merge in the light together.

Lines 61-68—Here the poet amplifies his sense of understanding as derived from careful listening.

Lines 69-70—This iteration of "Listen'd" and "Following you" offer the oral reader a model for approach. And the oral reader, by reason of being an interpreter, should well understand the poet: listen, and follow.

Lines 71-74—Frustration, symbolized in the efforts of the bird, deepens into self-pity. This concept is intensified by using the waves which soothe one another to contrast with the bird who finds nothing to soothe it.

Lines 75-76—The mood and feeling are intensified through contrasting the soothing waves with the lagging, heavy moon.

Lines 77-78—There is further intensification of the frustration through pointing up another facet of the sea's nature.

Lines 79-80—One feels the mounting frustration as the bird projects its desires into objects he thinks he sees in the night.

Lines 81-85—The bird shoots his voice over the waves. His frustration at being unanswered is mirrored in nature.

Lines 86-89—The he-bird thought he saw his mate in the night; now he thinks he sees her in the moon. Note how Whitman builds the intensity and anguish of his frustration.

Lines 90-92—Now the he-bird thinks he might see his mate on land. There is a growing intensification of the feeling that he sees his mate everywhere he looks. Notice the sheer beauty, the dip and rise of wings, the surge up and down of emotions, alternating between hope and despair. In line 9 the poet spoke of the "fitful risings and fallings" he heard. Through rhythm and contrasting symbols he bears out these risings and fallings with exquisite design.

Lines 93-94—The frantic eliciting of hope tempts the he-bird to believe his mate may rise with the stars.

Lines 95-98—The he-bird hopes his voice will reach his mate.

Lines 71-98—Note how, even in symbols, there has been a balanced rise and fall in both movement and images:

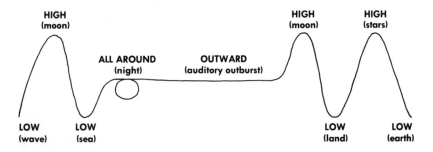

Lines 99-104—Now night, moon, and sea are all tied together as the he-bird seeks to hear his call answered from any point among all these symbols in nature.

Lines 105-110—In feverish hope the he-bird thinks he hears his mate. In almost breathless anticipation he pleads for quiet amid the rush, the noise of all nature which mirrors his own frustration.

Lines 111-114—The he-bird calls, trying to assume confidence—the kind of confidence one seeks to muster by whistling in the dark. He knows that hope is futile but he refuses to resign it.

Lines 115-118—Like a lover inventing excuses for the loved one who is late or never comes, the he-bird explains to himself why there is no answer.

Lines 119-120—The he-bird reaches the breaking-point in his emotion. He gives up.

Lines 121-124—Now the he-bird admits he has been singing uselessly.

Lines 125-126—Having given up, the bird is now unwilling to stop hoping; he continues to sing.

Lines 127-131—The bird meditates on the beauty of the past.

Lines 132-145—The aria sinks. All else continues. We return to the boy. The trio—boy, bird, sea—are brought together. Love releases the sense of frustration. The sea—"the savage old mother"—is about to answer the boy's questions.

Lines 146-153—The self-awareness of the poet expands as he asks whom the song was toward. He is beginning to identify his destiny.

Lines 154-161—The bird was a messenger that roused the boy to his destiny to be a poet.

Lines 162-169—Whitman has accepted the destiny of poet, but he senses that it is not the complete destiny. For complete self-awareness, he begs to be told more.

Lines 170-174—Ready to accept the final word he has sought, the boy (the poet) listens to hear the sea whisper this word.

Lines 175-183—The final word is *death,* not fearful but given tender attributes—delicious, melodious, low whispered, laving him softly all over.

Lines 184-192—The poet accepts the destiny of death and affirms its fusion with the destiny of poet, the union of self-awareness with awareness of the end of self.

Given opportunity—time for thinking and experiencing, space for setting down thought, libraries for study, colleagues for discussing and sharing— an analysis of this kind can be indefinitely extended, heightened, and refined.

Analysis of Techniques in Composition

The composition of a poem requires the poet to deal with numerous technical problems, either intuitively or consciously. Many of them are highly significant for the oral interpreter, and all of them in some degree significant since poetry is so strongly an oral art. Some comments on several of these techniques, as they appear in "Out of the Cradle," are offered here. These deal with alliteration, onomatopeia, tone color (or sound painting) and melody, and the organization of the poem.

Alliteration

The following instances are significant not as illustrations of alliteration as such but rather because the alliteration of the consonants mentioned enhances the mood of the poem and is consistent with it.

Line 4—[b] : *b*eyond, *b*ed, *b*areheaded, *b*arefoot.
Lines 7-9—[b] : *b*riers, *b*làckberries, *b*ird, *b*rother.
Lines 29-31—[k] : *c*rouch'd, *c*urious, *c*lose, *c*autiously.
Lines 95-98—[ð]: *th*roat (twice); *th*rough.

Onomatopoeia

Onomatopoeia is the use of words whose sound suggests their sense. It is useful to distinguish between *primitive* onomatopoeia, which reproduces the actual sound made by a natural source, and *artistic* onomatopoeia, which goes beyond reproducing the natural sound to suggest both the sound and the mental-emotional reaction to the sound.

Whitman employs primitive onomatopoeia throughout the poem, notably in these lines:

Line 16—twittering.
Line 57—slapping waves.
Line 106—murmur.
Line 116—whistle.
Line 123—throbbing.
Line 135—moans, moaning.
Lines 173, 177, 192—whispering, whisper'd.

Artistic onomatopoeia is especially notable in these lines:

Line 39—singing all the time, minding no time.
Line 77—sea pushes.
Line 107—husky nois'd sea.
Line 117—fluttering of the spray.
Line 143—incessantly crying.
Line 152—warbling echoes.
Line 182—laving me softly.

Tone Color and Melody

Whitman has caught the sound of the sea with recurrent use of sibilants either initially or internally. More than three-quarters of the lines contain the soft sea-suggesting sibilants [s], [ʃ], [ʃt], spelled with *s*, *c*, *sh*, and *ch*, and the use of the sibilant to suggest the sea is part of the poetic effort.

The *w* sound is brought out with marked beauty in lines 53-54. Note, too, that the [o] prolongs the sound of several words, giving strength and sweep to the [w].

In lines 41-45, short vowels hasten the utterance of words. They are appropriate in terms of the thought and emotion conveyed.

In lines 75-76 and 99-104, [o], [u], [ʌ], and [a:] prolong their words, giving an effect of heavy sorrow.

Throughout, minor climaxes are enhanced by the contrasts between longer and shorter vowel sounds (contrast especially lines 35-40 with lines 41-45).

The Artistic Proportioning of the Poem

"Out of the Cradle" is not symmetrical. Its artistic center is between lines 118 and 119. Whitman takes these 118 lines to present the story of the bird

—his joy, his loss, his hope of recovery, up to the final acceptance of despair. Then he balances the poem in the final 74 lines through heightening the intensity, the suspense, and final revelation of the boy's own questionings and the sea's repetitive answerings. The proportions observed in his introduction of the motifs of sea, bird, and boy, and in his bringing the three together at various intervals—lines 59-70, 132-161—enhance a sense of balance. But the supreme touch in the achievement of balance is noted in his first mention of "the word . . . more delicious than any" (line 14) and his consistently building, elaborating, structuring up to its second mention: "Lisp'd to me the low and delicious word death" (line 178), just 14 lines from the end, thereby balancing the effect at beginning and end.

Reasons for the Appeal of the Poem

Universality—The aesthetic, emotional, and thought content in "Out of the Cradle" combine to make this poem a significant commentary on life. Most of us at some time or other pause to reflect on death and the meaning of life. The intensity of the frustration and the resolution and the simplicity of the presentation serve to mark the beauty of the universal theme: the mystery of love and death.

Individuality—A very high degree of individuality is reflected in this poem. The use of the sea-bird-boy motifs personalizes the universal theme. The work is distinctly autobiographical and yet marked by so high a degree of artistic handling that each reader and listener can easily relate this to an individual experience which is meaningful to him. The form itself heightens the individuality and sharpens the attention of the observer and hearer.

Aesthetic or psychical distance — Whitman establishes and preserves aesthetic distance through the use of the motifs. The reader or listener stands apart and watches as the drama of the boy, the bird, and the sea unfolds. Neither the writer nor the reader becomes personally involved, losing himself in the poem.

4. Drama

The enactment of a drama on a stage is an experience appealing to the eye as well as to the ear. The audience takes its total impression of the play from the stage setting, from the movement and speech of the actors, from the lighting and sound effects, as well as from the costumes and properties— a combination of audiovisual elements. If instead of attending a stage play, the listener attends a readers'-theatre presentation of a drama, or an oral reading of a scene, he must imagine setting, characters, and movement in order to arrive at a complete concept of the work. The interpreter can do much to assist the audience in this visualization process through his introduction, for the listener will find the presentation meaningful in direct proportion to how well he has been prepared to look for certain aspects. It is especially helpful for the listener to know where the scene is being played and some of the particulars of the setting as they figure in the action or dialogue. The listener needs to know the characters, something of their motivation, and their relation to one another. The interpreter must judge to what extent he will outline the situation: in some instances the dialogue will reveal much; in other instances, background information will be essential.

Having found several selections of interest to himself, the oral reader will narrow his choice to serve his audience, deciding what readings will be of the greatest interest to the greatest number. Certain other considerations will also affect his final choice. Plays in which the major concern is theme or character will be more likely to lend themselves to effective oral reading than will plays which depend primarily upon action and situation. Farces and melodramas, therefore, are not usually good choices for reading aloud because the broad action and gestures, the exaggerated situation and dilemmas, all appeal to the eye and the oral aspects pall without the visual. If the spoken play is such that the full effect depends to a large extent on supplementary pantomime, the reader may do well to continue his search for suitable material. For example, consider the scene from *Cyrano de Bergerac* in which Cyrano describes his nose. The repartee, the wit, the action all make such heavy demands upon the eye that it is a shame to deprive the audience of the full theatrical effect of that scene.

The number of characters in a scene may influence a reader in his choice. Certainly the reader should confine himself to a scene which has only as many characters as he can successfully suggest. If one person is to do an entire scene, two to four characters are perhaps as many as the beginning reader can handle. The differences among characters may be suggested by changes in attitude. The thought and feeling of each character can be registered on the interpreter's face in the split second before as well as during the character's speech. The characters may also be made distinguishable through vocal changes in pitch, rate, and tone—provided these are truly suited to the character and do not call attention away from the major purpose of the piece. Though the character's name may be given the first time he speaks, it should not be necessary to tell the audience each time just who is speaking. Work for distinct clarification of each character in your oral interpretation.

READING DRAMATIC WORKS
Placement of Characters

One school of interpretation recommends placing the characters out against the back wall of the auditorium or classroom by having the reader direct his eyes to the extreme left or the extreme right or to points between according to the number of characters he has to portray. Another school of interpretation favors placing the characters immediately in front of the audience. Still another endorses having the reader turn to face other readers or to indicate the movement of characters on stage. Too much overt movement often disconcerts an audience because it is so close to acting that the listeners are either embarrassed or else want the reader to begin moving about. For many the procedure of placing the characters out behind and beyond the heads of the audience is effective largely because it promotes a kind of aesthetic distance which is satisfying to listeners who must involve themselves in a way quite different from those who attend the theatre to see the actors. If two or more persons are reading a scene, they should agree whether they will place characters out above the heads of the audience or whether they will turn and face one another when speaking. It is seldom clear or satisfying to an audience if the methods are mixed.

Use of Gestures

Whatever gesture supports the material, clarifies it, and illumines the literary work is acceptable. Whatever gesture calls attention to itself or to the interpreter and away from the work is not desirable. Different material will suggest different approaches. A reading from *The School for Scandal* featuring Mrs. Malaprop provides much more leeway for gestures and bodily movement than a reading from *The Glass Menagerie* featuring Laura. The broadness of the gesture will in turn depend upon the size of the room or auditorium, the size of the audience, the formality or informality of the situation, the sensitivity of the reader to his audience, and his interaction with them. Of one thing the reader can be sure: vocal variety— full variety in vocal range and rate—should be appropriately employed to differentiate among the characters. Facial expressions may also suggest changes in characters' tone and attitude. When used just a fraction of a moment prior to the speech as well as during the speech, facial expressions may enhance character development and clarify both motivation and conflict during reading.

Stage Directions

Try reading only those directions which are necessary or which clarify an otherwise confusing scene. If, for example, the character is pacing up and down during a speech and the reader can by his own general bodily alertness and bodily expression suggest such movement without himself moving, then it is clearly not necessary for him to say that the character paces. On the other hand, if a character enters in the middle of a scene and the dialogue does not make it plain who he is, then the reader should help his audience by naming the character and saying that he enters.

The Visible Script

Whether the reader should memorize his scene or read it is a question often raised in connection with the interpretation of drama.

Oral interpretation does demand a contact between performer and audience that is more direct than either acting or impersonation. Memorization followed by presentation without the script is clearly not oral interpretation. If you wish to do a monologue or impersonation, you do not need the book. If you wish to do a reading, refer to the book and turn the pages, at least occasionally. Many of the questions with respect to script, gestures, movement are really questions of taste. A reading might be done primarily to one side of or in front of a lectern, but unless the reader refers to his script from time to time the presentation is in some medium other than interpretation.

Preparation

In drama, perhaps more than in any other form of writing, students tend to omit or to read quickly over passages they do not understand. The interpreter must know the entire play before presenting a portion of it. He should be able to expound on the motivation of each individual character. He should study the play until he can justify each speech as it is written.

Several excerpts from drama follow. A brief commentary will prepare you for the scene presented. After each, you will find a series of questions designed to help you crystallize your interpretation.

RICHARD III / William Shakespeare

Richard the Third has been a much maligned character, generally portrayed as a despicable villain. In the scene that follows (I: ii), however, Richard Gloster is not wholly unattractive. His intelligence, wit, and persuasion during the interview with Anne reveal a personal charm that belies viciousness. Anne, full of bitter accusations and utter contempt for Richard in the first part of the scene, ultimately succumbs to his charm and power. Believing only what she wants to believe, she fails to see him as any less than repentant at the conclusion of the scene. The difference between the two characters as portrayed by one reader is essentially a difference in attitude. Strive by facial expression and bodily alertness to suggest the appropriate attitude as you portray one and then the other. Let thought and emotion govern your rate and pitch. To try consciously for a low or high pitch as a means of indicating the sex of the character is to make effect more paramount than cause.

Enter the Corpse of King HENRY *the Sixth, borne in an open Coffin.* GENTLEMEN, *bearing Halberds, to guard it,* TRESSEL, BERKLEY, *and Lady* ANNE, *as mourner.*

ANNE   Set down, set down your honourable load,
   If honour may be shrouded in a hearse,
   Whilst I a while obsequiously lament
   Th' untimely fall of virtuous Lancaster.—
   Poor key-cold figure of a holy king!
   Pale ashes of the house of Lancaster!
   Thou bloodless remnant of that royal blood,
   Be it lawful that I invocate thy ghost,
   To hear the lamentations of poor Anne,
   Wife to thy Edward, to thy slaughter'd son,
   Stabb'd by the self-same hand that made these wounds!
   Lo, in these windows, that let forth thy life,
   I pour the helpless balm of my poor eyes:—
   O, cursed be the hand that made these holes!
   Cursed the heart, that had the heart to do it!
   Cursed the blood, that let this blood from hence!
   More direful hap betide that hated wretch,
   That makes us wretched by the death of thee,
   Than I can wish to adders, spiders, toads,

Or any creeping venom'd thing that lives!
If ever he have child, abortive be it,
Prodigious, and untimely brought to light,
Whose ugly and unnatural aspect
May fright the hopeful mother at the view;
And that be heir to his unhappiness!
If ever he have wife, let her be made
More miserable by the death of him,
Than I am made by my young lord, and thee!—
Come, now toward Chertsey with your holy load,
Taken from Paul's to be interred there;
And still, as you are weary of this weight,
Rest you, whiles I lament king Henry's corse.

[*The* BEARERS *take up the Corpse and advance. Enter* GLOSTER.

GLOSTER   Stay you, that bear the corse, and set it down.

ANNE   What black magician conjures up this fiend,
    To stop devoted charitable deeds?

GLOSTER   Villains, set down the corse; or, by Saint Paul, I'll make a corse of him
    that disobeys.

GENTLEMAN   My lord, stand back, and let the coffin pass.

GLOSTER   Unmanner'd dog! stand thou when I command:
    Advance thy halberd higher than my breast,
    Or, by Saint Paul, I'll strike thee to my foot,
    And spurn upon thee, beggar, for thy boldness.

[*The* BEARERS *set down the Coffin.*

ANNE   What! do you tremble! are you all afraid?
    Alas! I blame you not; for you are mortal,
    And mortal eyes cannot endure the devil.—
    Avaunt, thou dreadful minister of hell!
    Thou hadst but power over his mortal body,
    His soul thou canst not have: therefore, be gone.

GLOSTER   Sweet saint, for charity, be not so curst.

ANNE   Foul devil, for God's sake, hence, and trouble us not;
    For thou hast made the happy earth thy hell,
    Fill'd it with cursing cries, and deep exclaims.
    If thou delight to view thy heinous deeds,
    Behold this pattern of thy butcheries.—
    O, gentlemen! see, see! dead Henry's wounds
    Open their congeal'd mouths, and bleed afresh!—
    Blush, blush, thou lump of foul deformity,
    For 'tis thy presence that exhales this blood
    From cold and empty veins, where no blood dwells:

Thy deed, inhuman and unnatural,
Provokes this deluge most unnatural.—
O God, which this blood mad'st, revenge his death!
O earth, which this blood drink'st, revenge his death!
Either, heaven, with lightning strike the murderer dead,
Or, earth, gape open wide, and eat him quick,
As thou dost swallow up this good king's blood,
Which his hell-govern'd arm hath butchered!

GLOSTER   Lady, you know no rules of charity,
Which renders good for bad, blessings for curses.

ANNE   Villain, thou know'st nor law of God nor man:
No beast so fierce, but knows some touch of pity.

GLOSTER   But I know none, and therefore am no beast.

ANNE   O wonderful! when devils tell the truth!

GLOSTER   More wonderful, when angels are so angry.—
Vouchsafe, divine perfection of a woman,
Of these supposed evils to give me leave
By circumstance but to acquit myself.

ANNE   Vouchsafe, diffus'd infection of a man,
For these known evils but to give me leave
By circumstance to curse thy cursed self.

GLOSTER   Fairer than tongue can name thee, let me have
Some patient leisure to excuse myself.

ANNE   Fouler than heart can think thee, thou canst make
No excuse current, but to hang thyself.

GLOSTER   By such despair I should accuse myself.

ANNE   And, by despairing, shalt thou stand excus'd
For doing worthy vengeance on thyself,
That didst unworthy slaughter upon others.

GLOSTER   Say, that I slew them not?

ANNE   Then say they were not slain.
But dead they are, and, devilish slave, by thee.

GLOSTER   I did not kill your husband.

ANNE   Why, then he is alive.

GLOSTER   Nay, he is dead; and slain by Edward's hand.

ANNE   In thy foul throat thou liest; queen Margaret saw
Thy murderous falchion smoking in his blood;
The which thou once didst bend against her breast,
But that thy brothers beat aside the point.

GLOSTER   I was provoked by her sland'rous tongue,
    That laid their guilt upon my guiltless shoulders.

ANNE   Thou wast provoked by thy bloody mind,
    That never dreamt on aught but butcheries.
    Didst thou not kill this king?

GLOSTER   I grant ye.

ANNE   Dost grant me, hedge-hog? then, God grant me too,
    Thou may'st be damned for that wicked deed!
    O! he was gentle, mild, and virtuous.

GLOSTER   The fitter for the King of heaven that hath him.

ANNE   He is in heaven, where thou shalt never come.

GLOSTER   Let him thank me, that holp to send him thither,
    For he was fitter for that place than earth.

ANNE   And thou unfit for any place but hell.

GLOSTER   Yes, one place else, if you will hear me name.

ANNE   Some dungeon.

GLOSTER   Your bed-chamber.

ANNE   Ill rest betide the chamber where thou liest.

GLOSTER   So will it, madam, till I lie with you.

ANNE   I hope so.

GLOSTER   I know so.—But, gentle lady Anne,—
    To leave this keen encounter of our wits,
    And fall something into a slower method,
    Is not the causer of the timeless deaths
    Of these Plantagenets, Henry, and Edward,
    As blameful as the executioner?

ANNE   Thou wast the cause, and most accurs'd effect.

GLOSTER   Your beauty was the cause of that effect;
    Your beauty, that did haunt me in my sleep,
    To undertake the death of all the world,
    So I might live one hour in your sweet bosom.

ANNE   If I thought that, I tell thee, homicide,
    These nails should rend that beauty from my cheeks.

GLOSTER   These eyes could not endure that beauty's wreck;
    You should not blemish it, if I stood by:
    As all the world is cheered by the sun,
    So I by that; it is my day, my life.

ANNE   Black night o'ershade thy day, and death thy life!

GLOSTER   Curse not thyself, fair creature; thou art both.

ANNE   I would I were, to be reveng'd on thee.

GLOSTER   It is a quarrel most unnatural,
  To be reveng'd on him that loveth thee.

ANNE   It is a quarrel just and reasonable,
  To be reveng'd on him that kill'd my husband.

GLOSTER   He that bereft thee, lady, of thy husband,
  Did it to help thee to a better husband.

ANNE   His better doth not breathe upon the earth.

GLOSTER   He lives that loves you better than he could.

ANNE   Name him.

GLOSTER   Plantagenet.

ANNE   Why, that was he.

GLOSTER   The self-same name, but one of better nature.

ANNE   Where is he?

GLOSTER   Here: [*She spits at him.*] Why dost thou spit at me?

ANNE   'Would it were mortal poison, for thy sake!

GLOSTER   Never came poison from so sweet a place.

ANNE   Never hung poison on a fouler toad.
  Out of my sight! thou dost infect mine eyes.

GLOSTER   Thine eyes, sweet lady, have infected mine.

ANNE   Would they were basilisks, to strike thee dead!

GLOSTER   I would they were, that I might die at once,
  For now they kill me with a living death.
  Those eyes of thine from mine have drawn salt tears,
  Sham'd their aspects with store of childish drops:
  These eyes, which never shed remorseful tear;
  No, when my father York, and Edward wept
  To hear the piteous moan that Rutland made,
  When black-fac'd Clifford shook his sword at him;
  Nor when thy warlike father, like a child,
  Told the sad story of my father's death,
  And twenty times made pause to sob and weep,
  That all the standers-by had wet their cheeks,
  Like trees bedash'd with rain; in that sad time
  My manly eyes did scorn an humble tear:
  And what these sorrows could not thence exhale,
  Thy beauty hath, and made them blind with weeping.
  I never sued to friend, nor enemy;
  My tongue could never learn sweet smoothing word;

But now thy beauty is propos'd my fee,
My proud heart sues, and prompts my tongue to speak.

[*She looks scornfully at him.*
Teach not thy lip such scorn; for it was made
For kissing, lady, not for such contempt.
If thy revengeful heart cannot forgive,
Lo! here I lend thee this sharp-pointed sword;
Which if thou please to hide in this true breast,
And let the soul forth that adoreth thee,
I lay it naked to the deadly stroke,
And humbly beg the death upon my knee.

[*He lays his Breast open: she offers at it with his Sword.*
Nay, do not pause; for I did kill king Henry:—
But 't was thy beauty that provoked me.
Nay, now despatch; 't was I that stabbed young Edward;—
But 't was thy heavenly face that set me on.

[*She lets fall the Sword.*
Take up the sword again, or take up me.

ANNE   Arise, dissembler: though I wish thy death, I will not be thy executioner.

GLOSTER   Then bid me kill myself, and I will do it. [*Taking up the Sword.*

ANNE   I have already.

GLOSTER   That was in thy rage:
Speak it again, and even with the word,
This hand, which for thy love did kill thy love,
Shall for thy love kill a far truer love:
To both their deaths shalt thou be accessary.

ANNE   I would I knew thy heart.

GLOSTER   'T is figur'd in my tongue.

ANNE   I fear me, both are false.

GLOSTER   Then, never man was true.

ANNE   Well, well, put up your sword.

GLOSTER   Say, then, my peace is made.

ANNE   That shalt thou know hereafter.

GLOSTER   But shall I live in hope? [*Sheathing his Sword.*

ANNE   All men, I hope, live so.

GLOSTER   Vouchsafe to wear this ring.

ANNE   To take, is not to give. [*She puts on the Ring.*

GLOSTER   Look, how my ring encompasseth thy finger,
Even so thy breast encloseth my poor heart;

Wear both of them, for both of them are thine.
And if thy poor devoted suppliant may
But beg one favour at thy gracious hand,
Thou dost confirm his happiness for ever.

ANNE   What is it?

GLOSTER   That it may please you leave these sad designs
To him that hath most cause to be a mourner,
And presently repair to Crosby-place.
Where (after I have solemnly interr'd,
At Chertsey monastery, this noble king,
And wet his grave with my repentant tears)
I will with all expedient duty see you:
For divers unknown reasons, I beseech you,
Grant me this boon.

ANNE   With all my heart; and much it joys me too,
To see you are become so penitent.—
Tressel, and Berkley, go along with me.

GLOSTER   Bid me farewell.

ANNE   'T is more than you deserve;
But since you teach me how to flatter you,
Imagine I have said farewell already.

Exeunt Lady ANNE, TRESSEL, *and* BERKLEY

QUESTIONS

1. What really prompts Anne to change her thought about Gloster?
2. Is Anne capable of believing that any man is thoroughly bad? Why?
3. To what extent does Gloster play on Anne's guilelessness? On her vanity?

LE BOURGEOIS GENTILHOMME / Molière [1]

The conversation in this scene is between Monsieur Jourdain and his Master of Philosophy. Jourdain, a wealthy man who has worked hard all his life, has neither title nor noble family heritage. He has determined to begin an educational program that will prepare him for the day when he can pay court to a fine lady. The Dancing Master and the Singing Master have given Jourdain their lessons, then quarreled with the Master of Philosophy. As the scene (IV: 2) opens, Jourdain is alone with the Master of Philosophy and is consoling him.

MASTER OF PHILOSOPHY, MONSIEUR JOURDAIN

---

[1]Translated by Jean De Sales Bertram.

MASTER OF PHILOSOPHY [*as he adjusts his collar*]   Come! To our lesson!

MONSIEUR JOURDAIN   Oh, Monsieur, I am sorry about the blows they have given you.

MASTER   It is nothing. A philosopher accepts things as they come. I shall compose a satire against them in the style of Juvenal. I will tear them to pieces in fine fashion. Enough of that. What would you like to study?

JOURDAIN   Everything I can, for I am desirous of being as learned as possible. Oh, it makes me mad to think my father and mother didn't let me study all the sciences when I was young.

MASTER   A noble sentiment! *Nam sine doctrina vita est quasi mortis imago.* You understand that, and you know Latin, no doubt.

JOURDAIN   Yes, but proceed as if I did not know. Explain it to me.

MASTER   It means "Without knowledge, life is virtually an image of death."

JOURDAIN   That Latin expresses a true thought.

MASTER   Do you not have some of the principles, the rudiments of knowledge?

JOURDAIN   Oh, yes! I know how to read and write.

MASTER   Where would you like for us to begin? Do you wish to learn logic?

JOURDAIN   What is this logic?

MASTER   It is that which instructs the three functions of the mind.

JOURDAIN   What are these three functions of the mind?

MASTER   The first, the second, and the third. The first is to comprehend clearly by means of the universals. The second is to judge rightly by means of categories. And the third is to make proper deductions by means of the figures Barbara, Celarent, Darii, Ferio, Baralipton, and the like.

JOURDAIN   Whoof! Those words are tongue twisters. That logic just doesn't come through. Let's study other things that are more fun.

MASTER   Do you wish to learn moral science?

JOURDAIN   Moral science?

MASTER   Yes.

JOURDAIN   What is this moral science?

MASTER   It treats of perfect contentment, instructing all men to restrain their passions, and—

JOURDAIN   No, not that. I'm as passionate as the devil. When I feel like it, I want to indulge myself. None of your moral science.

MASTER   Would you like to learn physics?

JOURDAIN   Physics? What's physics?

MASTER   Physics is that which explains the principles of natural things and the properties of matter; it discourses on the nature of the elements, of metals, minerals, rocks, plants, and animals, and it instructs us in the causes of all meteors, the rainbow, rockets, comets, lightning, thunder, thunderbolts, rain, snow, hail, wind, and whirlwinds.

JOURDAIN   There's too much hubbub in that; too much confusion.

MASTER   Then what do you want me to teach you?

JOURDAIN   Teach me orthography.

MASTER   With pleasure.

JOURDAIN   Then you can teach me the almanac so that I may know when there is a moon and when there is none.

MASTER   Agreed. In order to comply with your request and to treat the matter according to philosophy, we must begin at the beginning with an exact knowledge of the nature of the letters and of the different manner of pronouncing all of them. And on this subject I have to tell you that the letters are divided into vowels, called vowels because they are sounded by the voice, and into consonants, so called because they are co-sounded with the vowels and set off the various articulations of the sounds. There are five vowels or sounds: A, E, I, O, U.

MASTER   The sound A is formed with the mouth about half open: A.

JOURDAIN   A. A. Yes.

MASTER   The sound E is formed with the corners of the mouth stretched toward the ears. A, E.

JOURDAIN   A, E, A, E. Faith! Indeed! E-E-E-E! This is splendid!

MASTER   And the sound I is formed by making the sound AH and the sound E in smooth succession: AH-E, AH-E, I. A, E, I.

JOURDAIN   AH-E, AH-E, I. A, E, I. How true! Long live science!

MASTER   The sound O is formed with the lips rounded: O.

JOURDAIN   O, O. Nothing could be more correct. A, E, I, O, I, O. This is splendid! I, O, I, O.

MASTER   The opening of the lips must be just like the circle that writes O.

JOURDAIN   O, O, O. You're right! O! Ah, how grand to know something!

MASTER   The sound of the letter YOU is OO. This sound OO is made by almost closing the teeth and making the lips form a circle smaller than the circle for O. The lips are tense, puckered, and protruded: OO.

JOURDAIN   OO, OO. Nothing could be truer! OO.

MASTER   Your two lips protrude as if making a pout. If you want to deprecate what someone says, or to boo him mildly, you need only say OO.

JOURDAIN   OO, OO. How true! Had I studied earlier I would know all this.

MASTER   Tomorrow we will deal with the other letters, the consonants.

JOURDAIN   Are they as exciting as the vowels?

MASTER   Indeed so. The consonant D, for example, is pronounced by raising the tip of the tongue to touch the upper gum ridge. D.

JOURDAIN   D, D. Yes. Ah! Delightful! Delightful!

MASTER   The F is pronounced by forcing the upper teeth against the lower lip. Fa.

JOURDAIN   Fa. Fa. That's true! Oh, fie on my father and mother.

MASTER   And for the R, bring the tip of the tongue close to the gums, then let it give way to the pressure of air rushing over the tongue. AR, RA.

JOURDAIN   AR. AR. RA. AR, AR, AR, AR, RA. That's true. Ah! You're clever! And how much time I've lost! AR. AR. RA.

MASTER   All these particulars I will explain to you thoroughly.

JOURDAIN   Please do! I must let you in on a secret. I am in love with a person of high rank, and I would like for you to help me write something to her—a little note which I wish to let fall at her feet.

MASTER   Very well.

JOURDAIN   Something that will be quite gallant. Yes.

MASTER   Of course. Do you wish to write in verse?

JOURDAIN   No. No. No verses.

MASTER   Do you want only prose?

JOURDAIN   No. I do not want prose or verse.

MASTER   But it must be one or the other.

JOURDAIN   Why?

MASTER   Because, Monsieur, everything is expressed in either prose or verse.

JOURDAIN   Is there nothing but prose or verse?

MASTER   Nothing, Monsieur. All that is not prose is verse, and all that is not verse is prose.

JOURDAIN   And what is it when we speak?

MASTER   Prose.

JOURDAIN   What? When I say, "Nicole, bring me my slippers and give me my nightcap," that is prose?

MASTER   Yes, Monsieur.

JOURDAIN   Faith! For more than forty years I have been speaking prose without knowing it. I am very much obliged to you for having taught me this fact. I would like, then, to put this into a note to her: "Beautiful Lady, your beautiful eyes make me die of love." But I would like to say that in a gallant manner, turned in elegant phrases.

MASTER   Write that the fire of her eyes reduces your heart to cinders, that because of her night and day you suffer the fury of—

JOURDAIN   No. No. No. I don't want to say all that. I want to say only what I told you: "Beautiful Lady, your beautiful eyes make me die of love."

MASTER   You need to expand that statement. It is too short.

JOURDAIN   No. You heard me. In the note I want only those words which I spoke, but turned elegantly and arranged fashionably. I beg you to show me the different ways they can be put.

MASTER   First, they can be put as you said: "Beautiful Lady, your beautiful eyes make me die of love." Or "Of love to die make me, Beautiful Lady, your beautiful eyes." Or "Your eyes beautiful of love make me, Beautiful Lady, to die." Or "To die your beautiful eyes, Beautiful Lady, of love make me." Or "Make me your eyes beautiful to die, Beautiful Lady, of love."

JOURDAIN   Of all these ways which is best?

MASTER   What you have already said: "Beautiful Lady, your beautiful eyes make me die of love."

JOURDAIN   I have never studied, yet I said that in the first place. I thank you with all my heart, and I beg you to come tomorrow early.

MASTER   I will not fail to be here.

JOURDAIN   Now. What's this? Has my suit not yet come?

LACKEY   [*offstage*]   No, Monsieur.

JOURDAIN   That damnable tailor! He has kept me waiting this whole day while I've had so much business to attend to. He makes me mad. That hangman! I hope gets a four-day fever! The devil take him. The plague kill him. If I could get hold of that detestable tailor this very minute, why that dog, that traitor, I—

QUESTIONS

1. What motivates Jourdain in this scene? A sincere wish to learn? An interest in social advancement? His desire to impress someone else? Other reasons?

2. What motivates the Master of Philosophy? An eagerness to earn money? A wish to make fun of Jourdain? A sincere interest in Jourdain as an individual? Other reasons?

3. What is the focal point of the scene?

4. How does this scene advance the main theme and purpose of the whole play?

SAINT JOAN / George Bernard Shaw

Romanticizers have often sought to present Joan of Arc as a fragile, angelic figure. George Bernard Shaw saw her as a hardy, healthy, hearty peasant girl with a determined mind, simple speech, and sharp tongue when the occasion demanded. This passage of the play[2] presents Joan under trial before the Inquisition. The trial takes place in a town controlled by the English forces and in the court of Cauchon, the powerful bishop of Beauvais.

THE INQUISITOR [*kindly*] Sit down, Joan. [*She sits on the prisoner's stool*]. You look very pale today. Are you not well?

JOAN Thank you kindly: I am well enough. But the Bishop sent me some carp; and it made me ill.

CAUCHON I am sorry. I told them to see that it was fresh.

JOAN You meant to be good to me, I know; but it is a fish that does not agree with me. The English thought you were trying to poison me—

CAUCHON   } [*together*] { What!
THE CHAPLAIN }   { No, my lord.

JOAN [*continuing*] They are determined that I shall be burnt as a witch; and they sent their doctor to cure me; but he was forbidden to bleed me because the silly people believe that a witch's witchery leaves her if she is bled; so he only called me filthy names. Why do you leave me in the hands of the English? I should be in the hands of the Church. And why must I be chained by the feet to a log of wood? Are you afraid I will fly away?

D'ESTIVET [*harshly*] Woman: it is not for you to question the court; it is for us to question you.

COURCELLES When you were left unchained, did you not try to escape by jumping from a tower sixty feet high? If you cannot fly like a witch, how is it that you are still alive?

JOAN I suppose because the tower was not so high then. It has grown higher every day since you began asking me questions about it.

D'ESTIVET Why did you jump from the tower?

JOAN How do you know that I jumped?

D'ESTIVET You were found lying in the moat. Why did you leave the tower?

JOAN Why would anybody leave a prison if they could get out?

D'ESTIVET You tried to escape?

JOAN Of course I did; and not for the first time either. If you leave the door of the cage open the bird will fly out.

D'ESTIVET [*rising*] That is a confession of heresy. I call the attention of the court to it.

JOAN Heresy, he calls it! Am I a heretic because I try to escape from prison?

D'ESTIVET Assuredly, if you are in the hands of the Church, and you wilfully take yourself out of its hands, you are deserting the Church; and that is heresy.

JOAN It is great nonsense. Nobody could be such a fool as to think that.

D'ESTIVET You hear, my lord, how I am reviled in the execution of my duty by this woman. [*He sits down indignantly*].

CAUCHON I have warned you before, Joan, that you are doing yourself no good by these pert answers.

JOAN But you will not talk sense to me. I am reasonable if you will be reasonable.

THE INQUISITOR [*interposing*] This is not yet in order. You forget, Master Promoter, that the proceedings have not been formally opened. The time for questions is after she has sworn on the Gospels to tell us the whole truth.

JOAN You say this to me every time. I have said again and again that I will tell you all that concerns this trial. But I cannot tell you the whole truth: God does not allow the whole truth to be told. You do not understand it when I tell it. It is an old saying that he who tells too much truth is sure to be hanged. I am weary of this argument: we have been over it nine times already. I have sworn as much as I will swear; and I will swear no more.

COURCELLES My lord: she should be put to the torture.

THE INQUISITOR You hear, Joan? That is what happens to the obdurate. Think before you answer. Has she been shewn the instruments?

THE EXECUTIONER They are ready, my lord. She has seen them.

JOAN If you tear me limb from limb until you separate my soul from my body you will get nothing out of me beyond what I have told you. What more is there to tell that you could understand? Besides, I cannot bear to be hurt; and if you hurt me I will say anything you like to stop the pain. But I will take it all back afterwards; so what is the use of it?

LADVENU There is much in that. We should proceed mercifully.

COURCELLES But the torture is customary.

THE INQUISITOR It must not be applied wantonly. If the accused will confess voluntarily, then its use cannot be justified.

COURCELLES But this is unusual and irregular. She refuses to take the oath.

LADVENU [*disgusted*] Do you want to torture the girl for the mere pleasure of it?

COURCELLES [*bewildered*] But it is not a pleasure. It is the law. It is customary. It is always done.

THE INQUISITOR That is not so, Master, except when the inquiries are carried on by people who do not know their legal business.

COURCELLES   But the woman is a heretic. I assure you it is always done.

CAUCHON [*decisively*]   It will not be done today if it is not necessary. Let there be an end of this. I will not have it said that we proceeded on forced confessions. We have sent our best preachers and doctors to this woman to exhort and implore her to save her soul and body from the fire: we shall not now send the executioner to thrust her into it.

COURCELLES   Your lordship is merciful, of course. But it is a great responsibility to depart from the usual practice.

JOAN   Thou art a rare noodle, Master. Do what was done last time is thy rule, eh?

COURCELLES [*rising*]   Thou wanton: dost thou dare call me noodle?

THE INQUISITOR   Patience, Master, patience: I fear you will soon be only too terribly avenged.

COURCELLES [*mutters*]   Noodle indeed! [*He sits down, much discontentd*].

THE INQUISITOR   Meanwhile, let us not be moved by the rough side of a shepherd lass's tongue.

JOAN   Nay: I am no shepherd lass, though I have helped with the sheep like anyone else. I will do a lady's work in the house—spin or weave—against any woman in Rouen.

THE INQUISITOR   This is not a time for vanity, Joan. You stand in great peril.

JOAN   I know it: have I not been punished for my vanity? If I had not worn my cloth of gold surcoat in battle like a fool, that Burgundian soldier would never have pulled me backwards off my horse; and I should not have been here.

THE CHAPLAIN   If you are so clever at woman's work why do you not stay at home and do it?

JOAN   There are plenty of other women to do it; but there is nobody to do my work.

CAUCHON   Come! we are wasting time on trifles. Joan: I am going to put a most solemn question to you. Take care how you answer; for your life and salvation are at stake on it. Will you for all you have said and done, be it good or bad, accept the judgment of God's Church on earth? More especially as to the acts and words that are imputed to you in this trial by the Promoter here, will you submit your case to the inspired interpretation of the Church Militant?

JOAN   I am a faithful child of the Church. I will obey the Church—

CAUCHON [*hopefully leaning forward*]   You will?

JOAN   —provided it does not command anything impossible.

CAUCHON *sinks back in his chair with a heavy sigh.* THE INQUISITOR *purses his lips and frowns.* LADVENU *shakes his head pitifully.*

D'ESTIVET   She imputes to the Church the error and folly of commanding the impossible.

JOAN If you command me to declare that all that I have done and said, and all the visions and revelations I have had, were not from God, then that is impossible: I will not declare it for anything in the world. What God made me do I will never go back on; and what He has commanded or shall command I will not fail to do in spite of any man alive. That is what I mean by impossible. And in case the Church should bid me do anything contrary to the command I have from God, I will not consent to it, no matter what it may be.

THE ASSESSORS [*shocked and indignant*] Oh! The Church contrary to God! What do you say now? Flat heresy. This is beyond everything, etc., etc.

D'ESTIVET [*throwing down his brief*] My lord: do you need anything more than this?

QUESTIONS

1. Cite specific instances in her speeches that present Shaw's conception of Joan.
2. Outline the chief characteristics of each person as he appears in this scene.
3. How do you propose to differentiate among the characters? Justify your manner of presentation.

RIDERS TO THE SEA / John Millington Synge

In the final sequence of *Riders to the Sea,* Maurya mourns the loss of her sons. Her grief augments her fatigue and exhaustion so that she speaks with great effort.

MAURYA [*raising her head and speaking as if she did not see the people around her*] They're all gone now, and there isn't anything more the sea can do to me. . . . I'll have no call now to be up crying and praying when the wind breaks from the south, and you can hear the surf is in the east, and the surf is in the west, making a great stir with the two noises, and they hitting one on the other. I'll have no call now to be going down and getting Holy Water in the dark nights after Samhain, and I won't care what way the sea is when the other women will be keening. [*To* NORA]. Give me the Holy Water, Nora, there's a small sup still on the dresser.

NORA *gives it to her.*

MAURYA [*Drops* MICHAEL'S *clothes across* BARTLEY'S *feet, and sprinkles the Holy Water over him* It isn't that I haven't prayed for you, Bartley, to the Almighty God. It isn't that I haven't said prayers in the dark night till you wouldn't know what I'ld be saying; but it's a great rest I'll have now, and it's time surely. It's a great rest I'll have now, and great sleeping in the long nights after Samhain, if it's only a bit of wet flour we do have to eat, and maybe a fish that would be stinking. [*She kneels down again, crossing herself, and saying prayers under her breath.*]

CATHLEEN [*to an* OLD MAN]   Maybe yourself and Eamon would make a coffin when the sun rises. We have fine white boards herself bought, God help her, thinking Michael would be found, and I have a new cake you can eat while you'll be working.

THE OLD MAN [*looking at the boards*]   Are there nails with them?

CATHLEEN   There are not, Colum; we didn't think of the nails.

ANOTHER MAN   It's a great wonder she wouldn't think of the nails, and all the coffins she's seen made already.

CATHLEEN   It's getting old she is, and broken.

MAURYA *stands up again very slowly and spreads out the pieces of* MICHAEL'S *clothes beside the body, sprinkling them with the last of the Holy Water.*

NORA [*in a whisper to Cathleen*]   She's quiet now and easy; but the day Michael was drowned you could hear her crying out from this to the spring well. It's fonder she was of Michael, and would any one have thought that?

CATHLEEN [*slowly and clearly*]   An old woman will be soon tired with anything she will do, and isn't it nine days herself is after crying and keening, and making great sorrow in the house?

MAURYA [*puts the empty cup mouth downwards on the table, and lays her hands together on* BARTLEY'S *feet*]   They're all together this time, and the end is come. May the Almighty God have mercy on Bartley's soul, and on Michael's soul, and on the souls of Sheamus and Patch, and Stephen and Shawn *(bending her head)*; and may He have mercy on my soul, Nora, and on the soul of every one is left living in the world.

[*She pauses, and the keen rises a little more loudly from the women, then sinks away.*]

MAURYA [*continuing*]   Michael has a clean burial in the far north, by the grace of the Almighty God. Bartley will have a fine coffin out of the white boards, and a deep grave surely. What more can we want than that? No man at all can be living for ever, and we must be satisfied.

She kneels down again and the curtain falls slowly.

QUESTIONS

1. How would you describe Maurya's predominant emotion in this scene? Bitterness? Peacefulness? Quiet resignation? Other?

2. To whom is she speaking? To herself? To those in the room? To an unseen presence? Justify your answer.

3. Can you present this selection *aloud* as if you were *thinking* Maurya's thoughts for the first time?

HOW TO DEVELOP THE EAR AND THE VOICE

———◦•◦———

PREVIEW

Listening is a process of thinking about what is heard. You have already been given some suggestions in Part One about what to listen for in oral literature. Material in Part Two has sought to demonstrate that you can further train your ear to listen efficiently and intelligently by performing listening exercises in awareness of sounds you encounter every day and by listening to determine ideas, feelings, and attitudes in speech and readings. Develop standards of evaluation. They can help you focus your attention as you listen.

An effective way to improve your diction is to study the International Phonetic Alphabet. Your ear may be trained to become increasingly discriminating through practice in the accurate production of speech sounds and through facility in phonetic transcription. This ear training contributes immeasurably toward your development of good speech.

Controlled exhalation is a process of controlling the outward flow of breath so that you can sustain phonation as needed. In this connection make the most efficient use of breath in speech by vocalizing the instant of exhalation. A clear knowledge of how to use the voice efficiently aids oral reader and listener alike. No "techniques," however, can supersede the necessity for perceiving and experiencing the literature.

5. Ear Training and Listening

Reference has been made frequently in this text to ear training. The value of attuning the ear to the rhythms of poetry, prose, and drama cannot be overemphasized. The more sensitive the ear is to sounds—to the melody and rhythm of vowel sounds and the interruption of their smooth flow by the consonant sounds—the more effectively the reader can convey the emotional quality of those sounds. The ear that is trained to catch changes in quality, inflection, pitch, and rate serves as a valuable tool in perceiving even the slightest shift in the unfoldment of ideas.

Students of the voice can use tape recorders to study their own performance through repeated playbacks. Without a tape recorder, a good substitute may be improvised wherever two walls join together to make a corner. If the reader stands in the corner as close as he can to the walls, using his hands to cup his ears forward, he can hear himself very much as others hear him. This method is most effective if the student knows his material well enough to be free from the book. Holding the book with one hand and cupping one ear with the other hand is useful though not so effective as cupping both ears to magnify the sound.

Most of us have the idea that because we have ears and hear, we naturally listen. Listening and hearing are two different functions. We hear the ring of the alarm clock, the rush of water in the shower, the bubble-de-dup of coffee percolating, the screech of brakes, the click of the cash register, the clatter of dishes and silver in the cafeteria, the thump of shoes on concrete campus walks. Students hear most of these sounds every day. Until they react to these sounds, they only hear them. They listen to these sounds only when they think, react, and find their behavior influenced or changed by them. Listening, then, is a process of thinking about what is heard. In the selection that follows we find two people who fail to communicate with each other because they fail to listen to one another.

ON CONVERSATION / Ring Lardner [1]

The other night I happened to be comeing back from Wilmington, Del. to wherever I was going and was setting in the smokeing compartment or whatever they now call the wash room and overheard a conversation between two fellows who we will call Mr. Butler and Mr. Hawkes. Both of them seemed to be from the same town and I only wished I could repeat the conversation verbatim but the best I can do is report it from memory. The fellows evidently had not met for some three to fifteen years as the judges say.

"Well," said Mr. Hawkes, "if this isn't Dick Butler!"

"Well," said Mr. Butler, "if it isn't Dale Hawkes."

"Well, Dick," said Hawkes, "I never expected to meet you on this train."

"No," replied Butler. "I genally always take Number 28. I just took this train this evening because I had to be in Wilmington today."

"Where are you headed for?" asked Hawkes.

"Well, I am going to the big town," said Butler.

"So am I, and I am certainly glad we happened to be in the same car."

"I am glad too, but it is funny we happened to be in the same car."

It seemed funny to both of them but they successfully concealed it so far as facial expression was conserned. After a pause Hawkes spoke again:

"How long since you been back in Lansing?"

"Me?" replied Butler. "I ain't been back there for 12 years."

"I ain't been back there either myself for ten years. How long since you been back there?"

"I ain't been back there for twelve years."

"I ain't been back there myself for ten years. Where are you headed for?"

"New York," replied Butler. "I have got to get there about once a year. Where are you going?"

"Me?" asked Hawkes. "I am going to New York too. I have got to go down there every little while for the firm."

"Do you have to go there very often?"

"Me? Every little while. How often do you have to go there?"

"About once a year. How often do you get back to Lansing?"

"Last time I was there was ten years ago. How long since you was back?"

"About twelve years ago. Lot of changes there since we left there."

"That's the way I figured it. It makes a man seem kind of old to go back there and not see nobody you know."

"You said something. I go along the streets there now and don't see nobody I know."

"How long since you was there?"[2]

---

[1]"On Conversation" from *A General Commentary* is reprinted with the permission of Charles Scribner's Sons from *First and Last* by Ring Lardner. Copyright 1934 by Ellis A. Lardner; renewal copyright © 1962 Ring Lardner, Jr.

[2]This speech must be Butler's, since Hawkes answers the question. But the preceding speech must also be Butler's; check back to the last identified speeches above. Read the last two paragraphs as one speech by Butler.

"Me?" said Hawkes. "I only get back there about once every ten years. By the way what become of old man Kelsey?"

"Who do you mean, Kelsey?"

"Yes, what become of him?"

"Old Kelsey? Why he has been dead for ten years."

"Oh, I didn't know that. And what become of his daughter? I mean Eleanor."

"Why Eleanor married a man named Forster or Jennings or something like that from Flint."

"Yes, but I mean the other daughter, Louise."

"Oh, she's married."

"Where are you going now?"

"I am headed for New York on business for the firm."

"I have to go there about once a year myself—for the firm."

"Do you get back to Lansing very often?"

"About once in ten or twelve years. I hardly know anybody there now. It seems funny to go down the street and not know nobody."

"That's the way I always feel. It seems like it was not my old home town at all. I go up and down the street and don't know anybody and nobody speaks to you. I guess I know more people in New York now than I do in Lansing."

"Do you get to New York often?"

"Only about once a year. I have to go there for the firm."

"New York isn't the same town it used to be neither."

"No, it is changeing all the time. Just like Lansing. I guess they all change."

"I don't know much about Lansing any more. I only get there about once in ten or twelve years."

"What are you reading there?"

"Oh, it is just a little article in Asia. They's a good many interesting articles in Asia."

"I only seen a couple copies of it. This thing I am reading is a little article on 'Application' in the American."

"Well, go ahead and read and don't let me disturb you."

"Well I just wanted to finish it up. Go ahead and finish what you're reading yourself."

"All right. We will talk things over later. It is funny we happened to get on the same car."

There are many ways in which you can train your ear to hear with precision and your mind to attend with vigilance through the ear. Indeed, you can devise such ways rapidly once you start giving them some thought. Here are a few to begin.

1. Look back at the paragraph preceding the selection *On Conversation*. There, identified in relatively stereotyped phrases, are sounds that a student might hear during a forenoon. Try to describe similar sounds with more freshness and accuracy. For example, listen to your alarm clock tomorrow morning. Does it ring? Or buzz? Or snarl? Or hum? What is its pitch? Do

you hear its sound as a vowel? What vowel? Do you hear its sound as a consonant? One student gave his alarm clock away because it ruined his day by starting him off with a persistent [æ æ æ]. He said that one of the best things he ever did for himself was to buy a clock that sounded [hmmm].

Now think about your best friend. Could you recognize his footsteps? Listen to feet passing in the hall, approaching your room, or walking beside you on campus. How do they differ? Keep listening carefully. Within a week you should be able to identify several footsteps.

How many voices can you recognize? What distinguishes one from the other?

2. Write some descriptions of noises and sounds you hear during the day. Use a thesaurus and a dictionary to help you make your statement as accurate as possible. The more precise your thought about the sounds, the more precise your skill in hearing and listening.

3. In music courses you learn to identify structure—the motif, the various themes, the phrases. You can also, by persistent effort, train yourself to listen to the structure in literature. Reading aloud often enables you to improve your mental sense of hearing and listening.

4. Listen systematically to a series of oral events. Record what you hear, using the following list of items:

LISTENING CHECK LIST

Name of speaker (*as* John Doe, student)
Type of presentation (*as* Poetry reading)
Date of presentation
Speaker's vocal quality *(describe this as completely and accurately as you can)*
Speaker's main thoughts *(two or three)*
Speaker's attitude (*as* Earnest, Indifferent, Partisan, Hostile, Friendly)
Rating of speaker (*as* Excellent, Good, Satisfactory, Poor)
Reason for rating

Make notes of this type to report on activities which include listening to two recordings, two oral presentations in person by students, two television newscasters, two personalities on radio. Make them for eight consecutive days, one each day. Then notice what you have observed about your own listening habits—in speech and interpretation classes, in English classes, in ordinary conversation.

5. Listen to yourself. If you don't have a tape recorder, remember that a corner which you can face and to which you cup your ear will serve the purpose. Now rate yourself on the same list of items. Re-rate yourself each week. Don't be surprised if you hit a plateau for a while. Keep trying. Keep practicing. A few months' work will bring remarkable improvements, the

result of your being able to hear yourself, to evaluate and control your voice, to make your voice perform as your mind directs.

A student who had followed such a program of ear training and listening for some months was working late on a term paper. As the hands of the clock passed midnight, he sensed a change in the sounds outside. He made a few notes from time to time as he continued to write through the night. When he finished the paper, he organized and rewrote his listening notes to read:

All night my pen scratched across paper. In swift succession, the early morning hours hurried by. Slippered one o'clock came stealing through the grasses. She paused beneath my window to whisper, "Hush!"

Blatant two o'clock raced through the street and chased a tin can to the corner. He tapped on my windowpane and then ran on.

Three o'clock stirred in the trees and jarred a sparrow from his sleep. He protested; she answered flippantly. A cock crowed.

Creative listening—in the very midst of drudgery!

VOICE ATTRIBUTES

In the Listening Check List above you are asked to describe "vocal quality." What are you listening for when you listen for quality? Quality is one of four major aspects of sound which should be discussed now in order to help you deal adequately with this and other evaluation check lists that follow. Your attention is, accordingly, directed briefly to a consideration of quality, time, pitch, and loudness.

Quality

Quality, sometimes called *timbre,* is that characteristic of sound which distinguishes one voice from another, one musical instrument from another. There is, for example, a difference in the quality of sound produced by the oboe as compared with that produced by a French horn. If you play the E string on the violin the string vibrates as a whole and also in sections. The tone resulting from the vibration of the whole is called a *fundamental,* and the tones resulting from vibrations of the sections are called *overtones* or *harmonics.* Quality is the result of overtones accompanying the fundamental. During phonation you produce both a fundamental tone which vibrates at the rate of so many cycles per second and also many harmonic tones that vibrate at higher rates than the fundamental (multiples of the fundamental frequency). The human voice is capable of far more variations in quality than any musical instrument. The voice which produces a combination of sounds that is pleasing to the ear by reason of its harmonics is said to have a pleasing vocal quality. In the listening assignment for vocal quality you are not asked to determine the acoustics for each voice but rather to react (admittedly subjectively) to the individual's distinguishing character-istic (quality) of voice. The effective oral reader will vary quality according to the dictates of the intellectual and emotional content in order to empha-size various points. Quality is not a single element in itself but rather a com-plex and composite attribute of sound. A major aspect of quality is the resonance of the speaker's voice.

Resonance

The three main resonators of the human voice are the pharynx, the nasal cavity, and the mouth. Speech sounds are modified by the resonators accord-ing to the size and shape of the resonators, according to the size of their openings, and according to the texture of their structures. Even without performing specific experiments, most people are ready to agree that the quality of sound produced by tapping an inverted oatmeal carton would not be the same as that produced by tapping a metal container of the same size and shape. Three cartons of the same substance but of different sizes or shapes would yield different sounds. If you were to puncture one of them to provide an opening or openings, the quality of the sound would be further modified. The effect of such differences on resonance is important not only in musical instruments but also in the human voice.

The human pharynx as a resonator can be altered somewhat by the move-ment of the back of the tongue, by the epiglottis, or by a change in the mus-culature which lines the back walls of the pharynx. Muscles relaxed and resilient will provide one kind of sounding board; muscles tense and con-stricted, another; and the sound which "bounces off" these differing textures will also be of differing quality. The interdependence of the muscles—not only of the pharynx but also of the entire body—is such that it is virtually impossible to relax individual muscles and to tense others, especially if they are closely related. You can help keep your pharynx "in tune" by following the tension-relieving program outlined on pages 141-144 and by maintain-ing the tongue in the position and at the tension required for accurate pro-duction of the various speech sounds.

The nasal cavity is not subject to as much alteration as the pharynx. At the posterior opening, the soft palate (velum) should be lowered for the production of [m], [n], and [ŋ] but should be elevated for all other sounds, particularly the vowels even when they are sounded between any two of the three nasal consonants. Since the operation of the soft palate cannot be readily seen during the production of all sounds, it is not practical to try to govern its movement consciously. Attention should rather be given to forming the sounds correctly and articulating distinctly. Keeping healthy

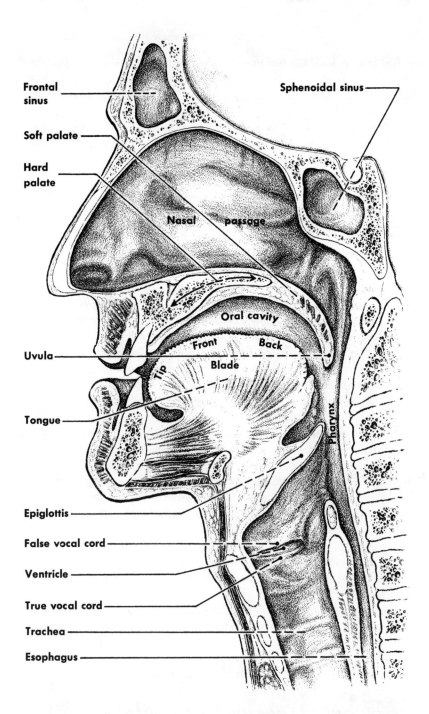

Frontal
sinus

Sphenoidal sinus

Soft palate

Hard
palate

Nasal   passage

Oral cavity

Front   Back

Blade

Uvula

Tip

Pharynx

Tongue

Epiglottis

False vocal cord

Ventricle

True vocal cord

Trachea

Esophagus

SAGGITAL SECTION OF HEAD, MOUTH, AND THROAT

and free from colds is the best one can do to maintain satisfactory operation of the anterior opening to the nasal chamber. Aside from such physiological phenomena as a deviated septum, polyps, or the like, there is no other way of altering this cavity.

The resonator most subject to alteration is the mouth. Adjustments may be made by the tongue with respect to its position and tension, by the jaw, by the lips, and by the teeth in their relation to the other articulators. Exercises for the development of oral resonance may be found on pages 124-126. Meanwhile, check the diagram on page 97 and learn the terms for the labeled portions. Reference will be made to these areas in later notations on the production of speech sounds, so you will need to know them.

Time

Time includes the rate at which one speaks, the number and length of pauses used, the duration of the vowel sounds. Fairbanks reports that an excellent oral reading rate for college men and women was found to be 160 to 170 words per minute.[3] Choose a passage of some 500 words and ask a friend to time you as you read aloud. How many words per minute did you average? Mark the same passage at intervals of 160 words. Try to read each portion in one minute. Was communication improved? Try a faster rate, then a slower rate. What is your reaction to these different rates? At which rate did you communicate most effectively to your friend? Do you find that your rate varies according to the emotional nature of the oral reading? Now consider the *pauses* in your oral interpretation. Do they follow a distinct pattern, or do they vary according to the content of the material? *Duration* is another aspect of time in speech. Do you say your vowels quickly, or prolong them? Can you control them? Poetry in particular is written with careful regard for vowel duration. Are you allowing sufficient duration of the vowels to achieve the effect which the poet desired?

Pitch

Pitch in speech is much like pitch in music; an oral reader's voice tones are high or low on the musical scale. A tone that is high in pitch is also high in *frequency;* a tone low in pitch is also low in frequency. Musicians and psychologists tend to speak of pitch, physicists and engineers of frequency. Differences in frequency are perceived by the human ear as changes in pitch. An *inflection* is a change in pitch during phonation. A reader's *range* is the total number of tones which he can produce with some degree of quality on an ascending and descending scale. If the lowest note that a

---

[3]Grant Fairbanks, *Voice and Articulation Drillbook,* 2nd ed., New York: Harper and Row, 1960; p. 115.

speaker can vocalize is second G below middle C and the highest note is the first G above middle C, then that individual has a speaking range of two full octaves or twenty-three semitones. *Habitual pitch* is the pitch to which the voice most frequently returns.

Ask a friend to help you determine your habitual pitch. With your friend seated at the piano ask him to listen as you speak or read and to strike those notes which you use the most. (If you find the process makes you self-conscious or causes constriction in the throat, stand to one side of the piano so as not to see the keys.) To which notes did your voice return most often? There you have your habitual pitch. How many notes did your voice produce? There you have your range—not necessarily your potential range but the range you actually used. If you find your range is less than one octave, or not much more you will want to practice the exercises on pages 123-124. Having determined your habitual pitch, you will want to discover your optimum pitch. Optimum pitch is that level of pitch at which you produce a clear, ringing tone and the greatest loudness with the least effort. Each individual will have his own optimum pitch, for that pitch appears to depend upon a variety of such personal factors as anatomy, structural relationships, breathing habits and patterns, and utilization of resonance.

Ask a friend to help you find your optimum pitch by striking notes on the piano as you sing down the scale until you reach the lowest note you can sing easily and with acceptable vocal quality. Now sing up the scale to the fourth whole tone from this lowest note and sustain [ɑ] on that note. Use that same single tone to chant a sentence. If you are uncertain how to chant, practice the vocal exercise on page 123. Then proceed to read or speak a few sentences naturally and have your friend observe whether that tone—the fourth whole note up from your lowest—was the one to which you most frequently returned. If so, does your throat feel freer? Does the tone sound clearer? Your task is to discover the frequency which your particular resonators are tuned to amplify. When you have made this individual discovery, you have determined your optimum pitch and so made a major step forward in achieving your true vocal potential. Your optimum pitch should become your habitual pitch. Further suggestions for achieving such a goal will be found on page 126 in the vocal exercise for tone placement. You may also consult Virgil Anderson's text[4] for other procedures in finding and developing optimum pitch.

Loudness

Loudness refers to the degree to which you can make yourself heard. This term is sometimes used interchangeably with *volume, projection,* and

---

[4]Virgil A. Anderson, *Training the Speaking Voice,* 2nd ed., New York: Oxford University Press, 1961; pp. 84-86.

strength. If you have difficulty achieving adequate loudness, consult your instructor.

Those desiring additional information on these four aspects of sound—quality, time, pitch, and loudness—may investigate references listed under sections "Phonetics and Practice Material" and "Acoustics of Speech" in Chapter 8.

EVALUATION CHECK LISTS

The oral reader expects to have his work evaluated—by peers, by instructors, by prospective employers, by himself. The evaluations will range from casual to searching, the methods from intuitive and subjective to systematic and objective. The systematic evaluators will use check lists and rating scales; with these the oral reader, the one who is being evaluated, should be familiar. He needs this familiarity in his capacity as listener as well as in his capacity as reader.

Here follows an assortment of such check lists for evaluating readers. They come from departments of drama, education, speech, and radio-television-film training. Knowing the items that evaluators watch and listen for, you can watch and listen for the same items and thereby improve the satisfaction you get from your oral reading and the satisfaction you give to your listeners.

Reading Aloud in General

1. The INTELLECTUAL MEANING was (completely, partially, not at all) communicated.
2. The EMOTIONAL MEANING was (completely, partially, not at all) communicated.
3. VOICE:
    a. The reader used (good, average, poor) variety of RATE.
    b. The reader made (good, average, poor) use of PAUSE.
    c. The reader used (good, average, poor) variety of PITCH.
    d. The reader's use of TONE COLOR or QUALITY was (appropriate, inappropriate) for the selection.
    e. The reader used (too much, the right amount of, too little) VOLUME.
    f. His SENSE STRESS on words and phrases was (appropriate, sometimes appropriate, inappropriate).
4. PHYSICAL APPEARANCE:
    a. EYE CONTACT (frequent, occasional, infrequent, none).
    b. FACIAL EXPRESSION (animated, somewhat animated, not animated sufficiently).
    c. POSTURE (appropriate, inappropriate).

Poetry Reading

1. Introduction (superior, good, average, poor)
2. Interpretation—as opposed to mere reading or singsong rendition (superior, good, average, poor)
3. Conception of:
    a. Sensory images (superior, good, average, poor)
    b. Emotional appeal (superior, good, average, poor)
    c. Intellectual values—idea (superior, good, average, poor)
    d. Wonder, magic, and enchantment (superior, good, average, poor)
4. Voice—clarity, distinctness, pleasantness (superior, good, average, poor)
5. Poise: (superior, good, average, poor)

Storytelling

1. Choice of story (superior, good, average, poor)
2. Introduction (s, g, a, p)
3. Interpretation:
    a. Directness (s, g, a, p)
    b. Sincerity (s, g, a, p)
4. Conception of dramatic values (s, g, a, p)
5. Voice—clarity, distinctness, pleasantness (s, g, a, p)
6. Poise (s, g, a, p)
7. Vitality (s, g, a, p)

Book Talk

1. Use of imagination (superior, good, average, poor)
2. Coverage of material:
    a. Scope of text (s, g, a, p)
    b. Illustrations (s, g, a, p)
    c. Quality of book (s, g, a, p)
    d. Use in curriculum (s, g, a, p)
3. Poise in handling of book (s, g, a, p)
4. Vocal quality—clarity, distinctness, pleasantness (s, g, a, p)
5. Speech:
    a. Unaffectedness (s, g, a, p)
    b. Freedom from grammatical errors (s, g, a, p)
6. Reading—evidence of perception and lively interest (s, g, a, p)
7. Enthusiasm (s, g, a, p)

Announcer Rating

(The rater grades the announcer 1, 2, 3, 4, or 5 on each item, 1 being the highest rating and 5 the lowest. The grades are totaled and averaged for an over-all rating.)

1. Appropriateness of style
2. Authority

3. Warmth
4. Flow
5. Vocal variety
6. Enunciation
7. Pronunciation
8. Meaning
9. Use of physical resources:
   a. Eye contact
   b. Body gestures
   c. Emphasis techniques

Oral Interpretation of Literature

(The oral reader is rated according to a five-number scale from 1 to 5, in which 1 = poor, 2 = below average, 3 = average, 4 = above average, 5 = excellent.)

choice of material
1. Understanding and comprehension of author's intent
2. Suitability in terms of reader's age, sex, and experience
3. Appropriateness for audience
4. Total effectiveness and clarity of cutting

delivery
1. Volume and physical projection
2. Eye contact with audience
3. Phrasing and use of pause
4. Rate of speaking
5. Rhythm of speaking
6. Vocal variety
7. Diction and pronunciation

stage presence
1. Poise and control
2. Gesture and movement
3. Facial expression
4. Physical characterizations

general effectiveness
1. Projection of thought content
2. Projection of emotional content
3. Degree of response shared with audience

Ranking Sheet for Oral-Interpretation Contests

(These are items used for rating contestants who are to be ranked in relation to one another. The rating scale is from 1 to 9, in which 9 signifies the most favorable reaction and 1 the least favorable.)

1. Understanding and projection of thought
2. Understanding and projection of emotional content
3. Use of voice:
   a. Quality
   b. Loudness
   c. Pitch
   d. Rate
   e. Flexibility
4. Pronunciation and articulation
5. Total bodily response
6. Platform poise:
   a. Ease
   b. Posture
   c. Use of reading stand
   d. Handling of script
7. General over-all effectiveness

You can use any or all of these check lists as guides for systematic listening, for evaluating your own performance, or for exchanging evaluations with your friends. You are likely to discover that the shorter lists are the easier to use. The more judgments required, the greater the difficulty for the evaluator; and fatigue contributes to discrepancies in ratings.

In practice, these check lists should be arranged for ease and rapidity of use, with space for the name and other data about the reader, evaluation symbols that can be underscored or circled, spaces for totaling and averaging, and other convenient features. Your own organization may print or mimeograph forms of this sort for you.

You may, from your own experience, be able to improve these check lists. For example, you may come to think that it is better to evaluate on a scale of uneven numbers (three or five or seven) rather than on a scale of even numbers (four or six or eight). You may find that it is easier to give recognition to small improvements if seven or nine levels are evaluated rather than three or five. You may discover that some attributes should be evaluated in addition to or instead of those in the lists. By giving thought to such matters you will very probably improve your performance as an oral reader in addition to perceiving what contributes to good and poor performance.

6. The Sounds of Speech

The chapter preceding this one was designed for training the ear in the skill of listening. But it must have become evident that listening and speaking cannot be separated. Learning to listen is an important preparation for learning to speak with skill, for learning to produce accurately and effectively the sounds of speech. Having listened to poor speakers and good speakers, you are prepared to know when you yourself speak fluently or hesitantly, clearly or indistinctly, effectively or ineffectively. Having trained your ear, you are ready to learn the details of how the sounds of speech are produced.

The sounds that make up words are given their form by the action of the speech organs. A person of college age is usually able to make the sounds of his language, but he does not necessarily know how to make them or how he makes them. To become skilled in the oral interpretation of literature he needs to perfect his skill in making and organizing these sounds. Toward this end, he needs to learn the manner in which muscular actions, both small and large, generate and form the sounds—the names of the muscles and other organs involved and the manner in which they function. He needs also to know the sounds of speech with greater exactness and greater specificity than do most people. The improved listening abilities developed in the preceding chapter contribute to these learnings and skills.

The names and places of the various organs that form speech sounds are shown in a diagram of the head, mouth, and throat in saggital section, page 97. You will need to be thoroughly familiar with these names and with the manner in which you use the organs, especially in order to understand the descriptions of the sound-production process given later in this chapter.

Before you begin studying the technical details of speech-sound production, take advantage of the fact that you are able to make the sounds and perform a brief experiment with your own speech mechanism. Open your mouth wide and say *AAAaaahhh*. Sustain this *ah* sound while you round your lips. What happens to the sound? Say *ah* again. Sustain the tone while slowly closing the jaw until the teeth are almost touching. What changes occurred in the sound? Try other vowel sounds. Can you feel as well as hear and see some changes in your speech sounds?

The more accurately you can form and produce speech sounds, the more efficiently will your total speech mechanism serve you. It therefore behooves you to put some time into the study of phonetics, the science of speech sounds. This study will introduce you to IPA, the International Phonetic Alphabet, which uses a separate symbol for each sound. You will learn the accurate formation for each sound, and through the aid of recordings your ear will receive further training in assessing your production of these sounds. Once you have mastered the symbols you can accurately transcribe any speech you hear.

THE ALPHABET OF SOUNDS

Two considerations should govern your study:

1. Remember that IPA is an alphabet of *sounds*. In phonetic transcription you write only what you hear. You will soon learn that your knowledge of everyday spelling, however accurate, has only limited usefulness when you set about transcribing words into IPA symbols. Though the IPA is much longer than the everyday alphabet, you will readily see the advantages of its use in developing accuracy and correctness in the spoken arts and speech science, for teaching, research, performance, even for some informal communication.

2. Learn this alphabet in small assignments day by day. Phonetics is not like a history or humanities course, where you can catch up on your reading. Master each symbol and the production of the sound it represents as you study it. Practice the forms until you begin to think the symbol when you hear the sound in face-to-face conversation, on the telephone, radio, and television. Practice for twelve minutes a day on five days a week is more beneficial than practice for one hour on Saturday alone.

Usage dictates standards in speech. General American is that form of good speech spoken by a majority of Americans. Good General American is required by the radio-television industry when it hires newscasters and others responsible for direct verbal communication to an audience. From the stage, however, one often hears other kinds of speech: one is called "Standard Southern British," another reflects the standards of good usage in Eastern United States. With the influence of television, we may observe more and more actors using General American in preference to other forms. This book emphasizes material for training in good General American; this same material, incidentally, will augment the student's diction and voice-training program in various areas of specialization such as theatre and drama, foreign languages, and education concerned with speech in the classroom.

Speech sounds and phonetic symbols are classified according to whether they are vowels, consonants, or diphthongs. A *vowel* may be defined as a speech sound in which voiced breath is allowed to flow continuously and without interruption from the mouth. The tone produced is determined by the position and tension of the tongue, lips, jaw, and soft palate. A *consonant* may be defined as a speech sound in which the passage of air is blocked or interrupted by the adjustment of the articulators. A diphthong is a vocalic unit produced by the articulators gliding from one vowel position to another during the phonation of a continuous breath. In *soil*, for example the *oi* is a diphthong; in *so ill*, the *o* and *i* are separate *vowels*, not a diphthong.

A list of the IPA symbols for the sounds of American English follows. Note that the symbols are enclosed in square brackets; this practice distinguishes them from ordinary-alphabet letters, and is used whenever there is the slightest risk of confusion. For example, the word spelled "sit" is pronounced [sɪt] and the word pronounced [sit] is spelled "seat."

Sometimes in transcription you will find, after a vowel symbol, another symbol of two dots, perhaps [i:]. This sign indicates that the vowel is elongated; it is not a sound symbol but a duration symbol; it would take longer to say [hi:t] than to say [hit].

The IPA symbols here are presented with key words that have each sound in initial, medial, and final positions insofar as they are employed in these positions. Say all these key words aloud, looking the while at the symbol representing the sound under consideration. Write the IPA symbols along with these key words. Try, however, to give up the key words as quickly as possible. Learn to see, hear, and use the symbols. Prolonged use of key words will keep your ears and mind on crutches and delay your progress in transcription. You can soon learn the symbols well enough to read them and to write them in words; you need to do each of these things in order to do the other, much as you need to sound musical notes in order to learn the reading of music.

INTERNATIONAL PHONETIC SYMBOLS (IPA) WITH KEY WORDS CONTAINING SOUNDS IN INITIAL, MEDIAL, AND FINAL POSITIONS

Vowel and Diphthong Symbols

[i]   eat, machine, we
[ɪ]   ill, will
[e] *or* [eɪ]   aid, bake, way
[ɛ]   ebony, web
[æ]   at, ham
[a]   ask, path

[ɑ]   ah, father
[aɪ]   aisle, bright, why
[aʊ]   out, mouse, how
[ɒ]   on, softly
[ɔ]   all, ball, withdraw
[ɔɪ]   oil, point, boy
[o] *or* [oʊ]   old, cold, Romeo
[ʊ]   book
[u]   ooze, whose, woo
[ju]   use, beauty, few
[ʌ]   up, cup
[ə]   away, buffalo, papa
[ɝ], [ɜ]   earth, turn, deter
[ɚ], [ə]   perceive, alter
[ɪə]   ear
[ɛə]   air
[ɔə], [oə]   oar
[ʊə]   poor
[:]   elongation of vowel; contrast [ɑ], [ɑ:]

Consonant Symbols

[p]   pet, pupil, mop
[b]   bee, able, bib
[t]   tea, motto, wait
[d]   do, widow, end
[k]   keep, wicket, back
[g]   go, meager, dog
[m]   me, humming, warm
[n]   not, any, bin
[ŋ]   hanger, wing
[f]   feel, deafen, doff
[v]   vow, divine, move
[θ]   thought, ether, breath
[ð]   though, bother, breathe
[s]   supper, eraser, house
[z]   zip, lazy, buzz
[ʃ]   sham, wishing, fresh
[ʒ]   treasure, garage
[h]   hat, behold
[tʃ]   choo-choo, teacher, coach
[dʒ]   jab, magic, badge
[w]   one, bewail

[l]   leaf, silly, bull
[r]   rattle, merry, bear
[j]   year, beyond
[hw]   when, everywhere

EXERCISE

List the letters of the alphabet: A, B, C, on through X, Y, Z in a column. Beside each, write its *name* in IPA symbols. See page 109 for the list of acceptable answers.

EXAMPLES OF PHONETIC TRANSCRIPTIONS

Now you may read ten lines from *Romeo and Juliet* in three forms: the everyday alphabet and two sample phonetic transcriptions. One transcription represents General American; the other transcription is Standard Southern British. A comparison of the two may suggest advantages and uses of the IPA beyond those already cited in this book.

Juliet's Speech: *Romeo and Juliet,* **IV :iii**

Farewell! God knows when we shall meet again.
I have a faint, cold fear thrills through my veins
That almost freezes up the heat of life.
I'll call them back again to comfort me.
Nurse!—What should she do here!
My dismal scene I needs must act alone.
Come, vial!
What if this mixture do not work at all?
Shall I be married then tomorrow morning?
No, no, this shall forbid it. Lie thou there.

General American Diction

fɛrwɛl	gɑd	noz	hwɛn	wi	ʃæl	mit	əgɛn
aɪ	hæv	ə	fent	kold	fɪr	θrɪlz	θru	maɪ
venz							
ðət	ɔlmost	frizɪz	ʌp	ðə	hit	əv	laɪf
aɪl	kɔl	ðəm	bæk	əgɛn	tə	kʌmfɚt	mi
nɝs	hwɒt	ʃud	ʃi	du	hɪr		
maɪ	dɪzmal	sin	aɪ	nidz	mʌst	ækt	əlon
kʌm	vaɪl						
hwɒt	if	ðɪs	mɪkstʃɚ	du	nɑt	wɝk	ət	ɔl
ʃæl	aɪ	bi	mærɪd	ðɛn	təmɔro	mɔrnɪŋ	
no	no	ðɪs	ʃæl	fɚbɪd	ɪt	laɪ	ðaʊ	ðɛr

Standard Southern British Stage Diction

fɛəwɛl	gɔːd	nouz	hwɛn	wi	ʃæl	miːt	əgeɪn
aɪ	hæv	ə	feɪnt	kould	fɪːə	θrɪlz	θruː	maɪ
veɪnz							
ðæt	ɔːlmoust	friːzɪz	ʌp	ðə	hiːt	əv	laɪf
aɪl	kɔːl	ðəm	bæk	əgeɪn	tə	kʌmfət	mi
nɜːs	hwɒt	ʃʊd	ʃi	duː	hɪə
maɪ	dɪzməl	siːn	aɪ	niːdz	məst	ækt	aloun
kʌm	vaɪl						
hwɒt	ɪf	ðɪs	mɪkstʃə	duː	nɒt	wɜːk	ət	ɔl
ʃæl	aɪ	bi	mærɪd	ðɛn	təmɔro	mɔːnɪŋ
nou	nou	ðɪs	ʃəl	fəbɪd	ɪt	laɪ	ðau	ðɛə

VOWELS AND DIPHTHONGS

Two primary questions to ask yourself while learning to form and produce the vowels are: (1) How are you altering the mouth as a resonating chamber? (2) What acoustical differences do you hear between and among vowel tones? This beginning course in phonetics does not require studying the physics of sound, though anyone wishing to pursue the study will find pertinent material in the bibliography at the end of this section. A discussion of how the vowels are produced follows. Some diphthongs are discussed with the vowel sounds below. Further discussion of diphthongs may be found on pages 114-115.

THE NAMES OF 26 LETTERS IN INTERNATIONAL PHONETIC SYMBOLS

A = [e] *or* [eɪ]	N = [en]
B = [bi]	O = [o] *or* [ou]
C = [si]	P = [pi]
D = [di]	Q = [kju]
E = [i]	R = [ɑr]
F = [ef]	S = [es]
G = [dʒi]	T = [ti]
H = [eɪtʃ] *or* [aɪtʃ]	U = [ju]
I = [aɪ]	V = [vi]
J = [dʒeɪ] *or* [dʒe]	W = [dʌblju]
K = [keɪ] *or* [ke]	X = [eks]
L = [el]	Y = [waɪ]
M = [em]	Z = [iz]

It is recommended that the student use a mirror to observe the articulators during formation of the sounds and that he prolong each tone sufficiently to feel the differences in the shape and position of the articulators involved. Following these visual and kinaesthetic observations, the student is urged to begin the second part of this work by training the ear.

For ear training, a series of lessons has been recorded that can be used with this book. Use these records if you can. Study one lesson at a time. Each lesson should be experienced at least three consecutive times before passing on to the next. The following program is recommended: On the first playing listen to the lesson all the way through; it is important that the ear be sensitized and trained to discriminate among the various vowels. On the second playing, participate by phonating according to instructions. The third time, utilize the lesson for dictation drill and for practice in phonetic transcription.

Production of Vowel Sounds and Diphthongs

[i]   *eat, machine, we*

The tongue is bunched high in the front of the mouth with the tip touching the back of the lower front teeth and the sides touching the molars. The teeth are close together, thus minimizing the jaw opening. The lips are parted and if the corners of the lips are turned up in a *slight* smile you should achieve a clear brilliant tone. If the lips are spread very wide, however, the tone is likely to be sharp and strident. The [i] is a longer sound than the [ɪ], described next.

[ɪ]   *ill, will*

Formation of the articulators is essentially the same as for [i] with these alterations: the tongue is not quite so high for [ɪ] as for [i]. The lower jawbone, or mandible, is a fraction lower and consequently slightly more relaxed than for [i]. The lips are also somewhat relaxed. The [ɪ] is a shorter sound than [i], immediately above.

[e], [eɪ]   *aid, bake, way*

The tongue is bunched in the front of the mouth but not quite so much as for [ɪ]. The lips are opened more and the jaw is lower than for [ɪ]. Care must be taken to focus this sound forward and not let it escape into the nasal chambers. Undue tension in the articulators may also cause a nasal quality. The soft palate should be elevated—standard procedure for all vowel sounds. The throat should be open and relaxed. In English one often hears the diphthong [eɪ] instead of the pure vowel tone, especially in words employing [e] as a final sound; for example: *pay day* [peɪ deɪ]. Prolongation of [e] usually results in [eɪ]. To the untrained ear [e] sounds very like [ɛ] so [bekən] may seem to be [bɛkən], which in this instance is a totally different word. Since [e] is a pure vowel in many languages those who may one day teach English as a foreign language or who plan to pursue an acting career should discriminate between [e] and [eɪ]. The [e] is a longer sound than [ɛ], which follows.

[ɛ]   *ebony, web*

The essential difference between the production of [e] and [ɛ] is that the tongue, jaw, and lips are less tense for [ɛ] than for [e] and the sound [ɛ] is shorter than [e], described above. The lower jaw is more open and the lips less retracted than for [e].

[æ]   *at, ham*

The tongue is low in the mouth. The jaw is lower than for [ɛ] and the lips are well parted. As with [e], care must be taken to keep tongue tension at a minimum. Undue tongue tension may well result in a flat-sounding tone. Attune your ear to a clear tone in producing [æ]. Note that [æ] is a shorter sound than [a], described next.

[a]   *ask, path*

The articulators are lax compared to the tension required for [æ]. The tongue is lower and tension further back. The lips are more relaxed and the jaw slightly lower than for [æ]. Note especially that [a] is a longer sound than [æ] immediately above. The [a] may be difficult for those who have not yet acquired it. Many persons use the [æ] or [ɑ] where [a] might be used by others. Those who consistently use [æ] are cautioned to keep [æ] a pure vowel tone free from nasality or "flatness." Those seeking a career in theatre may wish to cultivate the effective production of [a] for purposes of stage diction. They should, however, note that [a] is used only in a relatively small number of words. For a list of these words consult John Samuel Kenyon, *American Pronunciation*, 10th edition, Ann Arbor, Mich.: George Wahr Publishing Co., 1958.

[ɑ]   *ah, father*

The tongue is low, even flat on the floor of the mouth. The jaw is dropped lower for this vowel than for any other. The lips are relaxed. The throat is open. The [ɑ] is a longer sound than [a], above.

[aɪ]   *aisle, bright, why*

Though written [aɪ] in the International Phonetic Alphabet, this diphthong is produced by spreading the tone from either [a] or [ɑ] toward [i] or [ɪ]. In the speech of some people the sound is likely to be [ɑɪ], in that of others, [aɪ]. The second part of the single vocalic unit [aɪ] is not always a precise [ɪ] but a sound in the direction of [ɪ] or [i].

[aʊ]   *out, mouse, how*

This diphthong is produced by gliding quickly from [a] position to [ʊ] position or from [ɑ] to [ʊ]. Keep the soft palate up. Think of placing the tones forward. Do not confuse [aʊ] with its variant [æʊ]. The [æʊ] is a flat tone when compared to [aʊ].

[ɒ]   *on, softly*

Like [a], this sound may not be familiar to your ear. Just as [a] is a tone somewhere between [æ] and [ɑ], so [ɒ] is between [ɑ] and [ɔ]. Say [ɑ], then [ɔ]. Now say [ɑ], [ɒ], [ɔ]. The [ɒ] is a shorter sound than that for [ɑ]. While there is no lip rounding for [ɑ], there is slight rounding of the lips for [ɒ], more for [ɔ], and even more for [o]. Many persons tend to use [ɑ] instead of [ɒ]. Students of the theatre, however, would do well to practice its formation sufficiently to recognize and to produce it at will when required on stage. The sound is heard primarily in Eastern United States and Southern England.

[ɔ]   *all, ball, withdraw*

The tongue has now risen from its flat position for [ɑ] to a slightly higher position in the back of the mouth. The lips are rounded somewhat but not so much as for [o]. The [ɔ] is a longer sound than [ɒ], described above.

[ɔɪ]   *oil, point, boy*

The tongue glides swiftly from [ɔ] position toward [i] or [ɪ]. The other articulators make appropriate adjustments.

[o] [oʊ]   *old, cold, Romeo*

The lips are well rounded. The jaw is higher than for [ɔ]. The tongue is bunched in the back of the mouth and is slightly higher than for [ɔ]. The pure vowel [o] is not always heard in English. For example, when *o* occurs in an unstressed position as in *obey* one usually hears [o], but when *o* occurs in a stressed position as in *go* one usually hears [oʊ]. Those planning careers in languages should train their ear to detect the difference between [o] and [oʊ] in connected speech as well as in isolation, for [o] is a pure vowel in many languages. The [o] is a shorter sound than [oʊ].

[ʊ]   *book*

The tongue is raised in the back of the mouth, a little behind the position of greatest tension for [o]. The jaw is elevated somewhat more than for [o].

Though lip-rounding is required for this sound, there is less than for [o] or [u]. The [ʊ] is a shorter sound than [u], which follows.

[u]   *ooze, whose, woo*

The tongue position for [u] may be thought of as the reverse of that for [i], because the greatest bunching and hence the greatest tension of the tongue occurs in the rear of the mouth. Though the teeth are slightly separated, the lips are tense and thrust forward into a pucker. The lips must be rounded. The [u] is a longer sound than [ʊ], described above.

[ju]   *use, beauty, few*

The tongue glides from a position approximating that for [i] to the position for [u] during one sustained phonation. (See the discussion of the consonant [j].)

[ʌ]   *up, cup;*   [ə]   *away, buffalo, papa*

The sound often spelled *uh* is represented by two symbols, [ʌ] and [ə]. Two symbols are needed for this one sound because the *uh* is heard in stressed [ʌ] and unstressed [ə] positions, sometimes in the same word: *button, custom* [bʌtən], [kʌstəm]. The symbol [ə] is named *schwa*. The difference in stress is accompanied by enough difference in sound to require two symbols. What are some of the differences between [ʌ] and [ə]? Do you hear a change in the degree of loudness? Do you hear any other change? Identify the stressed syllable in the three words *oven, Duncan, musketeer*, and transcribe each word into phonetic symbols. Try

---

[mʌskətɪr].
Your transcription of the three words above should be [ʌvɛn] 'ˌ[dʌnkən]',

---

to think of other words that require both the [ʌ] and the [ə] in transcription. Check your results in Kenyon and Knott, *A Pronouncing Dictionary of American English*. The distinction will soon be clear to you and you will appreciate the need for both symbols.

[ɝ]   *earth, turn, deter;*   [ɚ]   *perceive*

This sound, which is spelled in many ways and sometimes with the combination *er*, is represented in the stressed position by [ɝ] and in the unstressed position by [ɚ]. The stressed sound [ɝ] occurs in *earth* [ɝθ], *turn* [tɝn], and *deter* [dɪtɝ]. The unstressed sound [ɚ] occurs in *perceive* [pɚsiv] and in *alter* [ɔltɚ].

[ɜ]   *heard, concern;*   [ə]   *perceive, alter*

Many speakers do not pronounce, even faintly, the postvocalic [r]—

that is, the [r] sound immediately following a vowel. Instead of saying *heard* [hɜ˞d], these people say *heard* [hɜd]; instead of *concern* [kənsɜ˞n], they say *concern* [kənsɜn]; instead of *purr* [pɜ˞], they say *purr* [pɜ]. The [ɜ] then is substitution for [ɜ˞] in the speech of some people. The *schwa* [ə], aside from its use described above as an unstressed counterpart of [ʌ], may in the speech of some people be substituted for [ɚ] and/or for the final [r]. Thus *perceive* [pɚsiv] becomes [pəsiv] and *alter* [ɔltɚ] becomes [ɔltə]. When substituted for the final [r], the *schwa* contributes four more diphthongs to the collection of speech sounds. For example: *hear* or *here* [hɪr] becomes [hɪə]; *their* or *there* [ðɛr] becomes [ðɛə]; *oar* [ɔr], [or] becomes [ɔə], perhaps [oə]; *poor* [pʊr] becomes [pʊə].

Additional Diphthongs and Triphthongs

There has been full discussion of the more important diphthongs

[eɪ] *as in* pay   [ɔɪ] *as in* oil
[aɪ] *as in* ice   [oʊ] *as in* home
[aʊ] *as in* house   [ju] *as in* you

A group of diphthongs used by some people results from failure to pronounce the postvocalic [r], for which the speaker substitutes the schwa [ə]:

[ɪə] *as in* ear, hear, pier
[ɛə] *as in* air, prayer, pear
[oə] *or* [ɔə] *as in* oar, bore, pour
[ʊə] *as in* tour, sure, poor

This generation of diphthongs by reason of substituting schwa [ə] for the postvocalic [r] may also give rise to triphthongs—series of three vowels pronounced in a single phonation. True triphthongs, however, are not often heard, since the tendency is to pronounce such series not as a single vocalic unit but as two. Nevertheless, two triphthongs may be mentioned:

[aɪə] *as in* wire
[aʊə] *as in* sour

Many speakers of American English feel a need for help in remembering diphthongs and their peculiar characteristics. One systematic method involves identifying the diphthongs by their endings:

[ɪ]	[eɪ], [aɪ], [ɔɪ]	(total 3)
[ə]	[ɪə], [ɛə], [oə] *or* [ɔə], [ʊə]	(total 4)
[ʊ]	[aʊ], [oʊ]	(total 2)
[u]	[ju]	(total 1)

Another useful method is to devise key phrases such as MAKE MY CHOICE for the three diphthongs ending in [ɪ], or HOUSE HOME for two ending in [ʊ]. What sort of phrase can you formulate for the diphthongs ending in [ə]?

You may usefully use any method that you need or find helpful.

CONSONANTS

Consonants may be classified (1) as to whether or not they are voiced, (2) as to the acoustical nature of their sounds, and (3) as to the place of articulation. Below are definitions of terms useful in classifying consonants.

UNVOICED CONSONANT—If phonation does not accompany the production of the sound, the consonant is said to be unvoiced. For example, [f] and [v] are formed similarly. For [f], however, the air is simply forced forward out of the mouth and over the obstruction formed by the teeth in contact with the lower lip.

VOICED CONSONANT—If the consonant is uttered aloud with the vocal folds in vibration, the consonant is said to be voiced. In the case of [v], the vocal folds vibrate and a voiced breath is emitted through the obstruction necessary to the proper formation of [v].

PLOSIVE—A consonant produced by the sudden expulsion of air as in [p], [b], [t], [d], [k], and [g].

FRICATIVE—A consonant produced by air meeting some obstruction and thereby resulting in a noise identified as friction. Hence the term fricative for [f], [v], [θ], [ð], [s], [z], [ʃ], [ʒ], [h].

AFFRICATE—A consonant which combines elements of the plosive and of the fricative is said to be an affricate as [tʃ] and [dʒ]. Some phoneticians list these two sounds under plosives.

NASALS—Sounds resonated in the nasal passages are known as nasals. There are only three: [m], [n], and [ŋ].

GLIDES or SEMIVOWELS—Both terms are used to designate those consonants requiring a movement or glide of one or more articulators during production of the sound. Because the resonance patterns of these consonants are similar to those of vowels, [w], [l], [r], and [j] are sometimes called semivowels.

BILABIAL (*two lips*)—Those consonants produced essentially by the lips: [p], [b], [m], [w].

LABIODENTAL (*lip-teeth*)—Those consonants produced by the lip in loose contact with the teeth: [f], [v].

LINGUADENTAL (*tongue-teeth*)—Those consonants produced by the tongue in loose contact with the teeth: [θ] and [ð].

LINGUA-ALVEOLAR (*tongue-gum ridge*)—Those consonants produced by the tongue in contact or approximation with the gum ridge just behind the front teeth: [t], [d], [n], [l], [s], [z], [tʃ], and [dʒ].

LINGUAPALATAL *(tongue-hard palate)*—Those consonants produced by elevating the tongue close to the hard palate to effect a fricative sound. [ʃ], [ʒ], [r], [j].

LINGUAVELAR *(tongue-soft palate)*—Those consonants produced by the tongue in contact with the velum, known also as the soft palate: [k], [g], [ŋ].

GLOTTAL *(glottis)*—Air is emitted through the narrowed glottis, the passageway between the vocal folds, but the vocal folds do not vibrate: [h].

There now follows a brief description of the procedure for producing the consonants, together with key words presenting the sounds in initial, medial, and final positions insofar as they are employed in those designated contexts. Individual procedure descriptions should be reviewed immediately prior to any study of consonants in the recording that may be used with this book.

Students desiring further information regarding the formation of speech sounds, faults associated with them, correctional methods, and drill materials will find a bibliography at the end of this section.

[p]   *pet, pupil, mop*

Air is stopped in the mouth by closing the lips. The breath is released in an explosion. The [p] is not voiced.

[b]   *bee, able, bib*

As for [p] except that [b] is voiced.

[t]   *tea, motto, wait*

The breath stream is obstructed by the tip of the tongue elevated to the gum ridge above the upper front teeth. Air is exploded upon release of the tongue but [t] is not voiced.

[d]   *do, widow, end*

As for [t] except that [d] is voiced.

[k]   *keep, wicket, back*

Air is blocked by the back of the tongue being pressed against the soft palate. The [k] is not voiced.

[g]   *go, meager, dog*

As for [k] except that [g] is voiced.

[m]   *me, humming, warm*

As the lips are brought together a voiced breath is phonated into the nasal passages. The sound does not begin until the lips are closed.

[n]   *not, any, bin*

Air is blocked by the tip of the tongue elevated to the upper gum ridge while a voiced breath is directed into the nasal passages. The [n] may be produced with the mouth open or closed.

[ŋ]   *hanger, wing*

As for [g] except that the soft palate is lowered against the back of the tongue as a voiced breath is phonated into the nasal passages.

[f]   *feel, deafen, doff*

The flow of air is restricted by the upper front teeth placed lightly against the lower lip. The [f] is not voiced.

[v]   *vow, divine, move*

As for [f] except that [v] is voiced.

[θ]   *thought, ether, breath*

The breath stream is obstructed by the tip of the tongue placed lightly against the edges of the upper front teeth. The [θ] is not voiced.

[ð)   *though, bother, breathe*

As for [θ] except that [ð] is voiced.

[s]   *supper, eraser, house*

The breath stream is obstructed by the sides of the tongue in contact with the upper teeth and gum ridge. The tongue should be kept as far forward as the canine teeth but the tip must never cover the incisors while a thin stream of air is forced through this obstruction. The [s] is unvoiced. Care should be taken to place the articulators in correct position and to avoid building up excess air pressure. The sound should not be prolonged. Prolongation of the vowel preceeding or following [s] may help some to avoid a whistle in the production of [s].

[z]   *zip, lazy, buzz*

As for [s] except that [z] is voiced.

[ʃ]   *sham, wishing, fresh*

The breath stream is interrupted by the middle of the tongue elevated toward the hard palate. The tongue tip is farther back and lower than for [s]. Lip rounding is required in the production of this unvoiced consonant.

[ʒ]   *treasure, garage*

As for [ʃ] except that [ʒ] is voiced.

[h]   *hat, behold*

To produce [h] the articulators must assume the position required for the sound which immediately follows [h]. Breath is then blown through the narrowed glottis before the second sound is phonated.

[tʃ]   *choo-choo, teacher, coach*

Begin with the position for [t] and merge rapidly with [ʃ] in a continuous motion which produces a single unit. The [tʃ] is not voiced.

[dʒ]   *jab, magic, badge*

As for [tʃ] except that [dʒ] is voiced.

[w]   *one, bewail*

Assume the position for [u]. Now glide rapidly to the adjacent sound with continuous voicing. For example speak *way* [weɪ] aloud by assuming the position for [u] and gliding rapidly to [eɪ].

[l]   *leaf, silly, bull*

The tongue is elevated in such a way that air passes around the sides of the tongue. Tongue position for [l] varies depending upon the sound adjacent to it. For example, the tongue will be raised far forward for the production of *leave* [liv], somewhat back for *coal* [kol]. Care should be taken not to omit or seem to "swallow" [l] in back positions, producing [koə] for [kol].

[r]   *rattle, merry, bear*

The midsection of the tongue is elevated toward the hard palate, lightly touching the inner sides of the back teeth forward to the bicuspids. The tongue tip is behind the upper gum ridge and may be pointed forward or upward. As air passes over the vocal folds they vibrate and the tongue moves into position for the adjacent sound, which may also require the adjustment of other articulators. If [r] precedes a vowel or appears between two vowels, it is pronounced. If [r] follows a vowel, it may or may not be pronounced. The [r] which appears in front of a vowel is termed the prevocalic [r]. The [r] which appears after a vowel is termed the postvocalic [r]. In the speech of most persons the final or postvocalic [r] differs from the prevocalic [r] in that the postvocalic or final [r] is pronounced with less retroflexion (less curling backward) of the tongue and consequently with less stress than the prevocalic or initial [r]. In Eastern American and Southern American speech, postvocalic [r] and final [r] may be dropped and the schwa [ə] substituted. Thus *forward* [fɔrwɚd] becomes [fɔːwɚd] and *bear* [bɛr] or [bær] becomes [bɛə] or [bæə].

[j]   *year, beyond*

Assume the position for [i]. Now glide rapidly to the adjacent sound. The [j] is voiced throughout its production. For example, speak *yell* [jɛl] aloud by assuming the position for [i] and gliding rapidly to [ɛ] with continuous voicing before sounding [l].

[hw]   *when, everywhere*

This sound requires that one take the lip formation for [w] but expel air as in [h] before moving into the [w].

7. Exercises

This section contains suggestions and directions for a variety of exercises concerning posture, breathing, and the training of the voice. You can well follow a systematic program in these exercises and keep a record of your performance and progress. The items for this record are given on pages 127 and 128.

POSTURE EXERCISES

If at all possible observe a baby lying on his back while cooing. What do you notice about his tone? Do the sounds impress your ear as being constricted, tense, and tight? Or is your impression that of a free, full, easily projected tone?

Before you retire tonight, lie on your back for a few moments, breathe deeply, and then repeat these two lines:

> Ah, to note the "bah-bah-bah" of two plump sheep.
> Sleep creeps and steals easily in my mind.

Now stand as you normally do and repeat the two sentences. What differences do you hear? Assume good posture and repeat the two sentences again. What differences do you hear now? What is the significance of this experiment?

To assume good posture, choose a smooth flat wall. Paneled walls, doors, and walls with molding extending several inches up from the floor are not as effective as a flat wall. Align your back against the wall, bringing your shoulders, hips, calves, and heels into contact with the wall. If you can do so (and most people cannot), make the small of your back touch the wall at the same time. If you cannot do so, then bend your knees and rotate your hips forward until the small of your back straightens out against the wall. Keeping it against the wall, gradually straighten your knees and try to stand erect. After you feel some improvement, measure the distance between the wall and the small of your back while the other parts of your body are in contact with the wall (insert a thin book, or a thick one, between your back and the wall). Practice to reduce this distance; you may need months, but do not become discouraged. Daily effort will help to bring your body into good alignment. Each time you have achieved the best alignment you can for the day, walk away from the wall with a free, easy gait, consciously trying to preserve the good posture you have attained against the wall. Walk about the room as you maintain this posture. Now stand still and move first one arm, then the other at the side, still keeping your back as straight as possible. Work out similar variations until you can maintain good posture without appearing stiff.

1. Do try to keep the chest up and the shoulders back at a natural elevation.

2. Do try to maintain good posture easily, naturally, without rigidity.

BREATHING EXERCISES

To develop a voice which will maintain the interest of your listeners and will inspire them with a desire to listen to you, you must first of all gain control of your breathing. One of the commonest faults among untrained voices is that of letting a portion of the breath supply escape before any sound is uttered. Vocalize the instant you begin exhalation.

Observe your own natural breathing pattern. What do you note about the rate of exhalation as compared with the rate of inhalation? Perform this experiment and try to explain its significance in terms of breath control for speech. Lie on the floor, back down, so that your spine does not sag. Place a book on your abdomen. Breathe deeply, taking in as much air as your lungs will hold, and note the extent to which your stomach is distended as if you had just eaten a great feast. Now exhale: Empty. Empty. Empty. Be sure you have exhausted your supply of air. Note that your stomach seems to collapse more and more, the more you exhale. There is no need to continue working with the book once you have become aware of the process of respiration. During inhalation the diaphragm contracts and moves downward whereas during exhalation the abdominal muscles contract and the diaphragm moves upward. The diaphragm is often referred to as the muscle of inhalation and the abdominal muscles as those of exhalation.

Controlled Exhalation

Breathe in and out at a normal rate. Immediately after inhalation, begin to control exhalation by consciously slowing down your rate of expiration. In coordinating your breathing with your phonation, which will be discussed shortly, you will become increasingly aware that different amounts of breath are needed, depending upon the demands of the phrase. In any event, try taking a fresh breath for each line. The amount of air you inhale is not nearly so important as the way you use that air. There is no need to contract any muscle excessively or to become rigid. The breath, however, must be supported. Maintain breath support by consciously letting the air out slowly.

Sometimes a student will try to control exhalation by excessively tightening the muscles of the abdomen and in so doing may achieve control rapidly, but such control has little value. Avoid excessive contraction or rigidity of the abdominal muscles. Excessive contraction induces changes in breathing which in turn affect tone. Avoid raising the chest and shoulders excessively; it is possible to damage your vocal mechanism by so doing. Avoid letting the chest or abdomen relax unduly; you will tire your voice and your tone will be faulty, even "flat."

Consult the Check List for Daily Exercises, page 128. Note the requirement for controlled-exhalation practice on short (1 to 5), average (1 to 10), and long (1-20) counts. These counts may be made at the rate of two numbers per second. The short counts are important. To achieve satisfactory loudness and to convey a proper sense of energy you will need to practice controlled exhalation even for short phrases. For speech purposes there is no need to "fill up" with great amounts of air and no virtue in your being able to hold your breath for long periods. Controlled exhalation is not designed to prepare you for skin diving but rather to help you support your breath and so gain control for orally interpreting material of varying phrase lengths.

Coordination of Phonation with Breathing

When you have achieved control at various counts, begin vocalizing the instant of exhalation by counting aloud one-two-three-four-five or any other set of numbers you have chosen.

From counting, progress to phrases and follow the same procedure. Speak aloud the following:

> Here they are!
> Where have you been?
> Why can't she come?
> When Betty heard the horn
>   she pushed open the window
>   and hailed the driver of the truck
>   to point to a parking area
>   where the delivery was to be made.

Take a fresh breath for each line. You discover you need varying amounts of breath depending upon the demands of the phrase. Now speak the last sentence as if it were written on one line. What phrasing have you adopted now?

CHANTING EXERCISES

For the development of strength and adequate loudness in the voice, practice the following exercise two minutes a day:

Assume the lowest pitch that is truly comfortable for you. Be careful that you do not force your pitch down unnaturally. You should feel no strain if you are doing the exercise properly. A low pitch for this exercise helps you to project your speech easily. Inhale up to the count of twenty. Using controlled exhalation (that is, consciously slowing down the rate at which you exhale), begin vocalizing immediately upon exhalation. Using one tone level throughout the exercise, chant aloud this sentence from *Macbeth:* "Hang out the banners on the outward walls." Dwell on the vowels as much as you can. Elide the final consonants with the initial vowels so that "Hang out" becomes "Hangout" and "banners on" becomes "bannerzon." Try to chant the sentence on one breath. If you find that you tend to run out of breath before the end of the sentence, do not force yourself to continue to the end. Stop. Take a deeper breath than before. If necessary, shorten the vowel sounds somewhat but continue to practice the sentence until you can chant it in the same time that it would take you to count to twenty slowly.

This exercise will be of considerable help to you only if you are careful to preserve the single tone level. Another interesting sentence to use for this exercise is: "Train twenty-one leaving on track one for Portland, Omaha, Chicago, and all points east." By alternating these two sentences you stimulate your ear and find mental fun in your routine practice. After you have carefully trained yourself to speak both sentences on one tone level you might vary the second by adding to the end "All aboard" and use a rising inflection on [bɔːrt] (as old-time station masters usually pronounced "board"). The rise at the end of the sentence provides a little fun for your exercise period. Do, however, delay use of the inflection until you have trained yourself to speak on one level and let no other syllables in the exercise vary from that level.

READING THE SCALES

Those who wish to develop range and melody in the speaking and reading voice would do well to spend a minimum of one minute per day reading the scales. The procedure is:

Read (do not sing) from the lowest tone you can vocalize to the highest and back down again. After a few times up and down, skip around in much the same manner as if you were singing "do-me-so-do."

Reading aloud from a newspaper is recommended for this exercise. Newspaper articles are often effective for exercise because the style of writing is usually objective, and a reader is not likely to be deterred by emotional involvement in the material.

Generally, newspaper or special material is best for drill work and exercises. It may be a mistake to use for practice the very selection you plan to read aloud. Avoid using your performance material for drill work because the selection you have chosen for your presentation must be interpreted with skill and artistry. No one can be the critic and the creator at the same time.

It is also helpful to sing a song or two before an oral reading performance. Songs with octave ranges stretch the voice nicely. "You Are My Lucky Star" is one good example; you may think of many others. Get the sheet music from your local music store if you don't know the air and lyric.

EXERCISES FOR THE CONTROL OF ORAL RESONANCE

Of the three resonators, the mouth is most capable of accommodating various adjustments. Changes in the tension or laxness of the jaw, variations of the lip spread during vocalization, and adjustments of the tongue all affect the sound produced.

Exercises for Control of Jaw Tension

The student with the rigid jaw is the one who parts his lips but slightly, just enough to permit some escape of sound. He often gives the impression of talking through his teeth because his jaw is so immobile. The oral reader with the tight jaw starts his performance with two handicaps. In proportion as the interpreter clenches his jaw, the beauty and melody of the vowel sounds are distorted and the amplification of sound minimized. To avoid having a rigid jaw, try the following exercise:

Holding your jaw as steady as possible with your teeth as close together as possible, part your lips just sufficiently for the following sounds to be emitted: [jo, ju, jɑ, je, jɛ]. Now let your jaw open as far as possible and speak the same sounds. What differences do you hear?

A change in the resonator effects a change in the sound itself. Clear well-modulated tones are far more likely to result when the jaw is governed by the appropriate tension than when it is either too tense or too relaxed. A rigid jaw suggests to the audience that the reader is unfriendly, disgruntled, or the bearer of some other negative quality. Those who find that they exhibit a rigid jaw would do well to spend a minimum of two minutes per day on this exercise:

Read aloud slowly. With exaggerated effort, let the jaw drop as far down as possible for *each word*. The exaggeration of physical effort and the attendant distortion of sounds usually succeeds in altering the undesirable rigidity so that the reader is soon able to present such positive qualities as enthusiasm, open friendliness, and a resonant voice.

Exercises for Control of Lip Spread

Those who have been following the exercises for the rigid jaw have had dramatic proof of changes in tone effected by mere alteration of jaw position. The lips are important, of course, as articulators for the bilabial consonants [p, b, m, w]. A wide spread of the lips, however, can alter vowel sounds. Some students consistently spread their lips very wide when they talk or read, with the result that much of what they present sounds flat and harsh and often does not project well. To increase the sensitivity of your own ear to the effect of the lips on vowel sounds try this experiment:

Stand in a corner or work with a tape recorder and listen to yourself say: "Eat the cheese if you please, but please squeeze the beets through the strainer." Say the sentence as you would in normal speech the first time. Then repeat the sentence, deliberately spreading your lips as widely as possible. Now say "Ah." Yawn and repeat "Ah." Analyze the position of your jaw and tongue as well as the placement of the tone as you say "Ah" again. Keeping the position of jaw and tongue for "ah," repeat the sentence again. What differences do you note?

Using your forefinger and middle finger to make a V, place the tips of your two fingers at the corners of your mouth and repeat the sentence again. Read several paragraphs or a column from a newspaper while you make the V with your fingers at your mouth. This exercise, practiced three minutes a day, is a distinct aid in the forward projection of tones and in minimizing distracting mannerisms of the mouth while talking or reading.

Exercises for Control of Tongue Position

Many speakers and readers would give excellent performances if they would do just one thing: control the tongue so that it does not tend to remain bunched in the back of the mouth for all speech sounds. Certain vowel sounds [u, ʊ] are produced with the tongue high in the back of the mouth; and certain consonant sounds [k, g, ŋ] are produced by bringing the back of the tongue into contact with the soft palate. These five sounds, however, constitute less than 12 per cent of the total sounds of General American speech and provide no justification for keeping the tongue in the rear of the mouth. Determine the extent to which you need to control your tongue by conducting the following experiment:

Stand in a corner or work with a tape recorder and listen to yourself as you read a few paragraphs from a newspaper. Read aloud as you customarily would with no other object than to listen to your normal voice. Now read aloud the same material but make a concentrated effort to keep your tongue in the back of your mouth as much as possible. What differences did you hear? Read aloud the same material a third time, this time concentrating on keeping your tongue as relaxed as possible on the floor of your mouth. What differences do you hear now? From what you heard, would you say that you tend to keep your tongue in the rear of your mouth more than you need to?

Read aloud the same passage, trying to control your tongue so that you achieve the proper tongue position required for the production of the sounds you are reading.

EXERCISES FOR TONE PLACEMENT

For tone placement and optimum pitch try this:

Follow the relaxation exercises in Part Three. Continue to do the exercises until you yawn voluntarily. After yawning several times, say [ɑ] and sustain the tone. Now quietly adjust your tongue, jaw, teeth, and lips for [i], without phonating; get the articulators ready. When they are in position, say [i]. Did one tone sound clearer and more vibrant than another? Could you feel the vibration from the tone in your mouth? In your head? In the bones of your face? Say each of the vowels. The instant you feel a vibration as far forward in the mouth as the gum ridge, stop. Try to reproduce the exact tone again. What vowel were you saying when you became kinaesthetically and acoustically aware of your tone? Say that same vowel again. Then in one continuous breath move on to another vowel sound, trying to keep the second in the same place as the first.

After you have done this exercise a few times, you will need the expert assistance and judgment of a competent teacher to get the best benefit from it. Once you and your teacher have witnessed by ear your correct placement of a tone, you will have an auditory guide to what (for want of a better term) is called "tone placement."

SOME SINGING EXERCISES

For Placement

Adjust the articulators for [ɑ]. Breathe in. Start singing [ɑ] the instant of exhalation. Sing [ɑ] twice on each note before moving to the next. Sing the entire line of sixteen notes on *one* breath.

For Pitch and Sustained Tone

[wi] [we] [wa] [wo] [wu]

Sing each phrase on one sustained breath: support the tone by consciously letting the air out slowly.

Sing [wi] [we] [wa] [wo] [wu] on the next tone in the chromatic scale and repeat this procedure through eight different tones going up the scale. Then reverse your process and work down the scale at least four notes below the note on which you began this complete exercise.

For Flexibility

Sing the two notes of each phrase on one breath for the following:

[do] [do]   [do] [do]   [do] [do]   [do][do]   [do][do]   [do] [do] [do][do]

KEEPING A RECORD OF YOUR PROGRESS

For your own information, encouragement, and guidance, you need to keep a record of the progress you make in the skills that relate to voice production. Here is a check list for periodic appraisal of your skills:

Check List on Posture, Breath Control, and Pitch

POSTURE:

When my head, shoulders, hips, calves, and heels touch the wall, the small of my back is —— inches from the wall.

BREATH CONTROL:

I have (excellent control) (little control) (no control) over the muscles of my abdomen when I exhale.

I can inhale to a count of ——.

I can exhale to a count of ——.

PITCH:

I can sing from —— to ——, a range of —— notes.

I normally speak in a range of —— notes.

You can use a check list of this kind in several ways. First, you can use it to record your achievements or status at any chosen date. You can also use it to set a goal for some future date. And you can use it to report to your instructor. But the value of keeping the record is for yourself.

You may find that the number of things you must practice is hard to remember. For example, you should do your exercises daily for posture control, breath control, chanting, scales, and many other skills. For this purpose also, the list is useful. Simply check, every day, the appropriate item when you have attended to it. Thus you can do at convenient times the brief exercises that should never be neglected, and you need not try to hold open a solid block of time for doing all of them at once.

Check List for Daily Exercises

	Exercise Performed on						
	S	*M*	*T*	*W*	*T*	*F*	*S*
POSTURE CONTROL:							
Lying down	___	___	___	___	___	___	___
Standing	___	___	___	___	___	___	___
BREATH CONTROL:							
Lying down with book	___	___	___	___	___	___	___
Short counts, to 5	___	___	___	___	___	___	___
Average counts, 1-6, . . . , 1-10	___	___	___	___	___	___	___
Long counts, 1-15, . . . , 1-20	___	___	___	___	___	___	___
Phrases	___	___	___	___	___	___	___
CHANTING:							
"Hang out . . ."	___	___	___	___	___	___	___
"Train 21 . . ."	___	___	___	___	___	___	___
SCALES:							
Not singing	___	___	___	___	___	___	___
Singing	___	___	___	___	___	___	___
ORAL RESONANCE:							
Jaw tension	___	___	___	___	___	___	___
Tongue position	___	___	___	___	___	___	___
Lip spread	___	___	___	___	___	___	___
TONE PLACEMENT	___	___	___	___	___	___	___
SINGING:							
Placement	___	___	___	___	___	___	___
Pitch and sustained tone	___	___	___	___	___	___	___
Flexibility	___	___	___	___	___	___	___

If you wish, you can transfer this kind of check list to a notebook or a wall chart. You can extend it to cover several weeks rather than a single week. You can increase the space in the blanks and thus make room for more data or comment than the simple check mark.

8. A Selected Bibliography
for Speech and Oral Interpretation

GENERAL

Brodnitz, Friedrich S. *Keep Your Voice Healthy*. Introduction by Olin Downes. New York: Harper and Bros., 1953. pp. 234. Written in conversational style by a medical doctor, this book presents scientific and technical information about voice science and medical treatment of vocal problems in terms a lay person can understand. Special attention is given to difficulties peculiar to singers and actors. Highly recommended.

Desfossés, Beatrice. *Your Voice and Your Speech,* rev. ed. New York: Hill and Wang, 1959. pp. 293. The subtitle of this book, "Self-training for Better Speaking," aptly expresses the approach of the author. Fine scholarship reflected in recognition of Mid-Atlantic and General American speech. Sources cited. Exercises, diagrams, and practice material well within the grasp of one who wishes to teach himself. Applications to acting, radio and television, choral speech, storytelling, poetry reading, and public speaking are suggested in separate chapters.

Gray, Giles Wilkeson, and Claude Merton Wise. *The Bases of Speech,* 3rd ed. New York: Harper and Bros., 1959. pp. 562. A classic reference for those interested in any or all of the following nine bases of speech: social, physical, physiological, neurological, phonetic, linguistic, psychological, genetic, semantic. Persons considering a career in speech but undecided as to an area of speciality would find this book particularly valuable. The importance and relationship of all areas to each other are stressed. Bibliography extensive.

Vennard, William. *Singing: The Mechanism and the Technic*. Ann Arbor, Mich.: Edwards Bros., 1950. (Distributed by University of California Bookstore, Los Angeles.) pp. 171. Though prepared especially for singers, this book is of value to students of speech as well. Scientific terms and concepts are presented in terms easily understood. Subject matter treated includes acoustics, breathing, registration, resonance, vowels, articulation, and coordination of all aspects of voice training. Throughout Vennard cites the findings and opinions of many, then indicates his own reactions. Highly recommended.

PHONETICS AND PRACTICE MATERIAL

Anderson, Virgil A. *Training the Speaking Voice,* 2nd ed. New York: Oxford University Press, 1961. pp. 453. Comprehensive presentation of theory and practice material for the development and training of the voice and for the improvement of articulation. Appendices provide information on the acoustics of speech and the measurement of auditory discrimination. Bibliography and index very helpful. Highly recommended.

Eisenson, Jon. *The Improvement of Voice and Diction.* New York: Macmillan Co., 1958. pp. 303. Basic information on the voice and exercises to prepare for speech production are treated in Part One. Part Two presents the study of individual speech sounds and offers extensive drills. Discussion of [r] is particularly helpful. Recommended.

Fairbanks, Grant. *Voice and Articulation Drillbook,* 2nd ed. New York: Harper and Row, 1960. pp. 196. Practice exercises for improvement of articulation and for development of effective time, pitch, intensity, phrasing, intonation, stress, and voice quality. Organization of material is based on phonetics and the acoustics of speech. This edition replaces the 1940 edition.

Kantner, Claude E., and Robert West. *Phonetics: An Introduction to the Principles of Phonetic Science from the Point of View of English Speech,* rev. ed. New York: Harper and Bros., 1960. pp. 433. A detailed study embracing kinesiologic phonetics, phonetic metamorphology, English speech styles in America, phonetic alphabets, and some suggestions for the application of phonetics to other subjects. Practice materials for transcription and reading are included in the appendices.

Kenyon, John Samuel. *American Pronunciation,* 10th ed. Ann Arbor, Mich.: George Wahr Publishing Co., 1958. pp. 265. Very valuable reference to use in conjunction with the Kenyon and Knott *Dictionary,* for which see the final group of entries in this bibliography.

Leutenegger, Ralph R. *The Sounds of American English: An Introduction to Phonetics.* Chicago: Scott, Foresman and Co., 1963. pp. 168. Designed for students beginning the study of phonetics. In addition to describing the position of the articulators for production of forty-eight different speech sounds, the text describes how to write the phonetic symbol for each sound. Exercises in transcription and crossword puzzles encourage application of the study.

Russell, G. Oscar. *Speech and Voice.* New York: Macmillan Co., 1931. pp. 250. Though almost forty years have elapsed since this book first appeared, it remains important because of X-rays revealing speech cavities and articulators during the production of speech sounds. The work is the result of some 3,000 experiments with approximately 400 subjects speaking English, French, German, Italian, and Spanish. The subjects represent all ages and include soprano, tenor, and baritone voices. Anatomical drawings are clear and detailed.

Thomas, Charles Kenneth. *An Introduction to the Phonetics of American English,* 2nd ed. New York: Ronald Press Co., 1958. pp. 273. Thomas recognizes regional variations in spoken American English, records and discusses these differences, and provides transcriptions of speech sounds used in Eastern New England, New York City, Philadelphia, the South, North Central area, Western Pennsylvania, Southern Mountain, Central Midland area, the Northwest, and the Southwest Coastal area. Extensive bibliography. Especially valuable to interpreters and actors requiring help in American dialects.

Van Riper, Charles. *Speech Correction: Principles and Methods,* 4th ed. Englewood Cliffs, N.J.: Prentice-Hall, 1963. pp. 528. Chapters 9 and 10 on articulation disorders—their nature, cause, and treatment—are of particular interest to students of phonetics. Though written from the point of view of the speech therapist working with children, the adult can adapt methods to his own level. A bibliography appears at the end of each chapter. The third edition, published in 1954, includes material on foreign dialects (pp. 479-491) which may be of interest to oral readers and actors.

Walsh, Gertrude. *Sing Your Way to Better Speech,* new rev. ed. Music arrangements by Roger Boardman. New York: E. P. Dutton and Co., 1947. pp. 213. Diction drills are made fun by the inclusion of rhymes and jingles set to the music of old folk tunes. All speech sounds are classified and often presented in pairs, as [p] and [b]. Each lesson systematically follows a five-point plan. There is no index, but the Table of Contents facilitates reference.

Wise, Claude Merton. *Applied Phonetics.* Englewood Cliffs, N.J.: Prentice-Hall, 1957. pp. 546. Actors attempting dialects for stage diction and speech correctionists will find this work of great value. In addition to regional variations in American speech, the following types of speech are treated: Standard Southern British, Cockney, Scottish, Irish, French, German, Yiddish, Italian, Spanish, Russian, Brazilian, and Portuguese.

ACOUSTICS OF SPEECH

Denes, Peter B., and Elliot N. Pinson. *The Speech Chain: The Physics and Biology of Spoken Language.* Bell Telephone Laboratories, Inc. Baltimore, Md.: Waverly Press, 1964. (Distributed by Williams and Wilkins Co., Baltimore, Md.) pp. 166. Written especially for the capable and interested student at the high-school level, this book presents the physics and biology of speech as an interdisciplinary subject. Equipment for demonstrations is listed, with address of producers and price.

Fant, Gunnar. *Acoustic Theory of Speech Production with Calculations Based on X-Ray Studies of Russian Articulations.* The Hague: Mouton and Co., 1960. pp. 323. Fant analyzes the production of six Russian vowels, their format frequency patterns, speech wave, and acoustic theory of resonance in their production. Highly mathematical and technical. Recommended only for the advanced student.

Fletcher, Harvey. *Speech and Hearing in Communication,* 2nd ed. New York: D. Van Nostrand Co., 1953. pp. 461. Fletcher's original work, *Speech and Hearing,* was published in 1929 after fifteen years of research in speech and hearing as related to the telephone. Conducted in the Research Laboratories of the Bell Telephone System, the work was continued for more than a decade after the first edition. Other laboratories contributed findings in succeeding years and Fletcher has brought the information together in the current book. Important information on the acoustics of speech and on hearing perception. Highly recommended.

Hoops, Richard A. *Speech Science: Acoustics in Speech.* Springfield, Ill.: Charles C Thomas, 1960. pp. 137. Writing in outline form, Hoops defines and briefly discusses sound, vibration, frequency, amplitude, wave motion, nature and effects of resonance, and vocal frequency in Part One. Part Two is devoted to time, intensity, and quality. Helpful to those who have problems understanding terms related to acoustics of speech. Study aids in the form of questions and a Glossary add to the value of the work. Chapter VII, "Vocal Frequency," is very helpful. Hoops presents theories and findings of various other scholars, indicating areas of agreement and disagreement.

Ladefoged, Peter. *Elements of Acoustic Phonetics.* Chicago: University of Chicago Press, 1962. pp. 118. In seven chapters the author discusses sound waves, loudness and pitch, quality, wave analysis, resonance, hearing, and the production of speech. Descriptions of simple experiments which the reader can try for himself, together with references to various easily understood examples, make this an excellent aid for the beginning student. Ladefoged clearly limits the scope of the book to what he calls "preliminaries to a theory." He does not attempt to report involved aspects of the physics of speech. Charts and diagrams in the last chapter are of particular interest to the beginning student of phonetics.

Pierce, John R., and Edward E. David, Jr. *Man's World of Sound.* Garden City, N.Y.: Doubleday and Co., 1958. pp. 287. In a highly readable analysis of the physics of sound, the authors demonstrate that an understanding of acoustics is vital to an understanding of man and his language.

Potter, Ralph K., George A. Kopp, and Harriet C. Green. *Visible Speech.* New York: D. Van Nostrand Co., 1947. pp. 441. Visible speech may be defined as a pattern of speech sounds which can be read by the eye. The authors describe their work at the Bell Telephone Laboratories and suggest applications of their research to the fields of speech education for the deaf, phonetics, speech correction, foreign languages, and vocal music. Recommended only for specialists in the aforementioned areas.

ANATOMY AND SPEECH

Palmer, John Milton, and Dominic A. La Russo. *Anatomy for Speech and Hearing.* New York: Harper and Row, 1965. pp. 216. Text, tables, and illustrations enable the student to understand interrelationships of the various anatomical parts employed in speech and hearing. Included are a Glossary and an Appendix on physiologic phonetics. The latter describes the musculature and action involved in the phonatory and resonance processes (pp. 204-205) and in the production of individual vowel and consonant sounds (pp. 206-214).

Shearer, William M. *Illustrated Speech Anatomy.* Springfield, Ill.: Charles C Thomas, 1963. pp. 85. Bone and muscle processes required for speech are clearly presented in text and diagrams. Work sheets for matching terms, writing short answers, making notes, and even applying knowledge gained to working a crossword puzzle all provide helpful review. Appendix 1 presents names, derivations, and meaning for terms referring to anatomical structures. Appendix 2 presents phonetic symbols. Highly recommended.

Penfield, Wilder, and Lamar Roberts. *Speech and Brain Mechanisms.* Princeton: Princeton University Press, 1959. pp. 286. The authors discuss the brain mechanisms of speech as well as the learning and teaching of language. Highly technical and scientific information is thoughtfully presented in terms the lay reader can understand. The final chapter, "The Learning of Languages," is of especial interest to parents and teachers.

VOCAL DISORDERS AND TREATMENT

Greene, Margaret C. L. *The Voice and Its Disorders.* New York: Macmillan Co., 1957. pp. 224. Margaret Greene has divided her book into two parts—one, the normal voice; and two, voice disorders. The latter comprises more than two-thirds of the book. The work is concise but comprehensive. An extensive bibliography and detailed index add to its value.

Levin, Nathaniel M. *Voice and Speech Disorders: Medical Aspects.* Foreword by Mary E. Switzer. Springfield, Ill.: Charles C Thomas, 1962. pp. 966. Thirty-five specialists contributed to this vast treatise on voice and speech disorders organized under four major headings: "Basic Mechanisms of Voice and Speech," "Otology and Audiology," "Pathology and Therapy of Voice and Speech," and "Habilitation and Rehabilitation." Scientific and technical terminology used throughout make the book more valuable to those who have some background in the various subjects than to those who are beginners in the field.

Luchsinger, Richard, and Godfrey E. Arnold. *Voice—Speech—Language.* Translated from the German by Godfrey E. Arnold and Evelyn Robe Finkbeiner. Belmont, Calif.: Wadsworth Publishing Co., 1965. pp. 812. Physiology, pathology, and therapy of respiration, phonation, voice, speech, and language are presented in detail from many different points of view. Students and teachers of voice training will want to study pp. 3-165 carefully.

Rieber, R. W., and R. S. Brubaker (ed.). *Speech Pathology: An International Study of the Science.* Amsterdam: North-Holland Publishing Co., 1966. pp. 656. Comprehensive presentation of recent developments in speech pathology. Part V reveals current trends in fifteen foreign countries.

PSYCHOLOGY, PSYCHIATRY, AND SPEECH

Eisenson, Jon, J. Jeffery Auer, and John V. Irwin. *The Psychology of Communication.* New York: Appleton-Century-Crofts, 1963. pp. 394. The importance and relationship of psychology to the communication process is treated in discussions of the nature, origin, and purposes of speech, of basic psychological principles, of the communicative process, of personality and speech. Applications of psychology to the speech of the individual and to speech in group communication are also noted. Begun as a revision of Eisenson's *The Psychology of Speech,* which first appeared in 1938, this work is wider in scope than the original. Valuable. Highly recommended.

Ostwald, Peter F. *Soundmaking: The Acoustic Communication of Emotion.* Springfield, Ill.: Charles C Thomas, 1963. pp. 186. The author, himself a psychiatrist, attempts to bridge some gaps between psychiatry and acoustics. Written in an easily understood prose, the work suggests correlation between acoustics and behavior and cites major problems in effecting such correlation. Bibliography, glossary, and index are valuable aids. An interesting and relatively short study for those who wish to investigate the relationships among psychiatry, speech, and acoustics.

SPEECH AND EDUCATION

Abernathy, Elton. *Fundamentals of Speech,* 2nd ed. Dubuque, Iowa: William C. Brown Co., 1964. pp. 240. Interestingly and concisely written, this book relates the study of speech to human everyday affairs and to such specific activities as oral reading, public speaking, and listening. Phonetics, voice production, language, and pronunciation are treated. Two appendices present material for parliamentary procedure and for correcting defective speech. Work sheets provide for application of theory to speech situations and for evaluation of student's progress. Bibliography appears at the end of each chapter. Recommended to teachers of all subjects because of the many possibilities for using speech throughout the curriculum.

Anderson, Virgil A. *Improving the Child's Speech.* New York: Oxford University Press, 1953. pp. 333. Valuable reference for parents, teachers, and all others who work with children. Relationships between speech development and social, emotional, and mental problems are discussed. Approaches to improvement are suggested. Generally written in nontechnical language.

Eisenson, Jon, and Mardel Ogilvie. *Speech Correction in the Schools,* 2nd ed. New York: Macmillan Co., 1963. pp. 399. Helpful to classroom teacher and speech correctionist in understanding each other's functions as related to the school-age child with speech problems. Basic information is followed by discussion of specific speech defects. Chapters 3, 7, and 8 on speech standards and language development of particular interest to teachers of all subjects. Recommended.

Fest, Thorrel B., and Martin T. Cobin. *Speech and Theater.* Washington, D.C.: The Center for Applied Research in Education, 1964. pp. 120. Fest and Cobin analyze the present relationship of speech and theater to our society today and indicate the need for dynamic integration of these subjects into the total educational curriculum. Recommended to all educators.

Mulgrave, Dorothy. *Speech for the Classroom Teacher,* 3rd ed. New York: Prentice-Hall, 1955. pp. 470. Written especially for teachers, the book offers comprehensive and useful material on the speech mechanism, language, speech arts, and speech pathology. Interested students are urged to compare this work with Fred Sorrenson, *Speech for the Teacher.*

Raubicheck, Letitia. *Speech Improvement.* New York: Prentice-Hall, 1952. pp. 225. Prepared especially for high-school students, this book deals with common speech problems. Part Four, "Foreign Accent," is valuable for foreign students trying to learn English.

Sorrenson, Fred S. *Speech for the Teacher.* New York: Ronald Press Co.,

1952. pp. 471. Regardless of his major subject, any teacher could find this book useful for improving his own speech. The reader is urged to examine both this and the Mulgrave book to determine which meets his own needs and interests.

Van Riper, Charles, and John V. Irwin. *Voice and Articulation*. Englewood Cliffs, N.J.: Prentice-Hall, 1958. pp. 566. Van Riper and Irwin have organized existing information on voice and articulation for the purpose of showing what is known and not known (as of 1958) on the subject. Some 868 references are utilized and the authors react to theories and findings. Chapters 9-15 (pp. 272-496) are of value to beginning students in phonetics, articulation, and oral interpretation.

Zedler, Empress Young. *Listening for Speech Sounds*. New York: Harper and Bros., 1955. pp. 145. This book is of value to parents as well as to teachers and speech clinicians. Stories about Tommy emphasize all basic speech sounds, encouraging the child to listen and reproduce correctly. For use with the elementary-school child.

LISTENING

Duker, Sam. *Listening Bibliography*. New York: The Scarecrow Press, 1964. pp. 211. Duker has prepared an annotated bibliography of 880 articles and books on the subject of listening. Introduction should be read carefully to ascertain the limits of this work.

Fessenden, Seth Arthur. *Designed for Listening: A Speaker-Listener Workbook*. Dubuque, Iowa: William C. Brown Co., 1951. pp. 93. Charts in this workbook provide space for students to score designated items according to their discrimination and comprehension of that to which they have listened in committees, panel discussions, sociodrama, problem-solving panels, oral reading, public speaking, and symposiums. Included in each of the seven sections is an evaluation chart to be prepared by the instructor.

Pronovost, Wilbert, and Louise Kingman. *The Teaching of Speaking and Listening in the Elementary School*. New York: Longmans, Green and Co., 1959. pp. 338. Emphasis is placed on listening for comprehension of ideas expressed though various types of oral communication including oral reading and dramatic activities. Numerous lesson plans offer helpful suggestions to teachers.

DICTIONARIES AND PRONUNCIATION REFERENCES

Bender, James F. *NBC Handbook of Pronunciation*, 3rd ed. rev. by Thomas Lee Crowell, Jr. New York: Thomas Y. Crowell Co., 1964. pp. 418.

Jones, Daniel. *Everyman's English Pronouncing Dictionary*, 12th ed. London: J. M. Dent & Sons, 1963. pp. 539.

Kenyon, John Samuel, and Thomas Albert Knott. *A Pronouncing Diction-ary of American English*. Springfield, Mass.: G. & C. Merriam Co., 1953. pp. 484.

Kökeritz, Helge. *Shakespeare's Pronunciation*. New Haven, Conn.: Yale University Press, 1953. pp. 516.

Robbins, Samuel D. *A Dictionary of Speech Pathology and Therapy*. Cam-bridge, Mass.: Distributed by Sci-Art Publishers, 1951. pp. 112.

Webster's Third New International Dictionary of the English Language, Unabridged. Philip Babcock Gove, ed.-in-chief. Springfield, Mass.: G. & C. Merriam Co., 1961. pp. 2662.

Wentworth, Harold. *American Dialect Dictionary*. New York: Thomas Y. Crowell Co., 1944. pp. 747.

Part Three

RELAXATION AND
PLATFORM POISE

9. Working for Comfort and Confidence

RELAXATION PROCEDURES

To relax is not to collapse, to become limp as a dish rag, or even to fall asleep. Relaxation means a loosening or lessening of tension and rigidity. One is truly relaxed when he is poised and ready, using only those muscles which are absolutely essential to the performance of some designated activity.

The oral reader must be poised and ready, taking care to lessen those tensions which would constrict and restrict the easy production of vocal tones. Relaxation is a state of mind as well as a state of physical being. By governing himself the oral reader can refuse to be occupied by personal anxieties, worries, and fears during preparation and performance. He must let himself be increasingly engrossed by the desire to share the ideas and feeling he has encountered in his readings.

In physical education classes and gymnastic work, many college students have already learned how to eliminate some bodily tensions by vigorous shaking of the wrists, rolling the head from side to side, simultaneously stretching arms over head and legs as far in front of the body as possible, raising shoulders up to ear level and then letting them drop to normal position. Exercises such as these, however, involve such large and broad movements that they cannot be done easily a few minutes before an oral-reading performance. A man's tie and coat, a woman's hair-do or her blouse neatly tucked into her skirt would soon be askew if not in utter disarray after a few minutes in such a gymnastic program of relaxation.

Assume that you are walking on the way to your class in oral interpretation, where you are scheduled to give an oral reading. What simple procedures of relaxation can you practice during your walk so that you will be poised and ready for a vibrant, stimulating platform presentation?

Breathe Deeply

Begin at once to breathe deeply. Take in a long, slow draught of air up to the count of twenty. Exhale. Be certain that you have expelled all of the used air before inhaling again. Empty. Empty. Empty until the air seems almost to be running out at the tips of your toes. Then inhale slowly again for as long a count as you can sustain, and exhale. You may find that it takes you twice or three times as long to exhale as to inhale. Continue to breathe deeply as you practice the remaining relaxation procedures. Notice that the purpose of deep breathing differs from that of controlled exhalation: the objective of controlled exhalation is to support your vocal tone during phonation whereas the objective of deep breathing is to exchange used air for fresh air as a means toward relaxing.

Loosen Tongue and Jaw

Let your tongue lie loosely on the floor of your mouth. Look at the sky for a moment. Note the natural tendency of the jaw to drop. Let it drop down until the lips are just barely together. Maintain this relaxed position of the jaw as you return your head to normal position and continue to breathe deeply.

A switchboard operator working a midnight-to-morning shift experimented with this exercise by making a conscious effort to keep her tongue and jaw relaxed during free moments for the full eight-hour period. In addition she mentally refused to let unnecessary tension be manifest around her mouth. As she governed her muscles, she gained a physical freedom. After the first night of this regime she was convinced that her fatigue in the past had been as much mental as physical, for at the end of this shift she reported that she felt "truly refreshed."

Maintain Good Posture

As you breathe deeply and relax your tongue and jaw, recognize that good posture contributes to your deriving maximum benefit from these techniques. If walking, assume an easy stride, keep your head up, shoulders back, and abdomen muscles firm. If sitting, choose a chair that permits you to place both feet flat on the floor, press your hips against the back of the chair, and otherwise support your back comfortably. Maintaining good posture— whether sitting, standing, or walking—is the best way to maintain proper position for all the organs involved in speech. Try to feel that a string in the very middle of your head is pulling you erect and holding you lightly, without conscious effort of your own. Continue breathing deeply and relaxing your jaw.

Loosen Hands and Wrists

Proceed now to relax your hands and wrists. A majority of tension problems resulting in headache, upset stomach, and unpleasant speech sounds find expression first in the hands and wrists. Watch yourself next time you feel tense. If you are holding a pen do you tend to grasp it more tightly than is actually necessary? Or if you are not holding anything, do you tend to curl your fingers into your palm and tighten them? Experiment for a moment: Clench your fists. Notice how your wrists also tighten. Hold this position for only a few minutes and the tension runs up your arm into your shoulders, across the back of your neck and up into your head. Keep the wrists relaxed if you would not start a vicious circle of tension and fatigue.

Even if you are carrying a load of books between classes, you can relax your hands and wrists. Young college men usually carry their books in their hand with the arm down. Try bending the elbow slightly to relax the strain at the wrist. Experiment with various methods until you can keep both wrists relatively relaxed. Young college women often carry their books in their arms. Try resting the books in the crook of your arm. Flex your wrists. Let your hands literally dangle for a moment.

If you are seated in class and waiting your turn to read, there are several ways in which you can lessen the tension. Palms up, rest one hand across the other in your lap. Palms down and fingers outspread, rest your hands on your thighs, or on the arm of your chair. Later, suggestions will be made for keeping wrists relaxed even during performance. Meanwhile, continue breathing deeply, relax your tongue and jaw, and keep your hands and wrists free from tension.

Loosen Shoulders

Now direct attention to your shoulders. Your shoulders should be back and straight as possible. If you tend to be round-shouldered, make a conscious effort to pull your abdomen muscles in, roll your hips under, straighten the small of your back, bring your head up; with this effort, your shoulders will tend first to rise and then drop into proper position. When thought is directed toward the shoulders, the tendency is either to make them so straight that they become rigid, or to raise them up toward the ears. The first movement serves only to add to your tension; the latter not only interferes with normal breathing but also constricts the vocal mechanism so that the production of a free easy tone is virtually impossible. As you walk or sit, deliberately square your shoulders. Now imagine that a 500-pound weight is being placed on each shoulder. Let your shoulders drop into a relaxed position and you will note they are back but down. Very likely you will become aware that your elbows are also less rigid.

Loosen Neck and Head

Now direct attention to your neck and head. Turn your head slowly from side to side as if you were looking at someone over each shoulder. If you feel a strong hard pull in your muscles, let your head drop forward as if you were looking for something on the ground. Now raise your head slowly. If you still feel tension in the neck and head, let your head drop heavily to the right so that your right ear almost touches your right shoulder. Raise your head slowly. Do the same on the left, and conclude by bringing your head into normal position.

Yawn

Chances are you will not need to concentrate on this next exercise. The combination of good posture with

> breathing deeply,
> relaxing tongue and jaw,
> relaxing hands and wrists,
> settling shoulders in proper position, and
> relaxing neck and head

invariably produces a Y—A—W—N. If these five relaxation techniques have not effected a yawn, then force one—a great big yawn. Now try to yawn with your lips only slightly parted. Are you aware of an open, airy sensation in your throat? Your pharynx and larynx are truly relaxed now, poised and ready to serve you.

No exercise can relax the immediate muscles involved in speech so quickly as a yawn. It is unfortunate that yawning has come to be a sign of boredom. Fish yawn to procure additional oxygen, and man has a physical need to yawn for the same reason. Furthermore, the additional oxygen promotes good circulation and normal heart action. Whenever you are truly relaxed, you yawn. To yawn spontaneously is to admit that you are poised and ready for your platform presentation.

Summary

The reader who is relaxed and who has poise on the platform is truly prepared to devote all his energies to the sharing of ideas, emotions, attitudes, and moods from literature. Relaxation and poise contribute to a reader's effectiveness, but cannot replace his comprehension and communication of that selection. A reader must know the answers to three important questions: (1) What ideas does this selection seek to present? (2) What can the oral interpretation of this selection do for my listeners? (3) Why do I believe oral interpretation is one of the best ways to communicate the qualities contained in this reading? To answer these questions is the most difficult part of the interpreter's work and artistry. Relaxation is but one means by which the student may arrive at his own creative answer.

PLATFORM POISE

What and *why* would seem to be questions of little interest to the beginning oral reader, who asks: (1) How do I start? (2) How about my hands and feet? (3) How far can I go with gestures during oral reading? The reader who has some positive means for appearing calm even though he is experiencing stage fright will very often gain quicker command over himself and present the author's concepts more effectively than the student who flounders in the social graces of sharing ideas though oral reading. It is the purpose of this particular chapter to suggest some answers to these "how" questions and to indicate some procedures for achieving platform poise.

You make an impression upon your audience the instant you begin moving toward the platform. By your gait, your carriage, and your attire, the audience forms some immediate reaction: that you are, for example, indifferent or enthusiastic, frightened or confident, unkempt or neat. Good posture, an easy stride, and a cheerful smile contribute to your expression of self-confidence. A positive impression helps the audience to relax and to receive your reading favorably. For oral reading audiences are especially friendly, eager to see the performer succeed, willing to be moved by the material that the interpreter brings. Approach the lectern with joy that you have this opportunity to exchange some stimulating views with a receptive audience.

Stance

Assume a stance which not only is comfortable for you but also is free from elements likely to distract your audience. The average reader tends to express his own inner concerns and fears by shifting his feet. Body shifts and movement unrelated to the material being read so hypnotize audiences that they may well be prepared to give an accurate account of foot patterns yet be unable to report what was read. You may be sure that your performance is a failure if your audience has been more interested in what you were doing, or in how you said something, than in what perspectives you were communicating.

Men make a good appearance if they stand to their full height with feet apart and planted firmly in a position which affords easy balance on the balls of the feet. Another comfortable position which affords easy balance for a man is to stand with one foot slightly ahead of the other.

Women, on the other hand, do not show themselves to best advantage in either of these positions because these full front positions to the audience invariably make the body look wider than it appears in any of the standard modeling positions. Both men and women need to remember that their audiences see them whole, that the whole body makes an impression as a unit. To present a graceful line, a woman may slightly turn a portion of her body just a fraction away from the audience, thus narrowing the body line and affording a more pleasing appearance. Two of the basic positions used in modeling may be of help here.

1. *Closed hesitation position:* Think of your front foot as the *pointer* and point that foot toward the audience. The back foot is the *base* which bears your weight. For the closed hesitation position direct the feet to the same position as the hands of the clock when they read eleven o'clock, or one o'clock. If your right foot is the pointer, address the right foot to the audience. The left foot then becomes the base and the arch of the left is drawn up beside the heel of the right foot, with the left toe pointing at about a fifteen-degree angle away from the right pointer. Or reverse the position so that the left foot is the pointer and the right foot is the base. Then with the arch of the right foot beside the heel of the left, the right toe points right at a slight angle away from the left toe. In either case, turn the knee of the pointing leg so that there is little or no space between the calves of the legs.

2. *Open hesitation position:* Starting from the closed hesitation position, shift your weight from the base to the pointer (that is, to the front foot pointing toward the audience). Move the base foot back at the same angle as in closed position. Return your weight to the base foot and tilt in the knee of the pointing leg as before. The knee position described is also achieved by rolling the pointing foot over slightly on its ball and in toward the leg or the base foot. Even with this last slight shift the pointer still addresses the audience.

It is never natural to stand rigidly in any one position. Either stance suggested above gives a woman considerable leverage and balance, allowing her to shift easily without calling undue attention to herself in the process.

You may find a posture, other than any discussed, which seems right for you. In any event, these comments may have helped you become aware of the contribution which physical poise can make to your total presentation. Many young men and women who look awkward do not realize the fact until they see themselves as others see them. Practicing a stance in front of a full-length mirror may, therefore, be worthwhile. But to practice reading aloud in front of a mirror often has a negative effect, making the interpreter self-conscious in terms of how he is presenting himself and thus diverting his thought from what he is responsible for communicating.

Hands

After the reader has found a comfortable and flattering stance, the inevitable question is: What to do with the hands? If you use a lectern, keep your wrists and hands relaxed by letting them rest lightly on the stand. Keep the fingers slightly separated to prevent their tightening. If a woman's hand is likely to be seen by the audience, she produces a graceful effect if the hand that rests on the stand is turned slightly in toward her body with the middle and ring finger together, the index and little finger slightly separated from the others. If you hold your book instead of using a stand, let it rest on the palm of one hand and with your other hand turn the pages or even rest your fingertips on the edges of the page to keep them from slipping past your place. For the sake of your audience do not put your hands in your pockets, nor fiddle with a pen or other object, nor drum your fingers on the stand or book during your reading. For your own sake do not grip the lectern or the book. Some readers in an effort to provide physical stability and security for themselves while reading will seize lectern or book in a strangle hold. The taut fingers and wrists inaugurate a cycle of increased tension from hand to head.

Materials

Take time to arrange your books and notes so that you are quite comfortable. Check the position of your materials so that you have effortless eye contact. Depending upon your height and your vision, you may want the book up closer to your face or in front slightly to one side. If you are very tall there may not be a lectern truly suitable for you, and you would probably be wise to rest the book in the palm of one hand. Other reasons may prompt you to hold the book in preference to using a lectern. In any event, be sure before you begin that you can see faces in the audience without having to bob your head as you look up from the book. Eye contact will add a directness to your presentation, and you too will benefit from observing the reaction of your audience.

Relations with the Audience

Before you say or read a word, make demands upon your audience. Every real artist does. The oral interpreter is as much an artist as a concert pianist or a ballet dancer. Breathe deeply a few times before you begin; by now you have learned to do so without any obvious movement. Look out at your audience. Meet their eyes with composure and, though you may not smile with your lips, you might try to smile with your eyes. Wait until your audience is ready to listen. You have something to offer. You have spent much time preparing this reading. You have every right to expect the audience to listen carefully to your sharing of ideas, attitudes, emotions, and moods from this literature.

Paderewski knew how to make demands upon his audience. Time after time this renowned concert pianist relived the following experience during his career: As he walked out upon the stage a thunderous applause greeted him. He bowed several times in acknowledgment. Then he turned to his piano. A flick of his coattails and he was seated. He made certain that the bench was adjusted properly. He raised his head. There was a rustle of programs. He waited. The noise subsided. He raised his hands and poised them over the keys. He waited another moment. The concert hall became absolutely quiet. All eyes were directed toward the piano. Every ear was ready to receive every note he produced. Then Paderewski began to play. Those moments of anticipation were richly rewarded. Everyone listened and thrilled to every moment of living music. You may not be Paderewski, but you are reading from the ideas and feelings of minds and spirits as exciting as Paderewski and the composers he interpreted. You may not be performing on a grand piano, but you are playing the most distinctive and unique instrument in the world: your voice. There is not another instrument exactly like your voice anywhere in the universe. Begin with the confidence that comes from careful preparation for performance. Begin by making demands upon your audience.

And when you have finished, do so graciously. You would not slam the door in a friend's face. You would see your friend to the door, to his car even, then stand and wave as he drove off. So, too, be not in haste to close your book. Complete your reading. Pause momentarily. Let the mood, the atmosphere, the ideas generated by your reading pervade your listeners. A moment or so, and then the reading is taking its own leave, leaving a breath of its own magic behind. You close your book quietly so as not to shatter the spell and walk—not run—from the lectern.

Gesture and Movement

Sooner or later every student of oral interpretation asks: "How far can I go?" meaning to what extent can he use facial expressions, gestures, or body movement and still keep his presentation within the realm of interpretation rather than acting. My answer to the student is to ask another question: "What does oral interpretation seek to achieve?" That is the basic question in this field of study. When you have answered that question the answer to "How far can I go?" is simply this: You can do whatever enables you to promote the idea, attitude, emotion, and mood of the selection.

Let me give an example of what I consider supreme artistry. In the scene where Juliet is waiting for the Nurse to return with news of Romeo, the oral reader is successful when, without moving half a step, he is able to suggest Juliet's frantic pacing so effectively that audiences believe they have seen a young girl moving back and forth in a courtyard.

Experience is the guide to trust. If from both the reader's and the audience's point of view, gestures and movement during a reading heightened the communication of ideas and emotions, then they must have been appropriate and effective. If, on the other hand, gestures and movement called attention to themselves or to the performer, causing the audience to forget what was said or making the audience more aware of *how* the reader achieved his purpose than of *what* was his purpose, then the gestures and movement were not proper, because they distracted the audience from the full meaning of the selection.

Since there is this risk of distraction, you may find it effective to use your voice and your facial expressions more than gesture and movement. Much of what you do depends on the style of the author you are interpreting, on the kind of program you are presenting, on the kind of audience you have, on the size of the room where you must perform, and on your own artistry. You must rely on a sense of what is in good taste. Time and experience are the best contributors to the formation of taste, so allow yourself plenty of each. Remember Eliza Doolittle? She *studied* how to speak correctly, how to walk, how to sit, how to stand, how to wear a beautiful gown. If you ask, "Will following the suggestions in this chapter make me a good interpreter?" your answer in Eliza's words is "Not bloody likely." Practice these suggestions for relaxation and physical poise. Live with them. You will grow more comfortable with them as time goes on. But above all, delve into the literature you read. Be convinced of your own reasons for wanting to share a selection with an audience. The practices recommended here will provide polish and setting for the gems you find in the literature.

Part Four

THE READING HOUR

PREVIEW

In arranging a program, you must consider your audience, your time limit, and the type of presentation to be made. Sometimes it is expedient to use an excerpt or to make a cutting from a very long piece. When you present only a portion of a work, be careful that the excerpt constitutes an accurate interpretation of the author's intent. When cutting, preserve the author's purpose and style. Marking the script helps you in your interpretation. During your reading, however, you may sense reactions to the material which guide you to effect impromptu changes. Marking the script is one way of organizing your thoughts and feelings about the literature.

Oral interpretation may be done by one reader or by a group of readers. Group readings include readers' theatre, ensemble or choric readings, and chamber theatre. Reading aloud may be presented in many different ways. Oral interpretation has values far beyond any sense of a formal presentation. There are rewards just in listening to and in reading literature aloud. Many readers may find they are developing their taste in literature, expanding their insights, and finding new enjoyment in books. Many want most sincerely to share these perceptions with others.

10. Planning the Reading Hour

A reading hour may be formal or informal, public or private, for many people or for a few. It may be part of your college work. It may be a family project—for the adults, for the children, or for the whole family. It may be a service to entertain or enlighten invalids and shut-ins, or a professional performance for an audience that pays for the intellectual or artistic experience. Workers in factories have employed readers to bring literature to them during repetitive tasks; women in knitting and sewing circles have taken turns reading to each other; religious communities have long used mealtimes to share the oral experience of literature.

Students of oral interpretation are presumably making ready for conducting reading hours as professionals; they can practice, study, and enjoy themselves in informal or impromptu oral reading periods. But the rewards of oral interpretation for nonprofessionals are not to be ignored or forgotten. Reading literature aloud and listening to others read it are experiences beyond those that come to the silent reader. These rewards include insight into the literature and into its effect on those who experience it as listeners or as readers. They contribute to skill in communicating: spoken, heard, written, or read.

The truly successful professional reading hour is always planned. Even impromptu reading periods require elements of planning, however brief: for example, choosing one piece to read rather than another, deciding whether to stand or sit while reading, adapting the reading to a few minutes or a half hour or whatever time is available—dozens of subtle ways.

AUDIENCE FACTORS

Your audience is an important consideration in guiding your choice of literature to be read aloud. If you are planning a formal program for an audience who will participate only by listening, you will want to know as much about that audience as you possibly can. Will your listeners be primarily students like yourself? Or will they be an intellectually elite group of professional people who expect stimulating ideas? Are you appearing before a civic club or at a church-fellowship dinner meeting? If there are to be special guests, who are they?

Sometimes an individual or a group of readers, with a reading already prepared, is invited to present it before an audience different from the one originally planned. If you have this opportunity, be sensitive to your audience. Planned and organized as your delivery may be, you will find that each audience is unique, that each has its own composite personality. Awareness of audience reaction will increase your own perception of the material during performance. The audience can be an important consideration in helping the reader to discover new depths in the literature he reads aloud.

FACTORS OF TIME, VARIETY, AND ORDER

Establish your time limit first. If you are responsible for the entire presentation or if you are assigned only a portion of the program, find out exactly how many minutes are allotted to you. Not until you know your audience and your time limit can you intelligently arrange your program. Even so, choose material first because you like it, second because you feel it will appeal to your audience, and third because it fits the schedule.

The "reading hour" may be as long as the attention the audience will give to the reading. A solo performer must be a highly skilled artist if he is to hold this attention beyond about one clock hour. Variety in literature as well as the use of more than one reader are likely to maintain interest longer than one reader presenting one long selection. If a long selection is to be read, try to find one that is likely to hold the interest of the listeners. Remember, heavy demands are placed upon the audience's imagination when listening to a reading.

The reader needs to paint the scene with words, to people the platform with characters whom he differentiates by changes in attitude, pitch, rate, and bodily alertness—altogether, to direct his energies in appealing to his listeners' senses and faculties through one medium alone—the ear. This taxing assignment may be more interesting to audience and reader alike if the program is arranged to provide relief at calculated fatigue points in the performance. The gravedigging scene in Hamlet, for an example from drama, offers a much-needed relief from the tensions in the tragedy and comes at just the precise point where playgoers need a rest from the existing line of action.

Some interpreters like to start with something light and amusing in order to place their listeners in a receptive frame of mind. Others prefer a few short pieces at the opening until the reader and the audience have adjusted to one another. Then they conclude with a longer and perhaps more serious selection than the initial offerings. Still others may be successful in delivering a long serious selection first, closing with something light and amusing. Much depends upon the artist himself, his audience, the occasion or theme of the presentation. Rules cannot be imposed; only guide lines can be suggested.

HOW TO MAKE A CUTTING

Very often a reader wants to use a particular selection but finds it too long for his purposes. He may cut it in one of two ways. Either he can excerpt it—simply lift a portion out from the whole. Or he can take a sentence here, a paragraph there, a phrase later on, and so weave these bits into an integrated whole. It is impossible to say when one method can or cannot be used, and when one method is better than another. But one positive statement can be made: If the author's intent or purpose has been distorted or destroyed, no cutting is good and no excerpt is satisfactory. The cutting must preserve not only the author's purpose but also his style. The excerpt must in itself be an accurate interpretation of the author's intent. For example, you might choose to read aloud from Harper Lee's *To Kill A Mockingbird*. If you read an excerpt from the sequence in which Scout and her brother Jem are returning home after the Halloween party (Chapter 28), you could count upon your audience's enjoying the passage as a suspense story in itself. But the audience could not be expected to accept your oral reading as much more than a good who-done-it unless they understood Atticus's position in the community at that particular time. The theme and purpose of the whole book are certainly strengthened as a result of the careful motivation of the characters. To recognize these motivations in an introduction would be to help the audience understand deeper relationships than could be otherwise evident in the mere reading of the excerpt.

A cutting, if properly done, would not usually have to be introduced as carefully as an excerpt. A cutting tends to explain itself while an excerpt necessitates your informing the audience what has happened up to the point of the excerpt. Here are some cuttings for you to study and examine. As you study them ask yourself: Why was one portion omitted? Why was another included? Why were some passages, originally far apart, connected in the cutting?

Suppose you are assigned a three-minute oral reading. You can find essays challenging for such an assignment. For example, examine and experiment with one of Francis Bacon's essays as cut for a three-minute reading. The essay is given in full with the marks for cutting. Study it to determine the intention of the cuts and judge the validity of the result. Is the cut version faithful to the intent of the essay? Does it distort or suppress any significant statement?

OF TRUTH: (with Markings for Cutting to Three Minutes) / Francis Bacon

"What is truth?" said jesting Pilate, and would not stay for an answer. Certainly there be that delight in giddiness, and count it a bondage to fix a belief, affecting free-will in thinking as well as in acting. And though the sects of philosophers of that kind be gone, yet there remain certain discoursing wits which are of the same veins, though there be not so much blood in them as was in those of the ancients. But it is not only the difficulty and labour which men take in finding out of truth, nor again, that when it is found, it imposeth upon men's thoughts that doth bring lies in favour, but a natural though corrupt love of the lie itself. One of the later school of the Grecians examineth the matter, and is at a stand to think what should be in it that men should love lies, where neither they make for pleasure as with poets, nor for advantage as with the merchant, but for the lie's sake. But I cannot tell; this same truth is a naked and open daylight that doth not show the masks and mummeries and triumphs of the world half so stately and daintily as candlelights. Truth may, perhaps, come to the price of a pearl that showeth best by day, but it will not rise to the price of a diamond or carbuncle that showeth best in varied lights. A mixture of a lie doth ever add pleasure. Doth any man doubt that if there were taken out of men's minds vain opinions, flattering hopes, false valuations, imaginations as one would, and the like, but it would leave the minds of a number of men poor shrunken things, full of melancholy and indisposition, and unpleasing to themselves? One of the fathers, in great severity, called poesy *Vinum Daemonum* because it filleth the imagination, and yet it is, but with the shadow of a lie. But it is not the lie that passeth through the mind, but the lie that sinketh in, and settleth in it, that doth the hurt, such as we spake before. But howsoever these things are thus in men's depraved judgments and affections, yet truth, which only doth judge itself, teacheth that the inquiry of truth, which is the love-making or wooing of it; the knowledge of truth, which is the presence of it; and the belief of truth, which is the enjoying of it, is the sovereign good of human nature. The first creature of God, in the works of the days, was the light of the sense; the last was the light of reason; and His Sabbath work ever since is the illumination of His Spirit. First He breathed light upon the face of the matter or chaos, then He breathed light into the face of man, and still He breathed and inspired light into the face of His chosen. The poet that beautified the sect that was otherwise inferior to the rest, saith yet excellently well: "It is a pleasure to stand upon the shore and to see ships tossed upon the sea; a pleasure to stand in the window of a castle and to see a battle and the adventures thereof below; but no pleasure is comparable to the standing upon the vantage ground of truth" (a hill not to be commanded, and where the air is always clear and serene) "and to see the errors, and wanderings, and mists, and tempests in the vale below." So, always, that this prospect be with pity, and not with swelling or pride. Certainly it is

~~heaven upon earth to have a man's mind move in charity, rest in providence, and turn upon the poles of truth.~~

~~To pass from theological and philosophical truth to the truth of civil business~~, it will be acknowledged, even by those that practise it not, that clear and round dealing is the honour of man's nature; and that mixture of falsehood is like alloy in coin of gold and silver, which may make the metal work the better, but it embaseth it. For these winding and crooked courses are the goings of the serpent, which goeth basely upon the belly, and not upon the feet. There is no vice that doth so cover a man with shame as to be found false and perfidious. And therefore Montaigne saith prettily, when he inquired the reason why the word of the lie should be such a disgrace and such an odious charge, saith he, "If it be well weighed, to say that a man lieth is as much to say as that he is brave towards God and a coward towards men." For a lie faces God and shrinks from man. Surely the wickedness of falsehood and breach of faith cannot possibly be so highly expressed as in that it shall be the last peal to call the judgments of God upon the generations of men, it being foretold that when Christ cometh, "He shall not find faith upon the earth."

If you are not familiar with Bacon's style and find that his way of expressing himself is not immediately clear to you, try this approach: read the essay all the way through once. Look up in the dictionary any words you do not understand. If the meaning is still not clear, check the *Oxford English Dictionary* or *A Shakespeare Glossary* to find the sense of the word in Bacon's day, for he was contemporary with Shakespeare. On your second silent reading, try to rephrase mentally some of his ideas into your own words. The third time you read, read aloud. You may want to read aloud the fourth time. Now make a quick outline—in your mind, or on paper if you think better that way—of the entire essay. Read through the outline and become aware of Bacon's total organization. Now read the essay aloud. For many of you this procedure may be real work, but as literature this piece represents a bit of the biography of man—of all men. The selection reveals some of the many ways in which truth was regarded four hundred years ago, some ways still evident today.

You may find delightful material for oral reading in *The Tatler* and *The Spectator*. "Frozen Words" would take ten minutes to read in the original. Here is a proposed cutting which can be read in five minutes.

FROZEN WORDS / From *The Spectator*—Joseph Addison

There are no books which I more delight in than in travels, especially those that describe remote countries, and give the writer an opportunity of showing his parts without incurring any danger of being examined or contradicted. Among all the authors of this kind, our renowned countryman, Sir John Mandeville, has distinguished himself by the copiousness of his invention and the greatness of his genius. The second to Sir John I take to have been Ferdinand Mendez Pinto, a person of infinite adventure and unbounded imagination. One reads the voyages of these two great wits with as much astonishment as the travels of Ulysses in Homer, or of the Red-Cross Knight in Spenser. All is enchanted ground, and fairy-land.

I have got into my hands, by great chance, several manuscripts of these two eminent authors, which are filled with greater wonders than any of those they have communicated to the public; and indeed, were they not so well attested, they would appear altogether improbable. I am apt to think the ingenious authors did not publish them with the rest of their works, lest they should pass for fictions and fables: a caution not unnecessary, when the reputation of their veracity was not yet established in the world. But as this reason has now no farther weight, I shall make the public a present of these curious pieces, at such times as I shall find myself unprovided with other subjects.

The present paper I intend to fill with an extract from Sir John's Journal, in which that learned and worthy knight gives an account of the freezing and thawing of several short speeches, which he made in the territories of Nova Zembla. I need not inform my reader, that the author of Hudibras alludes to this strange quality in that cold climate, when, speaking of abstracted notions clothed in a visible shape, he adds that apt simile,

> Like words congeal'd in northern air.

Not to keep my reader any longer in suspense, the relation put into modern language, is as follows:

"We were separated by a storm in the latitude of seventy-three, insomuch, that only the ship which I was in, with a Dutch and French vessel, got safe into a creek of Nova Zembla. We landed in order to refit our vessels and store ourselves with provisions. The crew of each vessel made themselves a cabin of turf and wood, at some distance from each other, to fence themselves against the inclemencies of the weather, which was severe beyond imagination. We soon observed, that in talking to one another we lost several of our words, and could not hear one another at above two yards distance, and that too when we sat very near the fire. After much perplexity, I found that our words froze in the air, before they could reach the ears of the persons to whom they were spoken. I was soon confirmed in this conjecture, when, upon the increase of the cold, the whole company grew dumb, or rather deaf; for every man was sensible, as we afterwards found, that he spoke as well as ever; but the sounds no sooner took air than they were condensed and lost. It was now a miserable spectacle to see us nodding and gaping at one another, every man talking, and no man heard. One might observe a seaman that could hail a ship at a league's distance, beckoning with his hand, straining his lungs, and tearing his throat; but all in vain.

"We continued here three weeks in this dismal plight. At length, upon a turn of wind, the air about us began to thaw. Our cabin was immediately filled with a dry clattering sound, which I afterwards found to be the crackling of consonants that broke over our heads, and were often mixed with a gentle hissing, which I imputed to the letter *s*, that occurs so frequently in the English tongue. I soon after felt a breeze of whispers rushing by my ear; for those, being of a soft and gentle substance, immediately liquefied in the warm wind that blew across our cabin. These were soon followed by syllables and short words, and at length by entire sentences, that melted sooner or later, as they were more or less congealed; so that we now heard every thing that had been *spoken* during the whole three weeks that we had been *silent,* ~~if I may use that expression.~~ It was now very early in the morning, and yet, to my surprise, I heard somebody say, 'Sir John, it is midnight, and time for the ship's crew to go to-bed.' This I knew to be the pilot's voice; and, upon recollecting myself, I concluded that he had spoken these words to me some days before, though I could not hear them until the present thaw. My reader will easily imagine how the whole crew was amazed to hear every man talking, and see no man opening his mouth. In the midst of this great surprise we were all in, we heard a volley of oaths and curses, lasting for a long while, and uttered in a very hoarse voice, which I knew belonged to the boatswain, who was a very choleric fellow, and had taken this opportunity of cursing and swearing at me, when he thought I could not hear him; for I had several times given him the strappado on that account, as I did not fail to repeat it for these his pious soliloquies, when I got him on ship-board.

"I must not omit the names of several beauties in Wapping, which were heard every now and then, in the midst of a long sigh that accompanied them; as, 'Dear Kate!' 'Pretty Mrs. Peggy!' 'When shall I see my Sue again!' This betrayed several amours which had been concealed until that time, and furnished us with a great deal of mirth in our return to England.

"When this confusion of voices was pretty well over, ~~though I was afraid to offer at speaking, as fearing I should not be heard~~, I proposed a visit to the Dutch cabin, which lay about a mile farther up in the country. My crew were extremely rejoiced to find they had again recovered their hearing; though every man uttered his voice with the same apprehensions that I had done.

"At about half-a-mile's distance from our cabin we heard the groanings of a bear, which at first startled us; but, upon inquiry, we were informed by some of our company, that he was dead, and now lay in salt, having been killed upon that very spot about a fortnight before, in the time of the frost. Not far from the same place, we were likewise entertained with some posthumous snarls and barkings of a fox.

"We at length arrived at the little Dutch settlement; and, upon entering the room, round it filled with sighs that smelt of brandy, and several other unsavory sounds, that were altogether inarticulate. My valet, who was an Irishman, fell into so great a rage at what he heard, that he drew his sword; but not knowing where to lay the blame, he put it up again. We were stunned with these confused noises, but did not hear a single word until about half-an-hour after; which I ascribed to the harsh and obdurate sounds of that language, which wanted more time than ours to melt and become audible.

"After having here met with a very hearty welcome, we went to the cabin of the French, who, to make amends for their three weeks' silence, were talking and disputing with greater rapidity and confusion than I ever heard in an assembly, even of that nation. Their language, as I found, upon the first giving of the

weather, fell asunder and dissolved. I was here convinced of an error, into which
I had before fallen; for I fancied, that for the freezing of the sound, it was necessary for it to be wrapped up, and, as it were, preserved in breath; but I found my
mistake when I heard the sound of a kit playing a minuet over our heads. I asked
the occasion of it; upon which one of the company told me that it would play
there above a week longer; 'for,' says he, 'finding ourselves bereft of speech, we
prevailed upon one of the company, who had his musical instrument about him, to
play to us from morning to night, ~~all which time was employed in dancing in order
to dissipate our chagrin, *et tuer le temps.*" [and kill the time]~~

Here Sir John gives very good philosophical reasons why the kit could not be
heard during the frost; but, as they are something prolix, I pass them over in
silence, and shall only observe, that the honorable author seems, by his quotations,
to have been well versed in the ancient poets, which perhaps raised his fancy
above the ordinary pitch of historians, and very much contributed to the embel-
lishments of his writings.

MARKING THE SCRIPT

Marking the book or script is one valuable way of organizing one's
thoughts and feeling about the literature. The oral interpreter who has
prepared for his reading by marking his script can approach his performance with the confidence that he is organized. Even then, during the
very reading, he may sense reactions from the audience that will guide him
to make changes.

In addition to the marking for cuttings, the oral reader does well to mark
the script for key words, pauses, pace, and other details of interpretation.
These must be instantly clear—there is no time during a reading for a study
of a long stage direction. You will develop your own marks as you gain
experience with oral reading and insight into the resources that you can
apply to it. Here is a minimum set of marks by which you can guide
yourself.

_____ Underscore key words. Keep these to a minimum. Try to choose
nouns and words of color more than verbs. As words of action
verbs will receive considerable emphasis anyway.

/   Slight pause.

//   Long pause.

⌒ Connect two words or phrases.

In scripts requiring a change of characters, assign a specific color marking to each character.

GROUP FORMS OF ORAL INTERPRETATION

In planning the reading hour, you need not be confined to thinking of all
the presentations as solo performances. Some materials are actually better

suited to oral interpretation by a group than by an individual. Such group readings may take several forms.

Readers' theatre is oral interpretation by two or more persons reading the same piece of prose, poetry, or drama. The material may be memorized, but the performers will use scripts, refer to them, and turn pages as the reading progresses. Lighting and sound effects may be used. The reading may be done on a bare stage against a cyclorama or curtain, on a platform against one wall, or with readers in the center and the audience seated around them, arena style. High stools and reading stands are often provided for the readers.

Ensemble reading, sometimes called *choric reading,* is oral interpretation by a group of persons who speak the lines in unison. Passages may be read by individuals but these merge as facets of the whole which is projected essentially by the group. Members of the chorus, or ensemble, are usually placed in the group according to their voices. Depending upon the demands of the literature, the group may be arranged in various types of groupings. Two are illustrated.

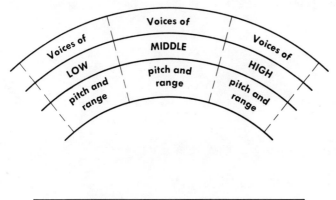

GROUPING OF VOICES FOR ENSEMBLE OR CHORIC READING

Choric readers often memorize their material and work without scripts, though presentations have been made with books in much the same way that a singing choir would appear with their music. This type of presentation requires hours of rehearsal, precise attention to articulation, careful agreement in rhythm and rate of speaking. A leader will often appear in front of the group, though readers proficient in this form of oral interpretation can designate leaders among themselves and learn to follow the leader of their particular voice grouping. Because the composition of voices in choric reading varies according to the literature, thus necessitating physical regrouping during the program, the readers usually stand rather than sit.

Chamber theatre is, according to some, not strictly oral interpretation. Others think of this form of reading as an imaginative combination of good interpretation and good acting in pantomime. In chamber theatre one reader is designated as the narrator—if the material demands, there may be additional narrators. The other readers move about on stage, handling imaginary props, and speaking only those lines assigned to them as specific characters. The form may be clear to you if you think of a television announcer engaged in on-the-spot reporting while those involved in the event he reports continue to move and speak to one another. As in other forms of oral interpretation, there are no sets, costumes, or props. Lighting and sound effects may be used.

In all of these forms of oral interpretation, the spoken word is the single most important aspect.

Part Five

SAMPLE PROGRAMS

———•••———

PREVIEW

The sample programs that conclude this book are offered as suggestions and examples to show how a program can be put together. They are not finished scripts for production, and moreover, if they are presented they may require the permission of the copyright holders, as mentioned in Chapter 11.

The sample programs include:

American Echoes in Literature (Chapter 11).
American Echoes in Historic Documents (Chapter 12).
A Cutting of a Short Work of Fiction (Chapter 13).
A Christmas Program (Chapter 14).
The Climax of a Novel as Readers' Theatre (Chapter 15).
A Long Poem (Chapter 16).

11. American Echoes in Literature

This program has two units of reading which can be presented in about an hour. The presentation time for each selection is indicated. If a two-hour production is desired, a verse drama entitled *The Fall of the City* by Archibald MacLeish might be added (see pages 187-188). The MacLeish piece requires thirty minutes, and when two intermissions of ten minutes each are allowed for setting up the stage between readings, the three units provide a full two-hour performance.

The first reading is made up of three sermons from James Weldon Johnson's *God's Trombones*. The complete book has seven sermons; an interpreter may wish to add or substitute one of the others. Mr. Johnson's introduction to these sermons is a valuable aid and should be studied by the interpreter before he prepares his reading.

The second reading is *The Devil and Daniel Webster*. What is used here is Charles Jackson's adaptation for radio, based on the original story by Stephen Vincent Benét.

Those who present oral interpretations of literature need to be aware of certain facts regarding literary property and its ownership. The laws of the United States and other countries, as well as numerous international treaties, protect writers and provide for the control of literary works, their publication, and their use. These laws and controls often seem intricate and complex, but they have a simple basis: a person's property cannot be used without his consent. In time a literary work becomes public property. For example, Benjamin Franklin's works published before the American Revolution are public properties whereas the works of James Weldon Johnson published in 1927 are private properties that will not become public until 1983 under current copyright law. Therefore anyone who undertakes to give a public oral interpretation of Mr. Johnson's "Listen Lord— A Prayer" or of the Benét-Jackson *The Devil and Daniel Webster* must have the permission of the writer. There may be a charge for this permission. This little that has been said about copyright and literary property is not intended to explain the whole subject but only to alert performers and producers to the matter.

The sample programs that comprise the remainder of this book, specifically, are not to be presented in public performances, especially performances for pay, without permission from the authors or publishers.

The sample program of American Echoes in Literature now follows.

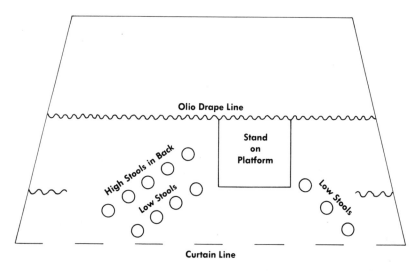

FLOOR PLAN FOR INTERPRETERS READING God's Trombones: "Listen, Lord—A Prayer"; "Go Down, Death—A Funeral Sermon"; "The Judgment Day."

THIS PLAN, AND OTHERS FOR THE SAMPLE PROGRAMS, IS A SUGGESTION FORMED BY EXPERIENCE ON A STAGE AVAILABLE AT SAN FRANCISCO STATE COLLEGE. THE GENERAL IDEA CAN BE MAINTAINED OR IMPROVED TO FIT OTHER PHYSICAL FACILITIES.

The house lights dim. A Voice in the darkness speaks:

NARRATOR: An American echo can send back many different sounds . . . much shouting . . . lusty singing . . . even a few soft sounds. The echoes we hear tonight have no implicit unity. Rather, like the separate sounds of a spring evening, they stand vivid in their uniqueness . . . a uniqueness that gives us a glimpse into various sections of this land of ours. The program tonight will take you to the Deep South with three sermons from James Weldon Johnson's *God's Trombones,* then to New England with Stephen Vincent Benét's *The Devil and Daniel Webster,* adapted by Charles Jackson. Our scenery will be painted with words. We're going to ask you to change, through your imaginations, our simple setting of stools and platform into a meeting house where men and women have gathered to hear an old-time preacher intone prayers and sermons. *Listen, Lord —A Prayer.*

Lights up on stage. The readers stroll in by twos and threes. Sound effects: musical background of "Swing Low, Sweet Chariot." The readers pantomime greetings to one another as if they were attending a revival meeting and take their time seating themselves. When the minister begins, they focus on him. For each of the sermons a different reader assumes the role of minister. During each reading there are appropriate responses from the "congregation."

LISTEN, LORD: A PRAYER[1] / James Weldon Johnson

O Lord, we come this morning
Knee-bowed and body-bent
Before thy throne of grace.
O Lord—this morning—
Bow our hearts beneath our knees,
And our knees in some lonesome valley.
We come this morning—
Like empty pitchers to a full fountain,
With no merits of our own.
O Lord—open up a window of heaven,
And lean out far over the battlements of glory,
And listen this morning.

Lord, have mercy on proud and dying sinners—
Sinners hanging over the mouth of hell,
Who seem to love their distance well.
Lord—ride by this morning—
Mount your milk-white horse,
And ride-a this morning—
And in your ride, ride by old hell,
Ride by the dingy gates of hell,
And stop poor sinners in their headlong plunge.

And now, O Lord, this man of God,
Who breaks the bread of life this morning—
Shadow him in the hollow of thy hand,
And keep him out of the gunshot of the devil.
Take him, Lord—this morning—
Wash him with hyssop inside and out,
Hang him up and drain him dry of sin.
Pin his ear to the wisdom-post,
And make his words sledge hammers of truth—
Beating on the iron heart of sin.
Lord God, this morning—
Put his eye to the telescope of eternity,

[1]From *God's Trombones* by James Weldon Johnson. Copyright 1927 by The Viking Press, Inc., 1955 by Grace Nail Johnson. Reprinted by permission of The Viking Press, Inc.

And let him look upon the paper walls of time.
Lord, turpentine his imagination,
Put perpetual motion in his arms,
Fill him full of the dynamite of thy power,
Anoint him all over with the oil of thy salvation,
And set his tongue on fire.

And now, O Lord—
When I've done drunk my last cup of sorrow—
When I've been called everything but a child of God—
When I'm done travelling up the rough side of the mountain—
O—Mary's Baby—
When I start down the steep and slippery steps of death—
When this old world begins to rock beneath my feet—
Lower me to my dusty grave in peace
To wait for that great gittin' up morning—Amen.

[Reading time: about 3 minutes

GO DOWN, DEATH: A FUNERAL SERMON[2] / James Weldon Johnson

Weep not, weep not,
She is not dead;
She's resting in the bosom of Jesus.
Heart-broken husband—weep no more;
Grief-stricken son—weep no more;
Left-lonesome daughter—weep no more;
She's only just gone home.

Day before yesterday morning,
God was looking down from his great, high heaven,
Looking down on all his children,
And his eye fell on Sister Caroline,
Tossing on her bed of pain.
And God's big heart was touched with pity,
With the everlasting pity.

And God sat back on his throne,
And he commanded that tall, bright angel standing at his right hand:
Call me Death!
And that tall, bright angel cried in a voice
That broke like a clap of thunder:
Call Death!—Call Death!
And the echo sounded down the streets of heaven

[2]From *God's Trombones* by James Weldon Johnson. Copyright 1927 by The Viking Press, Inc., 1955 by Grace Nail Johnson. Reprinted by permission of The Viking Press, Inc.

Till it reached away back to that shadowy place,
Where Death waits with his pale, white horses.

And Death heard the summons,
And he leaped on his fastest horse,
Pale as a sheet in the moonlight.
Up the golden street Death galloped,
And the hoofs of his horse struck fire from the gold,
But they didn't make no sound.
Up Death rode to the Great White Throne,
And waited for God's command.

And God said: Go down, Death, go down,
Go down to Savannah, Georgia,
Down in Yamacraw,
And find Sister Caroline.
She's borne the burden and heat of the day,
She's labored long in my vineyard,
And she's tired—
She's weary—
Go down, Death, and bring her to me.

And Death didn't say a word,
But he loosed the reins on his pale, white horse,
And he clamped the spurs to his bloodless sides,
And out and down he rode,
Through heaven's pearly gates,
Past suns and moons and stars;
On Death rode,
And the foam from his horse was like a comet in the sky;
On Death rode,
Leaving the lightning's flash behind;
Straight on down he came.

While we were watching round her bed,
She turned her eyes and looked away,
She saw what we couldn't see;
She saw Old Death. She saw Old Death
Coming like a falling star.
But Death didn't frighten Sister Caroline;
He looked to her like a welcome friend.
And she whispered to us: I'm going home,
And she smiled and closed her eyes.

And Death took her up like a baby,
And she lay in his icy arms,
But she didn't feel no chill.
And Death began to ride again—
Up beyond the evening star,

Out beyond the morning star,
Into the glittering light of glory,
On to the Great White Throne.

And there he laid Sister Caroline
On the loving breast of Jesus.

And Jesus took his own hand and wiped away her tears,
And he smoothed the furrows from her face,
And the angels sang a little song,
And Jesus rocked her in his arms,
And kept a-saying: Take your rest,
Take your rest, take your rest.

Weep not—weep not,
She is not dead;
She's resting in the bosom of Jesus.

[*Reading time: about 4½ minutes*

THE JUDGMENT DAY[3] / James Weldon Johnson

In that great day,
People, in that great day,
God's a-going to rain down fire.
God's a-going to sit in the middle of the air
To judge the quick and the dead.

Early one of these mornings,
God's a-going to call for Gabriel,
That tall, bright angel, Gabriel;
And God's a-going to say to him: Gabriel,
Blow your silver trumpet,
And wake the living nations.

And Gabriel's going to ask him: Lord,
How loud must I blow it?

And God's a-going to tell him: Gabriel,
Blow it calm and easy.
Then putting one foot on the mountain top,
And the other in the middle of the sea,
Gabriel's going to stand and blow his horn,
To wake the living nations.

Then God's a-going to say to him: Gabriel,
Once more blow your silver trumpet,
And wake the nations underground.

---

[3]From *God's Trombones* by James Weldon Johnson. Copyright 1927 by The
Viking Press, Inc., 1955 by Grace Nail Johnson. Reprinted by permission of The
Viking Press, Inc.

And Gabriel's going to ask him: Lord
How loud must I blow it?
And God's a-going to tell him: Gabriel,
Like seven peals of thunder.
Then the tall, bright angel, Gabriel,
Will put one foot on the battlements of heaven
And the other on the steps of hell,
And blow that silver trumpet
Till he shakes old hell's foundations.

And I feel Old Earth a-shuddering—
And I see the graves a-bursting—
And I hear a sound,
A blood-chilling sound.
What sound is that I hear?
It's the clicking together of the dry bones,
Bone to bone—the dry bones.
And I see coming out of the bursting graves,
And marching up from the valley of death,
The army of the dead.

And the living and the dead in the twinkling of an eye
Are caught up in the middle of the air,
Before God's judgment bar.

Oh-o-oh, sinner,
Where will you stand,
In that great day when God's a-going to rain down fire?
Oh, you gambling man—where will you stand?
You whore-mongering man—where will you stand?
Liars and backsliders—where will you stand,
In that great day when God's a-going to rain down fire?

And God will divide the sheep from the goats,
The one on the right, the other on the left.
And to them on the right God's a-going to say:
Enter into my kingdom.
And those who've come through great tribulations,
And washed their robes in the blood of the Lamb,
They will enter in—
Clothed in spotless white,
With starry crowns upon their heads,
And silver slippers on their feet,
And harps within their hands;—

And two by two they'll walk
Up and down the golden street,
Feasting on the milk and honey
Singing new songs of Zion,

Chattering with the angels
All around the Great White Throne.

And to them on the left God's a-going to say:
Depart from me into everlasting darkness,
Down into the bottomless pit.
And the wicked like lumps of lead will start to fall,
Headlong for seven days and nights they'll fall,
Plumb into the big, black, red-hot mouth of hell,
Belching out fire and brimstone.
And their cries like howling, yelping dogs,
Will go up with the fire and smoke from hell,
But God will stop his ears.

Too late, sinner! Too late!
Good-bye, sinner! Good-bye!
In hell, sinner! In hell!
Beyond the reach of the love of God.

And I hear a voice, crying, crying:
Time shall be no more!
Time shall be no more!
Time shall be no more!
And the sun will go out like a candle in the wind,
The moon will turn to dripping blood,
The stars will fall like cinders,
And the sea will burn like tar;
And the earth shall melt away and be dissolved,
And the sky will roll up like a scroll.
With a wave of his hand God will blot out time,
And start the wheel of eternity.

Sinner, oh, sinner,
Where will you stand
In that great day when God's a-going to rain down fire?

[*Reading time: about 5 minutes*

Intermission, about ten minutes, while reading stands and stools are placed in accordance with the floor plan illustrated. The intermission ends with readers in their places for—

THE DEVIL AND DANIEL WEBSTER[4] / Radio Version
by Charles Jackson from the Story by Stephen Vincent Benét

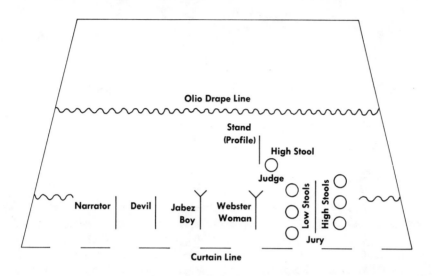

FLOOR PLAN FOR INTERPRETERS READING The Devil and Daniel Webster. STRAIGHT LINES INDICATE SINGLE READING STANDS. FORKED LINES INDICATE DOUBLE READING STANDS, OR PAIRS OF STANDS TURNED DIAGONALLY. ADDITIONAL STOOLS MAY BE USED.

CHARACTERS

A VOICE	BOY
DANIEL WEBSTER	THE DEVIL
NARRATOR	VOICE OF MISER STEVENS
JABEZ STONE	THE JUDGE
MRS. JABEZ STONE	THE JURY (SIX OR MORE)
WALTER BUTLER	

Microphones, music, and sound directions are for the radio script. Oral interpreters must work for the effects by methods fitting the medium. The sound effects bay be taped in advance, then played as needed during the reading; or a narrator may read appropriate comment. Characters who do not participate in the scene for long periods may sit with backs to the audience.

[4]Reprinted by permission of Brandt & Brandt, 101 Park Avenue, New York, N. Y. 10017.

SOUND   *Distant rolling thunder.*

VOICE [*a farmer calling loudly*]   Dan'l Webster—Dan'l Webster!

SOUND   *Thunder louder—sound of rushing wind . . . More thunder and rushing wind.*

VOICE [*louder*]   Dan'l Webster!

SOUND   *Loud crash of thunder: then*

WEBSTER [*far-away majestic voice*]   Neighbor, how stands the Union?

VOICE   The Nation stands as she stood—rockbottomed and copper-sheathed—one and indivisible . . .

SOUND   *Rolling thunder begins to fade—dying out by the time* WEBSTER *says:*

WEBSTER   So be it.

SOUND   *Thunder dies out.*

MUSIC   *Should be a rich, patriotic theme—coming in loud and strong for about ten seconds, then dying down and continuing low in background.*

NARRATOR [*good voice*]   Daniel Webster was the biggest man in the country. He never got to be President, but he was the biggest man. A man with a mouth like a mastiff, a brow like a mountain and eyes like burning anthracite: that was Dan'l Webster in his prime.—And the biggest case he argued never got written down in the books, for he argued it against the devil—nip and tuck and no holds barred. And *this* is the way we used to hear it told. . . .

MUSIC   *Fades out.*

SOUND   *Horse whinnies and snuffles.*

MRS. STONE'S VOICE [*calling off-mike—in the distance*]   Jabez—Jabez—Ja—bez!

JABEZ   What is it?

MRS. STONE [*off-mike—still in the distance*]   What are you settin' there for, Jabez?

JABEZ   Come nearer. There ain't no use for a lot of hollerin'.

MRS STONE [*coming nearer—into mike*]   I seen you from the kitchen window, Jabez Stone—settin' out here doin' nothin'. And you with all this plowing to do. What ails you, man?

JABEZ [*disgustedly*]   I'm plumb sick of the whole business! That's what I am.

MRS. STONE   What's the matter now?

JABEZ   Whoa there, Daisy!—Why, I just broke the plowshare on a rock that I swear wasn't there yesterday.

MRS. STONE   Well, now Jabez, there's no use crying over——

JABEZ   And then, as I was fixin' to look at the plowshare, the off horse began to cough—the ropy kind of cough that means sickness and horse-doctors.

MRS. STONE   I got my own troubles to worry about, what with two of the children down with the measles and me none too strong myself——

JABEZ [*almost in tears*]   Well, I'm sick and tired of the whole business. *Everything* goes wrong *all* the time.

MRS. STONE [*encouragingly*]   Now stop this, Jabez Stone. Why, you've got good land and a good farm.

JABEZ   Yeah, but it don't prosper me. If I plant corn, I get borers! If I plant potatoes, I get blight.

MRS. STONE [*consoling him*]   There's no use to go taking on so, Jabez, just because your old plow got broke on a rock. Stones crop up in *other* folks' fields——

JABEZ   And *boulders* crop up in mine. I'm the unluckiest man in the whole state of New Hampshire.

MRS. STONE   Now, Jabez—there's some folks bound to be like that—unlucky.

JABEZ   Well, this is the last straw—I vow it's enough to make a man want to sell his soul to the devil.

MRS. STONE [*alarmed*]   *Jabez Stone!*

JABEZ   And I *would,* too, for two cents.

MRS. STONE   Shame on you. Notice is always taken of things like that, Jabez. You'd better take that back.

JABEZ   I won't! For two cents and a change of luck I'd sell my soul to the devil.

MRS. STONE   Then I'm scared for you, Jabez Stone, and for us all—[*warningly*] Notice is always taken of things like that, sooner or later, just like the Good Book says . . .

MUSIC   *Comes up full, then fades out. It is later the same day.*

BOY   Pa, there's a man to see you outside.

JABEZ   Who is it, boy?

BOY   I don't know. I never see him before.

MRS. STONE   Tell him we're at supper and ask him in, son.

BOY   He said he couldn't come in. He wants to see you outside, Pa.

JABEZ [*thoughtfully*]   Oh, yes, oh, yes . . . Keep my soup warm for me, Mattie. [*His voice trailing off-mike, as he leaves the house*]   I'll be right back—I think.

SOUND   *Closing of door.*

MRS. STONE   What's he look like, Thomas? A stranger?

BOY   Queer like. He smiles all the time, and his teeth are awful white—and kind of pointed, too, and sharp.

MRS. STONE   How is he dressed?

BOY [*enjoying himself*]   All in black. Looks like a city feller, with a black hat, too, and pointed whiskers. Got a nice smart buggy, though—shiny and brand-new looking.—And Ma—the funniest thing. When he drove up in the yard, the dog took one look at him and run away howling, with his tail between his legs.

SOUND   *Door opens—as* JABEZ *enters.*

JABEZ   Never mind about the soup, Mattie. It's a lawyer feller, come to see me about a legacy. I and him are going to talk over some business—outside.

MRS. STONE   Better take a lantern with you, then, Jabez. Ain't it dark out there?

JABEZ   I ain't afraid.

MRS. STONE   Don't be stubborn, man. Take a lantern.

SOUND   *Door closes as we follow* JABEZ *into the night.*

JABEZ [*clears his throat: then*]   All right, stranger. Where do we go?

DEVIL [*engagingly—no leering at any time*]   We'll just walk down around behind the barn and make our little bargain, shall we, Jabez Stone?

JABEZ [*stubborn*]   Anywhere you say. I ain't afraid.

DEVIL   That's a nice farm you've got here, Jabez.

JABEZ   It ain't now . . .

DEVIL   But it will be—after our little deal. Is that what you mean?

JABEZ   That's up to you. Things couldn't be worse than the way they've been.

DEVIL   And so you're willing to do anything to change your luck—is that it?

JABEZ [*sullen*]   Yes.

DEVIL   Even to selling your soul?

JABEZ   I said it, didn't I?

DEVIL   Yes—I heard you this morning. Your good wife was right. Notice is always taken, sooner or later, just like the Good Book says. [*Laughs*]

JABEZ   I knew you was coming.

DEVIL [*all business*]   Well, then, here I am. Now for the papers. Just sign your name here—Jabez Stone, nice and plain like.

JABEZ   What are the terms?

DEVIL   Oh, yes—the terms. Why, for seven years you will prosper and grow rich—at the end of which time, I come to collect.

JABEZ   Collect what?

DEVIL   Why, your soul, Jabez Stone—your immortal soul. [*Laughs*]

JABEZ   Give me the pen!

DEVIL   Not so fast. You must prick your finger to sign. Give me your hand, Jabez.

JABEZ   No, I'll just hold it up.

DEVIL Any way you say, Jabez. Then I prick your finger with this little silver pin —so. Did it hurt?

JABEZ No.

DEVIL Don't worry about that wound, Jabez. It'll heal quick and clean—but you'll have a nice little white scar—just to remind you.

JABEZ [*grimly*] I won't need to be reminded.

DEVIL You might, Jabez. You might. And now you are ready to sign. You can write, I take it?

JABEZ Give me the paper.

DEVIL That's right—that's right. [*Pause while* JABEZ *signs the paper*] A mighty pretty hand, too.

JABEZ And now, if you'll excuse me, I'll be going.

DEVIL And I'll be going too, Jabez. Our deal and bargain is made, but I'll be back, after the seventh year. Meantime, you'll have *very* good luck. Oh, I'll see to that.

MUSIC *Comes up full to end the scene, then continues softly behind the narration.*

NARRATOR After that, all of a sudden, things began to pick up and prosper for Jabez Stone. His cows got fat and his horses sleek. His crops were the envy of the neighborhood, and lightning might strike all over the neighborhood, but it wouldn't strike *his* barn. Pretty soon he was one of the prosperous people of the country; they asked him to stand for selectman, and he stood for it; there began to be talk of running him for State Senate. All in all, you might say the Stone family was as happy and contented as cats in a dairy. And so they were—except for Jabez Stone . . .

MUSIC *Fades out.*

SOUND *Plowing noises, horse whinnies, harness rattling, fades into*

JABEZ Whoa, there, Daisy! Not so fast, Dandelion. Now, giddap!

SOUND *Plowing noises.*

DEVIL [*calling from the distance—off-mike*] Hello there, neighbor!

JABEZ Whoa, Daisy—Whoa, Dandelion! [*Pause*]

DEVIL [*coming close to mike*] I say—Hello, neighbor!

JABEZ [*sullen*] Don't call me neighbor.

DEVIL What are you staring at? Oh, it's my boots that seem to fascinate you. The very best money can buy.

JABEZ I don't like them.

DEVIL Why not? Too shiny for your taste?

JABEZ I don't like the looks of the toes. There aren't any.

DEVIL [*heartily*] Why, that shouldn't worry you, Jabez—no more than the little white scar on your finger there. It *hasn't* worried you, has it, Mr. Stone?

JABEZ   Oh, I've been contented enough—the first few years anyway.

DEVIL   I daresay.

JABEZ [*sadly*]   It's a great thing when bad luck turns. It drives most other things out of your head.

DEVIL   But there's always that little white scar to remind you.

JABEZ   Say, listen here, Mister—aren't you a year early?

DEVIL   I am—I am. There's one more year to go, before the seven are up—but I just dropped in for a friendly call, so to speak—to see how things are going.

JABEZ   Well, if there's still a year to go before you collect, then would you mind just——

DEVIL   Mr. Stone, you're a hummer. It's a very pretty property you've got there, Mr. Stone.

JABEZ   Well, some might favor it, and others might not.

DEVIL [*expansively*]   No need to belittle your industry! After all, we know what's been done, and it's all been according to contract and specifications. So when—ahem—the mortgage falls due next year, you shouldn't have any regrets.

JABEZ   Speaking of that mortgage, Mister—I'm beginning to have one or two doubts about it.

DEVIL   Doubts?

JABEZ   Why, yes—This being the U.S.A., and me always having been a religious man. [*Clears his throat, gets a bit bolder*] Yes sir, I'm beginning to have considable doubts as to that mortgage holding in—er—in court.

DEVIL [*chuckles*]   Well, if you're in doubt, let's have a look at the original document. [*Crackling sounds of stiff paper, as the devil thumbs through his document, muttering*] Sherwin, Slater, Stevens, Stone—Here it is— [*reading slowly*] "I, Jabez Stone, for a term of seven years—" —Oh, it's quite in order, I think.

VOICE OF MISER STEVENS [*filtered very squeaking and small as if from a tiny insect*]   Neighbor Stone—Neighbor Stone!

JABEZ [*terrified*]   What's that? That little white—a moth! It's saying—sounds like Miser Stevens—

VOICE OF MISER STEVENS [*the same squeaking again*]   Neighbor Stone—Neighbor Stone! Help me! For God's sake, help me!

JABEZ   It came out of your pocketbook! What's that in your handkerchief?

DEVIL [*dismissing the subject*]   That little moth—never mind, never mind—it's caught again. There, now I'll tie up the ends of the bandana—so!—and you won't be troubled any more.

JABEZ   What was it?—Oh, I think——

DEVIL   Sorry for the interruption. Now, as I was saying——

JABEZ   Hold on! That was Miser Stevens' voice! And you've got him in your handkerchief!

DEVIL   Oh, well, now that you know. It was very careless of me. [*Simpering*] Well, well—these little contretemps will occur.

JABEZ   I don't know what you mean by countertan—but that was Miser Stevens' voice! And he ain't dead! You can't tell me he is! He was just as spry and mean as a woodchuck, Tuesday!

DEVIL [*piously*]   In the midst of life, as they say . . .

SOUND   *Church bell begins to toll in the distance—off-mike.*

DEVIL   Listen! You hear? There it is now, tolling for Mister Stevens as you call him—and he *is* dead.

SOUND   *Tolling bells continue faintly in the background, through the rest of the scene.*

DEVIL   So it goes! These long-standing accounts—one really hates to close them. But business is business.

JABEZ [*awed voice*]   Are they all as small as that? As that little white moth I saw?

DEVIL   Small? Oh, I see what you mean. Why, they vary. Don't worry, Mr. Stone, you'll go with a very good grade. Now, a man like Daniel Webster, of course— well, we'd have to build a special box for him. And even at that, I imagine the wing-spread would astonish you. But in your case, as I was saying——

JABEZ [*in fear*]   Put that handkerchief away!

DEVIL   All right—if it annoys you. I'll put it away for a year. [*Portentously*] One year from today, Jabez Stone—and then . . .

SOUND   *Bells fade into*

MUSIC   *Comes up ending the scene—then continues softly behind narration.*

NARRATOR   But till you've made a bargain like that, you've no idea how fast a year can run. It seemed like it was only a week before the time was up. Till finally, Jabez Stone can't stand it any longer; and in the last evening of the year, he hitches up his horse and drives off to see Dan'l Webster. [MUSIC OUT] For Dan'l was born in New Hampshire, and it's well known that he has a particular soft spot for old neighbors. . . .

JABEZ [*almost tearfully*]   That's the story, then, Mister Webster, and ashamed I am to tell it. But it had to be told to someone, and who else should it be but you?

WEBSTER [*decisively*]   Well, I haven't pleaded a mortgage case in a long time, and I don't generally plead now, except before the Supreme Court—but if I can, I'll help you.

JABEZ   Then I've got hope for the first time in seven years. Oh, it's been awful— awful! The name of Jabez Stone has become known all over the state. I've been that prosperous. There's talk of running me for Governor—and it's dust and ashes in my mouth.

WEBSTER   You certainly have given yourself the devil's own row to hoe, Neighbor Stone, but I'll take your case.

JABEZ [*eagerly*]   You'll take it?

WEBSTER   Yes. I've been working up some speeches to make against John C. Calhoun and I've got seventy-five other things to do and the Missouri Compromise to straighten out, but I'll take your case. For if two New Hampshiremen aren't a match for the devil, we might as well give the country back to the Indians. When is he coming?

JABEZ   Tonight at midnight.

WEBSTER   Where?

JABEZ   At my house.

WEBSTER   Then we have no time to waste. You came here in a hurry yourself, didn't you?

JABEZ   Well, I admit I made time.

WEBSTER   You'll go back faster. [*Shouting*] Wilbur, hitch up Constitution and Constellation to the carriage. [*To* JABEZ] They're a pair of matched greys, Mr. Stone, and they step like greased lightning . . .

MUSIC   *Comes in loud, then continues behind the roar of thundering wheels, the clatter of horses' hoofs, and the crack of the whip as* WEBSTER *and* JABEZ *ride wildly through the night.*

JABEZ [*shouting above noise*]   You're going to kill these horses, Mr. Webster!

WEBSTER [*shouting*]   No, I won't! Not these two! I like doing things full-tilt— and so do they! Puts iron in your veins!

JABEZ [*shouting*]   There goes my hat!

WEBSTER [*shouting*]   What do you care! It isn't your soul, Jabez—we've still got that! [*Laughs.*]

MUSIC   *Comes up strong—then fades out.*

JABEZ   I'm still out of breath from that ride, Mister Webster.

WEBSTER   You'll recover, Neighbor Stone. Take a drink, man, while we're waiting for our friend to appear. There's no better company than a jug.

JABEZ   He'll be here soon.

WEBSTER   Your clock says only eleven-thirty.

JABEZ   Oh, Mr. Webster—listen! For God's sake, Mr. Webster, harness your horses and get away from this place as fast as you can!

WEBSTER [*putting the suggestion aside*]   You've brought me a long way, neighbor, to tell me you don't like my company.

JABEZ [*with great feeling*]   Miserable wretch that I am! I've brought you a devilish way, and now I see my folly! Let him take *me* if he wills! But you're the

Union's strength and New Hampshire's pride! He mustn't get *you,* Mister Webster! He mustn't get you!

WEBSTER I'm obliged to you, Neighbor Stone. But there's a jug on the table and a case in hand. And I never left a jug or case half finished in my life.

SOUND *Sharp knock on the door.*

WEBSTER Ah, I thought your clock was a trifle slow, Neighbor Stone—Come in!

SOUND *Opening of door . . . Faint sound of wind.*

JABEZ [*Gives a little cry.*]

WEBSTER Now, now, Jabez.

DEVIL [*with elaborate politeness*] Mr. Webster, I presume.

WEBSTER Attorney of record for Jabez Stone. Might I ask your name?

DEVIL I've gone by a good many. Perhaps Scratch will do for the evening. *Mister* Scratch. I'm often called that in these regions—You know the object of my errand?

WEBSTER I do.

DEVIL [*businesslike*] Well, then, I shall call upon you, as a law-abiding citizen, to assist me in taking possession of my property.

WEBSTER That is the nature of my errand here, too, this evening, Scratch. You shall not have this man!

DEVIL What, then, of the contract?

WEBSTER I have seen no contract.

DEVIL Then here it is. [*Crackling of stiff paper*] Here is the deed—and see, here is the signature.

WEBSTER It can't be right!

DEVIL But it is.

WEBSTER [*fencing*] Er—what will you take for that deed—just as it stands?

DEVIL I'll take what I came for—the soul of Jabez Stone.

WEBSTER But—wait a minute, man. This deed was made out some time ago, when the property was worth so much less. It can't hold now!

DEVIL But it does.

WEBSTER [*trying to find a way out*] But wait—Jabez Stone is no longer a poor farmer. The property has increased in value, and Jabez—why, state senators ought to be worth more!

DEVIL What have I to do with "oughts" and "should-be's"? I'm surprised at you, Daniel Webster! Stick to the letter of the law!

WEBSTER Do not put me off! I tell you, you shall not have this man's soul—do you hear me!

DEVIL   These spirited efforts on behalf of your client do you credit, Mr. Webster; but if you have no more argument to adduce, I'm rather pressed for time, and——

WEBSTER [*thundering*]   Pressed or not, you shall not have this man! Mr. Stone is an American citizen and no American citizen may be forced into the service of a foreign prince! We fought England for that in 1812!—and we'll fight all hell for it again!

DEVIL   Foreign! And who calls me a foreigner!

WEBSTER   Well, I never yet heard of the devil claiming American citizenship.

DEVIL   No? And who with better right? When the first wrong was done to the first Indian, I was there. When the first slaveship put out for the Congo, I stood on her deck. Am I not in your books and stories and beliefs, from the first settlements on? Am I not spoken of, still, in every church in New England? 'Tis true the North claims me for a Southerner, and the South for a Northerner, but I am neither. Why, I am merely an honest American like yourself—and of the best descent—for, to tell the truth, Mr. Webster, though I don't like to boast of it, my name is older in this country than yours.

WEBSTER   Aha! Then I stand on the Constitution! I demand a *trial* for my client!

DEVIL [*simpering*]   The case is hardly one for an ordinary court. And, indeed, the lateness of the hour——

WEBSTER   Let it be any court you choose, so long as it is an American judge and an American jury. Let it be the quick or the dead! I'll abide the issue!

DEVIL   Very well, you have said it! [*Claps his hands*] I need but clap my hands and you have your judge and jury.

SOUND   *Door crashes open with bang against the wall. The wind whistles into room. There is a tramping and shuffling of heavy feet as the jury enters.*

JABEZ [*terrified whisper*]   In God's name—who comes by so late! Who are these men?

DEVIL   The jury Mr. Webster demands! You must pardon the rough appearance of one or two; they have come a long way.

SOUND   *Tramping and shuffling of feet continues.*

WEBSTER   By heaven!

JABEZ [*in a low voice to* WEBSTER]   You know them?

WEBSTER [*replying to him in a low voice*]   It's plain who they are. Men who have long since sold themselves to the devil. For there's Walter Butler, the Loyalist, who spread fire and horror through the Mohawk Valley; and there is Simon Girty, the renegade, who saw white men burned at the stake.

JABEZ [*horrified*]   Look—his eyes are green—and there are stains of blood on his shirt . . .

WEBSTER [*continuing to* JABEZ] Here's King Philip, with the great gash in his head that gave him his death wound; and cruel Governor Dale, who broke men on the wheel. There's Morton of Merrymount, who so vexed the Plymouth Colony with his hate of the godly; and Teach, the bloody pirate, with his black beard curling on his breast. And see—here comes Reverend John Smeet with his strangler's hands, walking as daintily as he did to the gallows.

JABEZ Look—the red print of the rope is still around his neck . . .

WEBSTER Yes, Scratch has told the truth; they have all played a part in America.

DEVIL [*mockingly*] Are you satisfied with the jury, Mr. Webster?

WEBSTER Quite satisfied—though I miss General Arnold from the company.

DEVIL Benedict Arnold is engaged upon other business. And you asked for a justice, I believe? Here he is. Justice Hathorne is a jurist of experience. He presided at certain witch trials once held in Salem. There were others who repented of the business later, but not he.

JUDGE [*in a vicious voice*] Repent of such notable wonders and undertakings? Nay, hang them—hang them all!

JABEZ [*whimpering*] Oh—Mister Webster—that can't be the judge——

JUDGE [*loud*] Silence! The court is in order! [*Long pause*] Proceed with the case. Let the defendant take the stand.

JABEZ [*terrified*] Oh, I can't—I can't! Look at that man—there—and there—

JUDGE [*pounding gavel and shouting*] Order! What is the matter with the witness?

WEBSTER He is afraid of the jury, your honor.

JUDGE Then he'll have small chance, if he's afraid of the jury at the start.

WEBSTER May I speak for him, sir?

JUDGE Say on! We have other business yet to do this night.

WEBSTER The case is this, then, your honor. My poor neighbor here——

DEVIL I object!

JUDGE Objection sustained.

JURY *Cackles in a vicious manner, delighted with the unfairness of the* JUDGE.

WEBSTER This man, Jabez Stone, then, who happens to be my good neighbor——

DEVIL I object!

JUDGE Objection sustained!

JURY *Cackles again.*

WEBSTER This *man* is supposed to have sold his soul to the devil——

DEVIL I object!

JUDGE Objection sustained.

JURY   *Cackles and laughs with pleasure.*

WEBSTER   Sold his soul—for a period of seven years' good luck. Now those seven years are up, and this—this *gentleman* here in black—has come to collect. My client is unwilling, naturally, to give up his soul; for giving up his soul seems to him—as it does to me—an act completely outside the jurisdiction of this court, and thoroughly despicable besides.

DEVIL   I object!

JUDGE   Objection sustained.

JURY   *Laughs with glee.*

WEBSTER   That, then, is the case before the court. The defense rests—for a moment.

JUDGE   Very well. What is your argument, Scratch?

DEVIL   Simply this. I overheard this man, Jabez Stone, standing in the fields cursing his fate.

WEBSTER   I object.

JUDGE   Objection denied.

JURY   *Laughs and shouts, gloating over the plight of* JABEZ.

DEVIL   Cursing his fate because he had broken his plowshare on a rock. I heard him burst into tears and say, "I vow—for two cents—"

WEBSTER   I object.

JUDGE   Objection denied.

JURY   *Cackles again.*

DEVIL   So naturally I, being in the business, so to speak, called at his house that night and the bargain was made. It was sealed and signed, and if Jabez Stone denies that his signature is affixed to this paper, then let him show the jury the little white scar on his finger—if he dares.

WEBSTER   I object.

JUDGE   Objection denied.

JURY   *Laughs with fiendish glee.*

JUDGE   Proceed, Scratch.

DEVIL   Following the night of our bargain, Jabez Stone began to prosper—all as I had promised. Now the term of our contract is finished. The seventh year is ended tonight, and I have come to collect—all according to contract.

JUDGE   Collect what? Say it in words.

DEVIL   His soul.

WEBSTER   I object.

JUDGE   Objection denied.

JURY *Laughs with vicious delight.*

JUDGE Everything seems quite in order as far as I can see. Have you anything further to say, Mr. Webster, before we turn the case over to the jury?

WEBSTER [*after a pause and with quiet dignity*] I would like to say a few words, your honor—not for the sake of neighbor Stone, nor for my own sake—no, nor in argument or reply to Scratch here; but merely because the night seems good to me. Gentlemen, can you remember—recently for some of you, far, far, back for others—can you remember the freshness of a fine morning when you were young, and the taste of food when you were hungry, and the new day that's every day when you're a child? I'd like to feel these things again—and so, too, I think, would you. They are good things for any man. But without freedom, they sicken. Slavery—the loss of your soul—how the very thought revolts the heart! [*Fade to silence for suggesting a long-continued speech, then up.*] "Who is here so base that would be a bondman? If any, speak; for him have I offended." You've heard those words before? Yes, even in hell, if a man was a man, you'd know it. But because we forget this, sorrows, failures, meannesses, loneliness, persecutions, beset him along the endless journey of mankind. He gets tricked and trapped and bamboozled all along the way, but it is a great journey. And no devil that was ever sired can know the inwardness of it. It takes a man to do that.

I wish sometimes that I were clairvoyant, gentlemen. I would like to be able to put myself inside each man here and feel what part of the past, and what native ground, that man loves and clings to. But whatever it is, it is a part of your life—no man else's—*your* life that was dear to you and that was lived as *you* cared to live it. You could rush headlong into destruction if you chose, or till the field in bland contentment. Good or bad, your life was dear to you. Why? Because your *soul* was your *own,* and nobody was its master but yourself.

It seems we have been talking about the soul a great deal tonight, gentlemen. But not much, not really much, when you consider some things. For instance, I think it is a significant fact that the poet Shakespeare mentions the *body* two hundred and forty-one times, whereas he alludes to the *soul* five hundred and forty-one times. In other words, the word *soul* occurs in Shakespeare's plays exactly three hundred times more than the word *body,* or more than twice as often.

Furthermore, when the good bard does mention the body, it is nearly always a dead body he is referring to . . . whereas the soul—the *soul,* gentlemen . . . do I, or Shakespeare, need to remind you how *living* the soul is, how eternally alive! The very words "immortal" and "soul" go together. *O my immortal soul!*

Or, to leave the realm of literature for a moment and come back to earth where we belong, what about this, gentlemen; when we hear our good New Hampshire housewife exclaim: "Oh, my soul and body!" which one of the two does she mention first? And why? [*Pause of about four seconds . . . complete silence.*]

[*Gradually he builds to his climax*] Gentlemen, I don't care what you or anyone else might wish to do with neighbor Stone's life, but whatever you do, you cannot harm, you cannot *touch,* his soul. Even *Death* cannot do what Mr.

Scratch here presumes to do tonight. Say what you will, the soul shall be triumphant.

> "Imperious Caesar, dead and turned to clay,
> Might stop a hole to keep the wind away . . ."

But his soul, gentlemen . . . his *soul!* ranges the world, as long as the world shall last, or time itself, or *your immortal souls!*

JURY   *Cheers, stamps wildly, whistles.*

SOUND   *The* JUDGE *pounds his gavel to still the noise.*

WEBSTER   The defense rests.

Pause.

SOUND   JUDGE *pounds gavel again.*

JUDGE   The jury will retire to consider its verdict.

WALTER BUTLER   Your honor, I don't think we need to retire. The jury, I'm sure, has considered its verdict. [*Pause*] We find *for* the defendant, Jabez Stone.

JUDGE   Perhaps it's not strictly in accordance with the evidence . . . but even the damned may salute the eloquence of Mr. Webster.

SOUND   *A long crow of a rooster. There is a sudden scraping of chairs . . . a great rush of feet . . . sound of wind as all the ghastly* JURY *rush pell-mell out the door—the door slams.*

DEVIL   They've gone . . . just as they should, at cockcrow. And now we are alone again, we three.

WEBSTER   So we are, Scratch, so we are.

DEVIL   My congratulations, as between two gentlemen.

WEBSTER   I'll have that paper first, if you please.

SOUND   SCRATCH *hands paper to* WEBSTER, *who tears it in two.*

WEBSTER   And now . . . I'll have you!

DEVIL [*suddenly*]   Come, come, Mr. Webster . . . this sort of thing is ridic—ouch! . . . [*In pain as* WEBSTER *grabs him*] . . . ridiculous!

WEBSTER [*commandingly*]   Now you'll sit right down at that table and draw up a document, promising never to bother Jabez Stone nor his heirs nor assigns nor any other New Hampshireman till Doomsday! For any hell we want to raise in this state, we can raise ourselves, without assistance from strangers!

DEVIL [*still held by* WEBSTER]   *Ouch!* I agree . . .

WEBSTER   Feeling better now, Neighbor Stone?

JABEZ   I . . . I can't even speak.

WEBSTER   How about it, Scratch?

DEVIL   Here it is, Mr. Webster, proper and legal. And now, may I go?

WEBSTER   Go? Say, what can you do for me before I kick you out?

DEVIL   Well—I'm not a talented man, like yourself, Mr. Webster, but—I could tell your fortune for you.

WEBSTER   I don't take much stock in fortune-telling, ordinarily, but—well, it pleases me to listen. Here's my hand. No tricks, now!

DEVIL   Hum . . . An interesting palm, Mr. Webster. The future's not as you think it. It's dark. You have great ambitions, Mr. Webster.

WEBSTER   I have.

DEVIL   It almost seems within your grasp, but you will not attain it . . . Lesser men will; you will be passed over.

WEBSTER   And if I am, I'll still be Daniel Webster. Say on!

DEVIL   You have two strong sons. You look to found a line. But each will die in war, and neither reach greatness.

WEBSTER   Live or die, they are still my sons. Say on!

DEVIL   You have made great speeches. You will make more.

WEBSTER [*pleased*]   Ah—

DEVIL   But the last great speech you make will turn many of your own against you. Even in New England some will say you have turned your coat and sold your country, and their voices will be loud against you till you die.

WEBSTER [*anxiously*]   One question—I have fought for the Union all my life. Will I see that fight won against those who would tear it apart?

DEVIL   Not while you live. But it will be won. And after you are dead, there are thousands who will fight for your cause, because of words that you spoke.

WEBSTER [*with roar of laughter*]   Why, then, you long-barreled, slab-sided, lantern-jawed, fortune-telling note-shaver! Be off with you to your own place before I put my mark on you. For, by the thirteen original colonies, I'd go to the pit itself to save the Union!

SOUND   *Clatter of footsteps—sounds of* DEVIL *saying, "Ouch," as, prodded by* WEBSTER, *he goes out the door, which opens—then slams behind him.*

WEBSTER [*jovially*]   And now . . . we'll see what's left in the jug. It's spry work talking all night . . . I hope there's pie for breakfast, Neighbor Stone!

MUSIC   *Comes up, then continues behind the final speech.*

NARRATOR   And they say that whenever the devil comes near the town of Hartsfield even now, he gives it a wide berth. And he hasn't been seen in the state of New Hampshire from that day to this. Other states, maybe, but not New Hampshire!

MUSIC   *Up full to finish.*

[*Reading time: about 30 minutes*

THE FALL OF THE CITY / Archibald MacLeish

To extend this program to about two hours, Archibald MacLeish's *The Fall of the City* may be included. Its reading time is about thirty minutes and the preceding intermission may be about ten minutes. A floor plan is suggested here.

Scripts may be obtained from Dramatists Play Service, 400 Park Avenue South, New York, N. Y. 10016, in a paperback entitled *Three Short Plays. The Fall of the City* is on pp. 64-86.

These are radio scripts. As for *The Devil and Daniel Webster,* they must be adapted to the medium of oral interpretation.

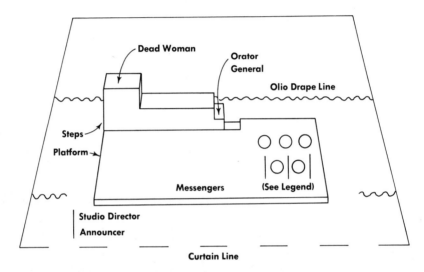

FLOOR PLAN FOR INTERPRETERS READING The Fall of the City.

AT STAGE LEFT FORWARD ARE GROUPED READING STANDS AND HIGH STOOLS
FOR PRIESTS, CROWD, CITIZENS, CHANTING VOICES, SINGLE VOICE,
DEEP VOICE, LOUD VOICE.

12. American Echoes in
Historic Documents

————————•◦•————————

There are many approaches to the American Echoes theme. All the readings might be related to one historical period, or grouped to cover a given chronological era, or chosen to represent specific areas of the country, or designed to express the significance of certain events. Of the countless possibilities one of the most exciting is the development of a program of historic documents. Such a documentary program might require both individual and group readings or even a combination of readings and music.

A university undertaking of this sort will involve the drama-speech department and the music department at the minimum. Research needs may draw in people from the history department, both to find materials and to assist with background information. Students or faculty members in the political-science department may furnish guidance with respect to the political documents. The English department may include critics and students who can contribute special insights into the literary pieces and thus offer opportunities to heighten the quality of the readings.

Should you choose to use both singers and readers, you will find a suggested floor plan on page 190. Following is a brief anthology of selections.

THE DECLARATION OF INDEPENDENCE / Ensemble Reading Prepared for this Book

The Declaration of Independence can be an exciting offering as an ensemble piece. The interrelationships of the American colonists together with the dynamics of their ideas and feelings may be effectively projected to an audience through some arrangement which utilizes individual voices for stating objections to the conduct of the king. The entire group of readers (designated "Chorus") together speaks the first two paragraphs and the last paragraph. Individual voices speak the mid-portion. This central section can be handled by as few as seven voices or as many as twenty-one. One

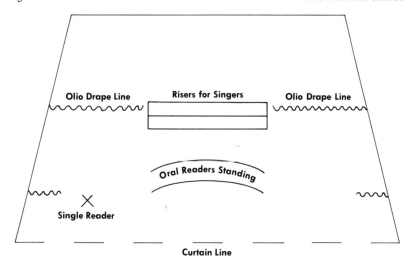

FLOOR PLAN FOR ARRANGEMENT OF READERS AND SINGERS
INTERPRETING American Echoes in Historic Documents

must recognize, however, that the more voices the more difficult it will be to coordinate the whole and polish the performance. Each voice must pick up cues quickly, giving the effect of literally breaking in upon one another. It may help the "voices" to visualize a crowd scene in a village square of 1776, with various members of the crowd speaking out in anger. Certainly the oral reading should make the words come alive.

CHORUS   In Congress, July 4, 1776. The Unanimous Declaration of the Thirteen United States of America.

When in the Course of human events, it becomes necessary for one people to dissolve the political bands which have connected them with another, and to assume among the powers of the earth, the separate and equal station to which the Laws of Nature and of Nature's God entitle them, a decent respect to the opinions of mankind requires that they should declare the causes which impel them to the separation.

We hold these truths to be self-evident, that all men are created equal, that they are endowed by their Creator with certain unalienable Rights, that among these are Life, Liberty and the pursuit of Happiness.—That to secure these rights, Governments are instituted among Men, deriving their just powers from the consent of the governed,—That whenever any Form of Government becomes destructive of these ends, it is the Right of the People to alter or to abolish it, and to institute new Government, laying its foundation on such principles and organizing its powers in such form, as to them shall seem most likely to effect their Safety and Happiness. Prudence, indeed, will dictate that Governments long established should not be changed for light and transient causes; and accordingly all experience hath shown, that mankind are more disposed to suffer, while evils are sufferable, than to right themselves by abolishing the forms to which they are accustomed. But when a long train of abuses and usurpations, pursuing invariably the same Object evinces a design to reduce them under absolute Despotism, it is their right, it is their duty, to throw off such Government, and to provide new Guards for their future security.—Such has been the patient sufferance of these Colonies; and such is now the necessity which constrains them to alter their former Systems of Government. The history of the present King of Great Britain is a history of repeated injuries and usurpations, all having in direct object the establishment of an absolute Tyranny over these States. To prove this, let Facts be submitted to a candid world.—

VOICE 1   He has refused his Assent to Laws, the most wholesome and necessary for the public good.

VOICE 2   He has forbidden his Governors to pass Laws of immediate and pressing importance, unless suspended in their operation till his Assent should be obtained;

VOICE 3   and when so suspended, he has utterly neglected to attend to them.

VOICE 4   He has refused to pass other Laws for the accommodation of large districts of people, unless those people would relinquish the right of Representation in the Legislature,

VOICE 5   a right inestimable to them and formidable to tyrants only.

VOICE 6   He has called together legislative bodies at places unusual, uncomfortable, and distant from the depository of their public Records, for the sole purpose of fatiguing them into compliance with his measures.

VOICE 7   He has dissolved Representative Houses repeatedly, for opposing with manly firmness his invasions on the rights of the people.

VOICE 1   He has refused for a long time, after such dissolutions, to cause others to be elected;

VOICE 2   whereby the Legislative powers, incapable of Annihilation, have returned to the People at large for their exercise;

VOICE 3   the State remaining in the mean time exposed to all the dangers of invasion from without, and convulsions within.

VOICE 4   He has endeavored to prevent the population of these States; for that purpose

VOICE 5   obstructing the Laws for Naturalization of Foreigners;

VOICE 6   refusing to pass others to encourage their migration hither,

VOICE 7   and raising the conditions of new Appropriations of Lands.

VOICE 1   He has obstructed the Administration of Justice, by refusing his Assent to Laws for establishing Judiciary powers.

VOICE 2   He has made Judges dependent on his Will alone, for the tenure of their offices, and the amount and payment of their salaries.

VOICE 3   He has erected a multitude of New Offices, and sent hither swarms of Officers to harrass our people, and eat out their substance.

VOICE 4   He has kept among us, in times of peace, Standing Armies, without the Consent of our legislatures.

VOICE 5   He has affected to render the Military independent of and superior to the Civil power.

VOICE 6   He has combined with others to subject us to a jurisdiction foreign to our constitution, and unacknowledged by our laws; giving his Assent to their Acts of pretended Legislation:

VOICE 7   For quartering large bodies of armed troops among us:

VOICE 1   For protecting them, by a mock Trial, from punishment for any Murders which they should commit on the Inhabitants of these States:

VOICE 2   For cutting off our Trade with all parts of the world:

VOICE 3   For imposing Taxes on us without our Consent:

VOICE 4   For depriving us in many cases, of the benefits of Trial by Jury:

VOICE 5   For transporting us beyond Seas to be tried for pretended offences:

VOICE 6   For abolishing the free System of English Laws in a neighbouring Province, establishing therein an Arbitrary government, and enlarging its Boundaries so as to render it at once an example and fit instrument for introducing the same absolute rule into these Colonies:

VOICE 7   For taking away our Charters, abolishing our most valuable Laws, and altering fundamentally the Forms of our Governments:

VOICE 1   For suspending our own Legislatures, and declaring themselves invested with power to legislate for us in all cases whatsoever.

VOICE 2   He has abdicated Government here, by declaring us out of his Protection and waging War against us.

VOICE 3   He has plundered our seas, ravaged our Coasts, burnt our towns, and destroyed the lives of our people.

VOICE 4   He is at this time transporting large Armies of foreign Mercenaries to compleat the works of death, desolation and tyranny, already begun with circumstances of Cruelty & perfidy scarcely paralleled in the most barbarous ages, and totally unworthy the Head of a civilized nation.

VOICE 5   He has constrained our fellow Citizens taken Captive on the high Seas to bear Arms against their Country, to become the executioners of their friends and Brethren, or to fall themselves by their Hands.

VOICE 6   He has excited domestic insurrections amongst us, and has endeavoured to bring on the inhabitants of our frontiers, the merciless Indian Savages, whose known rule of warfare, is an undistinguished destruction of all ages, sexes and conditions.

VOICE 7   In every stage of these Oppressions We have Petitioned for Redress in the most humble terms: Our repeated Petitions have been answered only by repeated injury.

VOICE 1   A Prince, whose character is thus marked by every act which may define a Tyrant, is unfit to be the ruler of a free people.

VOICE 2   Nor have We been wanting in attentions to our Brittish brethren. We have warned them from time to time of attempts by their legislature to extend an unwarrantable jurisdiction over us.

VOICE 3   We have reminded them of the circumstances of our emigration and settlement here.

VOICE 4   We have appealed to their native justice and magnanimity,

VOICE 5   and we have conjured them by the ties of our common kindred to disavow these usurpations, which, would inevitably interrupt our connections and correspondence.

VOICE 6   They too have been deaf to the voice of justice and of consanguinity.

VOICE 7   We must, therefore, acquiesce in the necessity, which denounces our Separation, and hold them, as we hold the rest of mankind, Enemies in War, in Peace Friends.—

CHORUS   We, Therefore, the Representatives of the United States of America, in General Congress, Assembled, appealing to the Supreme Judge of the world for the rectitude of our intentions, do, in the Name, and by Authority of the good People of these Colonies, solemnly publish and declare, That these United Colonies are, and of Right ought to be Free and Independent States; that they are Absolved from all Allegiance to the British Crown, and that all political connection between them and the State of Great Britain, is and ought to be totally dissolved; and that as Free and Independent States, they have full Power to levy War, conclude Peace, contract Alliances, establish Commerce, and to do all other Acts and Things which Independent States may of right do.—And for the support of this Declaration, with a firm reliance on the protection of Divine Providence, we mutually pledge to each other our Lives, our Fortunes and our sacred Honor.

THE MONROE DOCTRINE

This portion of the discussion of foreign relations, in President Monroe's Message to Congress of December 2, 1823, contained the original statement of a guiding principle of United States foreign policy.

The citizens of the United States cherish sentiments the most friendly, in favor of the liberty and happiness of their fellow-men on that side of the Atlantic. In the wars of the European Powers, in matters relating to themselves, we have never taken any part, nor does it comport with our policy so to do. It is only when our rights are invaded, or seriously menaced, that we resent injuries, or make preparation for our defence. With the movements in this hemisphere, we are, of necessity, more immediately connected, and by causes which must be obvious to all enlightened and impartial observers. The political system of the allied Powers is essentially different, in this respect, from that of America. This difference proceeds from that which exists in their respective Governments. And to the defence of our own, which has been achieved by the loss of so much blood and treasure, and matured by the wisdom of their most enlightened citizens, and under which we have enjoyed unexampled felicity, this whole nation is devoted. We owe it, therefore, to candor and to the amicable relations existing between the United States and those Powers, to declare, that we should consider any attempt on their part to extend their system to any portion of this hemisphere, as dangerous to our peace and safety. With the existing colonies or dependencies of any European Power, we have not interfered, and shall not interfere. But, with the Governments who have declared their independence, and maintained it, and whose independence we have, on great consideration, and on just principles, acknowledged, we could not view any interposition for the purpose of oppressing them, or controlling, in any other manner, their destiny, by any European Power, in any other light than as the manifestation of an unfriendly disposition towards the United States. In the war between those new Governments and Spain, we declared our neutrality at the time of their recognition, and to this we have adhered, and shall continue to adhere, provided no change shall occur, which, in the judgment of the competent authorities of this Government, shall make a corresponding change, on the part of the United States, indispensable to their security.

The late events in Spain and Portugal, show that Europe is still unsettled. Of this important fact, no stronger proof can be adduced than that the allied Powers should have thought it proper, on any principle satisfactory to themselves, to have interposed, by force, in the internal concerns of Spain. To what extent such interposition may be carried, on the same principle, is a question, in which all independent Powers, whose Governments differ from theirs, are interested; even those most remote, and surely none more so than the United States. Our policy, in regard to Europe, which was adopted at an early stage of the wars which have so long agitated that quarter of the globe, nevertheless remains the same, which is, not to interfere in the internal concerns of any of its Powers; to consider the Government *de facto* as the legitimate Government for us; to cultivate friendly relations with it, and to preserve those relations by a frank, firm, and manly policy; meeting, in all instances, the just claims of every Power; submitting to injuries from none. But, in regard to those continents, circumstances are eminently and conspicuously different. It is impossible that the allied Powers should extend their political system to any portion of either continent, without endangering our peace and happiness; nor can any one believe that our Southern brethren, if left to themselves, would adopt it of their own accord. It is equally impossible, therefore, that we should behold such interposition, in any form, with indifference. If we look to the comparative strength and resources of Spain and those new Governments, and their distance from each other, it must be obvious that she can never subdue them. It is still the true policy of the United States to leave the parties to themselves, in the hope that other Powers will pursue the same course.

A HOUSE DIVIDED AGAINST ITSELF CANNOT STAND / Abraham Lincoln[1]

The occasion of this famous speech was the Republican State Convention in Illinois, June 18, 1858.

Gentlemen of the Convention.—If we could first know where we are, and whither we are tending, we could then better judge what to do, and how to do it. We are now far on into the fifth year, since a policy was initiated, with the avowed object, and confident promise, of putting an end to slavery agitation. Under the operation of that policy, that agitation has not only not ceased, but has constantly augmented. In my opinion, it will not cease, until a crisis shall have been reached, and passed. "A house divided against itself can not stand." I believe this Government can not endure permanently, half slave and half free. I do not expect the Union to be dissolved—I do not expect the house to fall—but I do expect it will cease to be divided. It will become all one thing, or all the other. Either the opponents of slavery will arrest the further spread of it, and place it where the public mind shall rest in the belief that it is in course of ultimate extinction, or its advocates will push it forward, till it shall become alike lawful in all the States—old as well as new—North as well as South.

[Several pages omitted.

The nearest approach to the point of declaring the power of a State over slavery, is made by Judge Nelson. He approaches it more than once, using the precise idea, and almost the language, too, of the Nebraska Act. On one occasion his exact language is, "except in cases where the power is restrained by the Constitution of the United States, the law of the State is supreme over the subject of slavery within its jurisdiction."

In what cases the power of the State is so restrained by the United States Constitution, is left an open question, precisely as the same question, as to the restraint on the power of the Territories, was left open in the Nebraska Act. Put that and that together, and we have another nice little niche, which we may, ere long, see filled with another Supreme Court decision, declaring that the Constitution of the United States does not permit a State to exclude slavery from its limits. And this may especially be expected if the doctrine of "care not whether salvery be voted down or voted up," shall gain upon the public mind sufficiently to give promise that such a decision can be maintained when made.

Such a decision is all that slavery now lacks of being alike lawful in all the States. Welcome or unwelcome, such decision is probably coming, and will soon be upon us, unless the power of the present political dynasty shall be met and overthrown. We shall lie down pleasantly dreaming that the people of Missouri are on the verge of making their State free; and we shall awake to the reality, instead, that the Supreme Court has made Illinois a slave State.

---

[1]Abridged for this book.

To meet and overthrow the power of that dynasty, is the work now before all those who would prevent that consummation. That is what we have to do. But how can we best do it?

There are those who denounce us openly to their own friends, and yet whisper softly, that Senator Douglas is the *aptest* instrument there is, with which to effect that object. They do not tell us, nor has he told us, that he wishes any such object to be effected. They wish us to infer all, from the facts that he now has a little quarrel with the present head of the dynasty; and that he has regularly voted with us, on a single point, upon which he and we have never differed.

They remind us that *he* is a very *great man,* and that the largest of us are very small ones. Let this be granted. But "a *living dog* is better than a *dead lion*." Judge Douglas, if not a *dead* lion for this work, is at least a *caged* and *toothless* one. How can he oppose the advances of slavery? He don't care anything about it. His avowed mission is impressing the "public heart" to care nothing about it.

A leading Douglas Democrat newspaper thinks Douglas' superior talent will be needed to resist the revival of the African slave-trade. Does Douglas believe an effort to revive that trade is approaching? He has not said so. Does he *really* think so? But if it is, how can he resist it? For years he has labored to prove it a *sacred right* of white men to take negro slaves into the new Territories. Can he possibly show that it is less a sacred right to buy them where they can be bought cheapest? And, unquestionably, they can be bought cheaper in Africa than in Virginia.

He has done all in his power to reduce the whole question of slavery to one of a mere right of property; and as such, how can he oppose the foreign slave-trade—how can he refuse that trade in that "property," shall be "perfectly free"—unless he does it as a *protection* to the home production? And as the home *producers* will probably not ask the protection, he will be wholly without a ground of opposition.

Senator Douglas holds, we know, that a man may rightfully be wiser to-day than he was yesterday—that he may rightfully change when he finds himself wrong. But, can we for that reason run ahead and infer that he will make any particular change, of which he himself has given no intimation? Can we safely base our action upon any such vague inferences?

Now, as ever, I wish not to misrepresent Judge Douglas' position, question his motives, or do aught that can be personally offensive to him. Whenever, *if ever,* he and we can come together on *principle,* so that our great cause may have assistance from his great ability, I hope to have interposed no adventitious obstacle.

But clearly, he is not now with us—he does not pretend to be—he does not promise ever to be. Our cause, then, must be intrusted to, and conducted by its own undoubted friends—those whose hands are free, whose hearts are in the work —who do care for the result.

Two years ago the Republicans of the nation mustered over thirteen hundred thousand strong. We did this under the single impulse of resistance to a common danger, with every external circumstance against us. Of strange, discordant, and even hostile elements, we gathered from the four winds, and formed and fought the battle through, under the constant hot fire of a disciplined, proud and pampered enemy. Did we brave all then to falter now?—*now*—when that same enemy is wavering, dissevered and belligerent?

The result is not doubtful. We shall not fail—if we stand firm, we shall not fail. *Wise counsels* may *accelerate* or *mistakes delay* it, but, sooner or later, the victory is *sure* to come.

LABOR ARBITRATION / Grover Cleveland

President Grover Cleveland, in a special message to Congress on April 22, 1886, proposed that the government of the United States assume a function in the promotion of improved relations between labor and employer interests.

Under our form of government the value of labor as an element of national prosperity should be distinctly recognized, and the welfare of the laboring man should be regarded as especially entitled to legislative care. In a country which offers to all its citizens the highest attainment of social and political distinction its workingmen can not justly or safely be considered as irrevocably consigned to the limits of a class and entitled to no attention and allowed no protest against neglect.

The laboring man, bearing in his hand an indispensable contribution to our growth and progress, may well insist, with manly courage and as a right, upon the same recognition from those who make our laws as is accorded to any other citizen having a valuable interest in charge; and his reasonable demands should be met in such a spirit of appreciation and fairness as to induce a contented and patriotic co-operation in the achievement of a grand national destiny.

While the real interests of labor are not promoted by a resort to threats and violent manifestations, and while those who under the pretext of an advocacy of the claims of labor wantonly attack the rights of capital, and for selfish purposes or the love of disorder sow seeds of violence and discontent, should neither be encouraged nor conciliated, all legislation on the subject should be calmly and deliberately undertaken, with no purpose of satisfying unreasonable demands or gaining partisan advantage.

The present condition of the relations between labor and capital are far from satisfactory. The discontent of the employed is due in a large degree to the grasping and heedless exactions of employers and the alleged discrimination in favor of capital as an object of governmental attention. It must also be conceded that the laboring men are not always careful to avoid causeless and unjustifiable disturbance.

Though the importance of a better accord between these interests is apparent, it must be borne in mind that any effort in that direction by the Federal Government must be greatly limited by constitutional restrictions. There are many grievances which legislation by Congress can not redress, and many conditions which can not by such means be reformed.

I am satisfied, however, that something may be done under Federal authority to prevent the disturbances which so often arise from disputes between employers and the employed, and which at times seriously threatens the business interests of the country; and, in my opinion, the proper theory upon which to proceed is that of voluntary arbitration as the means of settling these difficulties.

But I suggest that instead of arbitration chosen in the heart of conflicting claims, and after each dispute shall arise, there be created a commission of labor, consisting of three members, who shall be regular officers of the Government, charged among other duties with the consideration and settlement, when possible, of all controversies between labor and capital.

A commission thus organized would have the advantage of being a stable body, and its members, as they gained experience, would constantly improve in their ability to deal intelligently and usefully with the questions which might be submitted to them. If arbitrators are chosen for temporary service as each case of dispute arises, experience and familiarity with much that is involved in the question will be lacking, extreme partisanship and bias will be the qualifications sought on either side, and frequent complaints of unfairness and partiality will be inevitable. The imposition upon a Federal court of a duty so foreign to the judicial function as the selection of an arbitrator in such cases is at least of doubtful propriety.

The establishment by Federal authority of such a bureau would be a just and sensible recognition of the value of labor, and of its right to be represented in the departments of the Government. So far as its conciliatory offices shall have relation to disturbances which interfere with transit and commerce between the States, its existence would be justified under the provisions of the Constitution which gives to Congress the power "to regulate commerce with foreign nations and among the several States." And in the frequent disputes between the laboring men and their employers of less extent, and the consequences of which are confused within State limits and threaten domestic violence, the interposition of such a commission might be tendered upon the application of the Legislature or executive of a State under the constitutional provision which requires the General Government to "protect" each of the States "against domestic violence."

If such a commission were fairly organized the risk of a loss of popular support and sympathy resulting from a refusal to submit to so peaceful an instrumentality would constrain both parties to such disputes to invoke its interference and abide by its decisions. There would also be good reason to hope that the very existence of such an agency would invite application to it for advice and counsel, frequently resulting in the avoidance of contention and misunderstanding.

If the usefulness of such a commission is doubted because it might lack power to enforce its decisions, much encouragement is derived from the conceded good that has been accomplished by the railroad commissions which have been organized in many of the States, which, having little more than advisory power, have exerted a most salutary influence in the settlement of disputes between conflicting interests.

In July, 1884, by a law of Congress, a Bureau of Labor was established and placed in charge of a Commissioner of Labor, who is required to "collect information upon the subject of labor, its relations to capital, the hours of labor, and the earnings of laboring men and women, and the means of promoting their material, social, intellectual, and moral prosperity."

The commission which I suggest could easily be ingrafted upon the bureau thus already organized by the addition of two more commissioners and by supplementing the duties now imposed upon it by such other powers and functions as would permit the commissioners to act as arbitrators when necessary between labor and capital, under such limitations and upon such occasions as should be deemed proper and useful.

Power should also be distinctly conferred upon this bureau to investigate the causes of all disputes as they occur, whether submitted for arbitration or not, so that information may always be at hand to aid legislation on the subject when necessary and desirable.

CONSERVATION OF RIVERS AND FORESTS /
Theodore Roosevelt

The message of President Theodore Roosevelt, read in the Senate on December 3, 1907, devoted two long sections to the importance of using wisely the inland waterways and the forests of the United States.

[INLAND WATERWAYS]

The conservation of our natural resources and their proper use constitute the fundamental problem which underlies almost every other problem of our National life. We must maintain for our civilization the adequate material basis without which that civilization can not exist. We must show foresight, we must look ahead. As a nation we not only enjoy a wonderful measure of present prosperity but if this prosperity is used aright it is an earnest of future success such as no other nation will have. The reward of foresight for this Nation is great and easily foretold. But there must be the look ahead, there must be a realization of the fact that to waste, to destroy, our natural resources, to skin and exhaust land instead of using it so as to increase its usefulness, will result in undermining in the days of our children the very prosperity which we might by right to hand down to them amplified and developed. For the last few years, through several agencies, the Government has been endeavoring to get our people to look ahead and to substitute a planned and orderly development of our resources in place of a haphazard striving for immediate profit. Our great river systems should be developed as National water highways; the Mississippi, with its tributaries, standing first in importance, and the Columbia second, although there are many others of importance on the Pacific, the Atlantic and the Gulf slopes. The National Government should undertake this work, and I hope a beginning will be made in the present Congress; and the greatest of all our rivers, the Mississippi, should receive especial attention. From the Great Lakes to the mouth of the Mississippi there should be a deep waterway, with deep waterways leading from it to the East and the West. Such a waterway would practically mean the extension of our coast line into the very heart of the country. It would be of incalculable benefit to our people. If begun at once it can be carried through in time appreciably to relieve the congestion of our great freight-carrying lines of railroads. The work should be systematically and continuously carried forward in accordance with some well-conceived plan. The main streams should be improved to the highest point of efficiency before the improvements of the branches is attempted; and the work should be kept free from every taint of recklessness or jobbery. The inland waterways which lie just back of the whole eastern and southern coasts should likewise be developed. Moreover, the development of our waterways involves many other important water problems, all of which should be considered as part of the same general scheme. The Government dams should be used to produce hundreds of thousands of horsepower as an incident to improve navigation; for the annual value of the unused water-power of the United States perhaps exceeds the annual value of the products of all our mines.

[FORESTS.]

Optimism is a good characteristic, but if carried to an excess it becomes foolishness. We are prone to speak of the resources of this country as inexhaustible; this is not so. The mineral wealth of the country, the coal, iron, oil, gas, and the like, does not reproduce itself, and therefore is certain to be exhausted ultimately; and wastefulness in dealing with it to-day means that our descendants will feel the exhaustion a generation or two before they otherwise would. But there are certain other forms of waste which could be entirely stopped. The waste of soil by washing, for instance, which is among the most dangerous of all wastes now in progress in the United States, is easily preventable, so that this present enormous loss of fertility is entirely unnecessary. The preservation or replacement of the forests is one of the most important means of preventing this loss. We have made a beginning in forest preservation, but it is only a beginning. At present lumbering is the fourth greatest industry in the United States; and yet, so rapid has been the rate of exhaustion of timber in the United States in the past, and so rapidly is the remainder being exhausted, that the country is unquestionably on the verge of a timber famine which will be felt in every household in the land. There has already been a rise in the price of lumber, but there is certain to be a more rapid and heavier rise in the future. The present annual consumption of lumber is certainly three times as great as the annual growth; and if the consumption and growth continue unchanged, practically all our lumber will be exhausted in another generation, while long before the limit to complete exhaustion is reached the growing scarcity will make itself felt in many blighting ways upon our National welfare. About 20 per cent of our forested territory is now reserved in National forests; but these do not include the most valuable timber lands, and in any event the proportion is too small to expect that the reserves can accomplish more than a mitigation of the trouble which is ahead of the nation. Far more drastic action is needed. Forests can be lumbered so as to give to the public the full use of their mercantile timber without the slightest detriment to the forest, any more than it is a detriment to a farm to furnish a harvest; so there is no parallel between forests and mines, which can only be completely used by exhaustion. But forests, if used as all our forests have been used in the past and as most of them are still used, will be either wholly destroyed, or so damaged that many decades have to pass before effective use can be made of them again. All these facts are so obvious that it is extraordinary that it should be necessary to repeat them. Surely, when these facts are so obvious, there should be no delay in taking preventive measures. Yet we seem as a nation to be willing to proceed in this matter with happy-go-lucky indifference even to the immediate future. It is this attitude which permits the self-interest of a very few persons to weigh for more than the ultimate interest of all our people. There are persons who find it to their immense pecuniary benefit to destroy the forests by lumbering. They are to be blamed for thus sacrificing the future of the Nation as a whole to their own self-interest of the moment; but heavier blame attaches to the people at large for permitting such action, whether in the White Mountains, in the southern Alleghenies, or in the Rockies and Sierras. A big lumbering company, impatient for immediate returns and not caring to look far enough ahead, will often deliberately destroy all the good timber in a region, hoping afterwards to move on to some new country. The shiftless man of small means, who does not care to become an actual home-maker but would like immediate profit, will find it to his advantage to take up timber land simply to turn it over to such a big company, and leave it valueless for future settlers. A big mine owner, anxious only to develop his mine at the moment, will care only to cut all the timber that he wishes without regard to the future—probably not looking ahead to the condition of the country when the forests are exhausted, any more than he does to the condition when the mine is worked out. I do not blame these men nearly as much as I blame the supine public opinion, the indifferent public opinion, which permits their action to go unchecked.

These several suggestions for a program of historic documents run to the beginning of the twentieth century. For program material of more recent date, consult your taste and draw on histories and libraries.

13. A Cutting of a Short Work of Fiction

An effective reading suitable for church suppers, fellowship meetings, and family gatherings is a cutting from *Rip Van Winkle,* by Washington Irving. That you may better understand some of the intricacies of cutting, the entire story is included with alterations duly noted. This cutting requires about thirty minutes for performance. Uncut, the story would take about fifty to fifty-five minutes.

RIP VAN WINKLE: A POSTHUMOUS WRITING OF DIEDRICH KNICKERBOCKER / Washington Irving

[The following Tale was found among the papers of the late Diedrich Knickerbocker, an old gentleman of New York, who was very curious in the Dutch history of the province, and the manners of the descendants from its primitive settlers. His historical researches, however, did not lie so much among books as among men; for the former are lamentably scanty on his favorite topics; whereas he found the old burghers, and still more their wives, rich in that legendary lore so invaluable to true history. Whenever, therefore, he happened upon a genuine Dutch family, snugly shut up in its low-roofed farmhouse, under a spreading sycamore, he looked upon it as a little clasped volume of black-letter, and studied it with the zeal of a book-worm.

The result of all these researches was a history of the province during the reign of the Dutch governors, which he published some years since. There have been various opinions as to the literary character of his work, and, to tell the truth, it is not a whit better than it should be. Its chief merit is its scrupulous accuracy, which indeed was a little questioned on its first appearance, but has since been completely established; and it is now admitted into all historical collections as a book of unquestionable authority.

The old gentleman died shortly after the publication of his work; and now that he is dead and gone, it cannot do much harm to his memory to say that his time might have been much better employed in weightier labors. He, however, was apt to ride his hobby his own way; and though it did now and then kick up the dust a little in the eyes of his neighbors, and grieve the spirit of some friends, for whom he felt the truest deference and affection, yet his errors and follies are remembered "more in sorrow than in anger," and it begins to be suspected that he never intended to offend. But however his memory may be appreciated by critics, it is still held dear by many folk whose good opinion is well worth having; particularly by certain biscuit-makers, who have gone so far as to imprint his likeness on their New-Year cakes; and have thus given him a chance for immortality, almost equal to being stamped on a Waterloo Medal, or a Queen Ann's Farthing.]

Whoever has made a voyage up the Hudson must remember Kaatskill mountains. They are a dismembered branch of the great Appalachian family, and are seen away to the west of the river, swelling up to a noble height, and lording it over the surrounding country. Every change of season, every change of weather, indeed, every hour of the day, produces some changes in the magical hues and shapes of these mountains, and they are regarded by all the good wives, far and near, as perfect barometers. When the weather is fair and settled, they are clothed in blue and purple, and print their bold outlines on the clear evening sky; but sometimes, when the rest of the landscape is cloudless, they will gather a hood of gray vapors about their summits, which, in the last rays of the setting sun, will glow and light up like a crown of glory.

At the foot of these fairy mountains, the voyager may have descried the light smoke curling up from a village, whose shingle-roofs gleam among the trees, just where the blue tints of the upland melt away into the fresh green of the nearer landscape. It is a little village, of great antiquity, having been founded by some of the Dutch colonists in the early times of the province, just about the beginning of the government of the good Peter Stuyvesant, (may he rest in peace!) and there *where stand* were some of the houses of the original settlers, standing within a few years built of small yellow bricks brought from Holland, having latticed windows and gable fronts, surmounted with weathercocks.

In that same village, and in one of these very houses, (which, to tell the precise truth, was sadly time-worn and weather-beaten,) there lived, many years since, while the country was yet a province of Great Britain, a simple, good-natured fellow, of the name of Rip Van Winkle. He was a descendant of the Van Winkles who figured so gallantly in the chivalrous days of Peter Stuyvesant, and accompanied him to the siege of Fort Christina. He inherited, however, but little of the martial character of his ancestors. I have observed that he was a simple, good-natured man; he was, moreover, a kind neighbor, and an obedient, hen-pecked husband. Indeed, to the latter circumstance might be owing that meekness of spirit which gained him such universal popularity; for those men are most apt to be obsequious and conciliating abroad, who are under the discipline of shrews at home. Their tempers, doubtless, are rendered pliant and malleable in the fiery furnace of domestic tribulation; and a curtain-lecture is worth all the sermons in the world for teaching the virtues of patience and long-suffering. A termagant wife may, therefore, in some respects, be considered a tolerable blessing; and if so, Rip Van Winkle was thrice blessed.

Certain it is, that he was a great favorite among all the good wives of the village, who, as usual with the amiable sex, took his part in all family squabbles; and never failed, whenever they talked those matters over in their evenings gossipings, to lay all the blame on Dame Van Winkle. The children of the village, too, would shout with joy whenever he approached. He assisted at their sports, made their playthings, taught them to fly kites and shoot marbles, and told them long stories of ghosts, witches, and Indians. Whenever he went dodging about the village, he was surrounded by a troop of them, ~~hanging on his skirts, clambering on his back, and playing a thousand tricks on him with impunity;~~ and not a dog would bark at him throughout the neighborhood.

The great error in Rip's composition was an insuperable aversion to all kinds of profitable labor. It could not be from the want of assiduity or perseverance; for he would sit on a wet rock, with a rod as long and heavy as a Tartar's lance, and fish all day without a murmur, even though he should not be encouraged by a single nibble. He would carry a fowling-piece on his shoulder for hours together, trudging through woods and swamps, and up hill and down dale, to shoot a few squirrels or wild pigeons. He would never refuse to assist a neighbor even in the roughest toil, and was a foremost man at all country frolics for husking Indian corn, or building stone fences; the women of the village, too, used to employ him to run their errands, and to do such little odd jobs as their less obliging husbands would not do for them. In a word, Rip was ready to attend to anybody's business but his own; but as to doing family duty, and keeping his farm in order, he found it impossible.

In fact, he declared it was of no use to work on his farm; it was the most pestilent little piece of ground in the whole country; everything about it went wrong, and would go wrong, in spite of him. His fences were continually falling to pieces; his cow would either go astray, or get among the cabbages; weeds were sure to grow quicker in his fields than anywhere else; the rain always made a point of setting in just as he had some out-door work to do; so that, ~~though his patrimonial estate had dwindled away under his management, acre by acre, until~~ there was little more left than a mere patch of Indian corn and potatoes, yet it was the worst conditioned farm in the neighborhood.

His children, too, were as ragged and wild as if they belonged to nobody. His son Rip, an urchin begotten in his own likeness, promised to inherit the habits, with the old clothes, of his father. He was generally seen trooping like a colt at his mother's heels, equipped in a pair of his father's cast-off galligaskins, which he had much ado to hold up with one hand, as a fine lady does her train in bad weather.

Rip Van Winkle, however, was one of those happy mortals, ~~of foolish, well-oiled dispositions,~~ who take the world easy, eat white bread or brown, whichever can be got with least thought or trouble, and would rather starve on a penny than work for a pound. If left to himself, he would have whistled life away in perfect contentment; but his wife kept continually dinning in his ears about his idleness, his carelessness, and the ruin he was bringing to his family. Morning, noon, and night, her tongue was incessantly going, and everything he said or did was sure to produce a torrent of household eloquence. Rip had but one way of replying to all lectures of the kind, and that, by frequent use, had grown into a habit. He shrugged his shoulders, shook his head, cast up his eyes, but said nothing. This, however, always provoked a fresh volley from his wife; so that he ~~was~~ would fain ~~to draw off his~~

~~forces, and~~ take to the outside of the house—the only side which, in truth, belongs to a hen-pecked husband.

Rip's sole domestic adherent was his dog Wolf, who was as much hen-pecked as his master; for Dame Van Winkle regarded them as companions in idleness, and even looked upon Wolf with an evil eye, as the cause of his master's going so often astray. True it is, in all points of spirit befitting an honorable dog, he was as courageous an animal as ever scoured the woods; but what courage can withstand the ever-enduring and all-besetting terrors of a woman's tongue? The moment Wolf entered the house his crest fell, his tail drooped to the ground, or curled between his legs, he sneaked about with a gallows air, casting many a sidelong glance at Dame Van Winkle, and at the least flourish of a broomstick or ladle he would fly to the door with yelping precipitation.

Times grew worse and worse with Rip Van Winkle as years of matrimony rolled on; a tart temper never mellows with age, and a sharp tongue is the only edged tool that grows keener with constant use. For a long while he used to console himself, when driven from home, by frequenting a kind of perpetual club of the sages, philosophers, and other idle personages of the village, which held its sessions on a bench before a small inn ~~designated by a rubicund portrait of His Majesty George the Third.~~ Here they used to sit in the shade through a long, lazy summer's day, talking listlessly over village gossip, or telling endless sleepy stories about nothing. But it would have been worth any statesman's money to have heard the profound discussions that sometimes took place, when by chance an old newspaper fell into their hands from some passing traveller. How solemnly they would listen to the contents, as drawled out by Derrick Van Bummel, the schoolmaster, a dapper learned little man, who was not to be daunted by the most gigantic word in the dictionary; and how sagely they would deliberating upon public events some months after they had taken place.

The opinions of this junto were completely controlled by Nicholas Vedder, patriarch of the village, and landlord of the inn, at the door of which he took his seat from morning till night, just moving sufficiently to avoid the sun and keep in the shade of a large tree; so that the neighbors could tell the hour by his movements as accurately as by a sun-dial. It is true he was rarely heard to speak, but smoked his pipe incessantly. His adherents, however (for every great man has his adherents), perfectly understood him, and knew how to gather his opinions. When anything that was read or related displeased him, he was observed to smoke his pipe vehemently, and to send forth short, frequent, and angry puffs; but when pleased, he would inhale the smoke slowly and tranquilly, and emit it in light and placid clouds; and sometimes, taking the pipe from his mouth, and letting the fragrant vapor curl about his nose, would gravely nod his head in token of perfect approbation.

From even this stronghold the unlucky Rip was at length routed by his termagant wife, who would suddenly break in upon the tranquillity of the assemblage and call the members all to naught; nor was that august personage, Nicholas Vedder himself, sacred from the daring tongue of this terrible virago, who charged him outright with encouraging her husband in habits of idleness.

Poor Rip was at last reduced almost to despair; and his only alternative, to

escape from the labor of the farm and clamor of his wife, was to take gun in hand
and stroll away into the woods. Here he would sometimes seat himself at the foot
of a tree, and share the contents of his wallet with Wolf, with whom he sym-
pathized as a fellow-sufferer in persecution. "Poor Wolf," he would say, "thy
mistress leads thee a dog's life of it, but never mind, my lad, whilst I live thou
shalt never want a friend to stand by thee!" Wolf would wag his tail, look wist-
fully in his master's face, and if dogs can feel pity, I verily believe he reciprocated
the sentiment with all his heart.

In a long ramble of the kind on a fine autumnal day, Rip had unconsciously
scrambled to one of the highest parts of the Kaatskill mountains. He was after his
favorite sport of squirrel-shooting, and the still solitudes had echoed and re-
echoed with the reports of his gun. Panting and fatigued, he threw himself, late
in the afternoon, on a green knoll, covered with mountain herbage, that crowned
the brow of a precipice. From an opening between the trees he could overlook all
the lower country for many a mile of rich woodland. He saw at a distance the
lordly Hudson, far, far below him, moving on its silent but majestic course, with
the reflection of a purple cloud, or the sail of a lagging bark, here and there
sleeping on its glassy bosom, and at last losing itself in the blue highlands.

On the other side he looked down into a deep mountain glen, wild, lonely, and
shagged, the bottom filled with fragments from the impending cliffs, and scarcely
lighted by the reflected rays of the setting sun. For some time Rip lay musing on
this scene; evening was gradually advancing; the mountains began to throw their
long blue shadows over the valleys; he saw that it would be dark long before he
could reach the village, and he heaved a heavy sigh when he thought of encounter-
ing the terrors of Dame Van Winkle.

As he was about to descend, he heard a voice from a distance, hallooing, "Rip
Van Winkle, Rip Van Winkle!" He looked round, but could see nothing but a
crow winging its solitary flight across the mountain. He thought his fancy must
have deceived him, and turned again to descend, when he heard the same cry
ring through the still evening air: "Rip Van Winkle! Rip Van Winkle!"—at the
same time Wolf bristled up his back, and giving a low growl, skulked to his
master's side, looking fearfully down into the glen. Rip now felt a vague apprehension stealing over him; he looked anxiously in the same direction, and perceived a strange figure slowly toiling up the rocks, and bending under the weight
of something he carried on his back. He was surprised to see any human being in
this lonely and unfrequented place; but supposing it to be some one of the neighborhood in need of his assistance, he hastened down to yield it.

On nearer approach he was still more surprised at the singularity of the
stranger's appearance. He was a short, square-built old fellow, with thick bushy
hair, and a grizzled beard. His dress was of the antique Dutch fashion,—a cloth
jerkin strapped around the waist—several pairs of breeches, the outer one of
ample volume, decorated with rows of buttons down the sides, and bunches at
the knees. He bore on his shoulders a stout keg, that seemed full of liquor, and
made signs for Rip to approach and assist him with the load. Though rather shy
and distrustful of this new acquaintance, Rip complied with his usual alacrity;
and mutually relieving one another, they clambered up a narrow gully, apparently

the dry bed of a mountain torrent. As they ascended, Rip every now and then heard long, rolling peals, like distant thunder, that seemed to issue out of a deep ravine, or rather cleft, between lofty rocks, toward which their rugged path conducted. He paused for an instant, but supposing it to be the muttering of one of those transient thunder-showers which often take place in mountain heights, he proceeded. Passing through the ravine, they came to a hollow, like a small amphitheatre, surrounded by perpendicular precipices, over the brinks of which impending trees shot thir branches, so that you only caught glimpses of the azure sky and the bright evening cloud. During the whole time Rip and his companion had labored on in silence; for though the former marvelled greatly what could be the object of carrying a keg of liquor up this wild mountain, yet there was something strange and incomprehensible about the unknown, that inspired awe and checked familiarity.

On entering the amphitheatre, he found ~~new objects of wonder presented themselves. On a level spot in the centre was~~ a company of odd-looking personages playing at ninepins. They were dressed in a quaint, outlandish fashion; some wore short doublets, others jerkins, with long knives in their belts, and most of them had enormous breeches, of similar style with that of the guide's. Their visages, too, were peculiar: one had a large beard, broad face, and small piggish eyes; the face of another seemed to consist entirely of nose, and was surmounted by a white sugar-loaf hat, set off with a little red cock's tail. They all had beards, of various shapes and colors. There was one who seemed to be the commander. He was a stout old gentleman, with a weather-beaten countenance; he wore a laced doublet, broad belt and hanger, high crowned hat and feather, red stockings, and high-heeled shoes, with roses in them. The whole group reminded Rip of the figures in an old Flemish painting, in the parlor of Dominie Van Shaick, the village parson, ~~and which had been brought over from Holland at the time of the settlement.~~

What seemed particularly odd to Rip was, that, though these folks were evidently amusing themselves, yet they maintained the gravest faces, the most mysterious silence, and were, withal, the most melancholy party of pleasure he had ever witnessed. Nothing interrupted the stillness of the scene but the noise of the balls, which, whenever they rolled, echoed along the mountains like rumbling peals of thunder.

As Rip and his companion approached them, they suddenly desisted from their play, and stared at him with such fixed, statue-like gaze, and such strange, uncouth, lack-lustre countenances, that his heart turned within him, and his knees smote together. His companion now emptied the contents of the keg into large flagons, and made signs to him to wait upon the company. He obeyed with fear and trembling; they quaffed the liquor in profound silence, and then returned to their game.

By degrees Rip's awe and apprehension subsided. He even ventured, when no eye was fixed upon him, to taste the beverage, ~~which he found had much of the flavor of excellent Hollands.~~ He was naturally a thirsty soul, and was soon tempted to repeat the draught. One taste provoked another; and he reiterated his visits to the flagon so often that at length his senses were overpowered, his eyes swam in his head, his head gradually declined, and he fell into a deep sleep.

On waking, he found himself on the green knoll whence he had first seen the old man of the glen. He rubbed his eyes—it was a bright sunny morning. The birds were hopping and twittering among the bushes, and the eagle was wheeling aloft, and breasting the pure mountain breeze. "Surely," thought Rip, "I have not slept here all night." He recalled the occurrences before he fell asleep. The strange man with a keg of liquor—the mountain ravine—the wild retreat among the rocks— the woe-begone party at ninepins—the flagon—"Oh! that flagon! that wicked flagon!" thought Rip, "what excuse shall I make to Dame Van Winkle?"

He looked round for his gun, but in place of the clean, well-oiled fowling-piece, he found an old firelock lying by him, the barrel encrusted with rust, the lock falling off, and the stock worm-eaten. He now suspected that the grave roisters of the mountains had put a trick upon him, and, having dosed him with liquor, had robbed him of his gun. Wolf, too, had disappeared, but he might have strayed away after a squirrel or partridge. He whistled after him, and shouted his name, but all in vain; the echoes repeated his whistle and shout, but no dog was to be seen.

He determined to revisit the scene of the last evening's gambol, and if he met with any of the party, to demand his dog and gun. As he rose to walk, he found himself stiff in the joints ~~and wanting in his usual activity.~~ "These mountain beds do not agree with me," thought Rip, "and if this frolic should lay me up with a fit of the rheumatism, I shall have a blessed time with Dame Van Winkle." With some difficulty he got down into the glen: he found the gully up which he and his companion had ascended the preceding evening; but to his astonishment a mountain stream was now foaming down it, leaping from rock to rock, and filling the glen with babbling murmurs. He, however, made shift to scramble up its sides, working his toilsome way through thickets of birch, sassafras, and witch-hazel, and sometimes tripped up or entangled by the wild grape-vines that twisted their coils or tendrils from tree to tree, and spread a kind of network in his path.

At length he reached ~~to where the ravine had opened through the cliffs to~~ the amphitheatre; but no traces of such opening remained. The rocks presented a high, impenetrable wall, over which the torrent came tumbling in a sheet of feathery foam, and fell into a broad deep basin, black from the shadows of the surrounding forest. Here, then, poor Rip was brought to a stand. He again called and whistled after his dog; he was only answered by the cawing of a flock of idle crows sporting high in air about a dry tree that overhung a sunny precipice; and who, secure in their elevation, seemed to look down and scoff at the poor man's perplexities. What was to be done? the morning was passing away, and Rip felt famished for want of his breakfast. He grieved to give up his dog and gun; he dreaded to meet his wife; but it would not do to starve among the mountains. He shook his head, shouldered the rusty firelock, and, with a heart full of trouble and anxiety, turned his footsteps homeward.

As he approached the village he met a number of people, but none whom he knew, which somewhat surprised him, for he had thought himself acquainted with every one in the country round. Their dress, too, was of a different fashion from that to which he was accustomed. They all stared at him with equal marks of surprise, and whenever they cast their eyes upon him, invariably stroked their chins. The constant recurrence of this gesture induced Rip, involuntarily, to do the same, when, to his astonishment, he found his beard had grown a foot long!

He had now entered the skirts of the village. A troop of strange children ran at his heels, hooting after him, and pointing at his gray beard. The dogs, too, not one of which he recognized for an old acquaintance, barked at him as he passed. The very village was altered; it was larger and more populous. There were rows of houses which he had never seen before, and those which had been his familiar haunts had disappeared. Strange names were over the doors—strange faces at the windows—everything was strange. His mind now misgave him; he began to doubt whether both he and the world around him were not bewitched. Surely this was his native village, which he had left but the day before. There stood the Kaatskill mountains—there ran the silver Hudson at a distance—there was every hill and dale precisely as it had always been. Rip was sorely perplexed. "That flagon last night," thought he, "has addled my poor head sadly!"

It was with some difficulty that he found the way to his own house, which he approached with silent awe, expecting every moment to hear the shrill voice of Dame Van Winkle. He found the house gone to decay—the roof fallen in, the windows shattered, and the doors off the hinges. A half-starved dog that looked like Wolf was skulking about it. Rip called him by name, but the cur snarled, showed his teeth, and passed on. This was an unkind cut indeed. "My very dog," sighed poor Rip, "has forgotten me!"

He entered the house, which, to tell the truth, Dame Van Winkle had always kept in neat order. It was empty, forlorn, and apparently abandoned. This desolateness overcame all his connubial fears—he called loudly for his wife and children—the lonely chambers rang for a moment with his voice, and then all again was silence.

He now ~~hurried forth, and~~ hastened to his old resort, the village inn, but it too was gone. A large rickety wooden building stood in its place, with great gaping windows, some of them broken and mended with old hats and petticoats, and over the door was painted, "The Union Hotel, by Jonathan Doolittle." Instead of the great tree that used to shelter the quiet little Dutch inn of yore, there now was reared a tall naked pole, with something on the top that looked like a red nightcap, and from it was fluttering a flag, on which was a singular assemblage of stars and stripes;—all this was strange and incomprehensible. He recognized on the sign, however, the ruby face of King George, under which he had smoked so many a peaceful pipe; but even this was singularly metamorphosed. The red coat was changed for one of blue and buff, a sword was held in the hand instead of a sceptre, the head was decorated with a cocked hat, and underneath was painted in large characters, GENERAL WASHINGTON.

There was, as usual, a crowd of folk about the door, but none that Rip recollected. The very character of the people seemed changed. There was a busy, bustling, disputatious tone about it, instead of the accustomed ~~phlegm and~~ drowsy tranquillity. He looked in vain for the sage Nicholas Vedder, with his broad face, double chin, and fair long pipe, uttering clouds of tobacco-smoke instead of idle speeches; or Van Bummel, the schoolmaster, doling forth the contents of an ancient newspaper. In place of these, a lean, bilious-looking fellow, with his pockets full of handbills, was haranguing vehemently about rights of citizens—

elections—members of congress—liberty—Bunker's Hill—heroes of seventy-six—and other words, which were a perfect Babylonish jargon to the bewildered Van Winkle.

The appearance of Rip, with his long, grizzled beard, his rusty fowling-piece, his uncouth dress, and an army of women and children at his heels, soon attracted the attention of the tavern-politicians. They crowded round him, eying him from head to foot with great curiosity. The orator bustled up to him, and, drawing him partly aside, inquired "On which side he voted?" Rip stared in vacant stupidity. Another short but busy little fellow pulled him by the arm, and, rising on tiptoe, inquired in his ear, "Whether he was Federal or Democrat?" Rip was equally at a loss to comprehed the question; when a knowing, self-important old gentleman, in a sharp cocked hat, made his way through the crowd, putting them to the right and left with his elbows as he passed, and planting himself before Van Winkle, with one arm akimbo, the other resting on his cane, his keen eyes and sharp hat penetrating, as it were, into his very soul, demanded in an austere tone, "What brought him to the election with a gun on his shoulder, and a mob at his heels; and whether he meant to breed a riot in the village?"—"Alas! gentlemen," cried Rip, somewhat dismayed, "I am a poor quiet man, a native of the place, and a loyal subject of the King, God bless him!"

Here a general shout burst from the by-standers—"A tory! a tory! a spy! a refugee! hustle him! away with him!" It was with great difficulty that the self-important man in the cocked hat restored order; and, having assumed a tenfold austerity of brow, demanded again of the unknown culprit, what he came there for, and whom he was seeking? The poor man humbly assured him that he meant no harm, but merely came there in search of some of his neighbors, who used to keep about the tavern.

"Well—who are they?—name them."

Rip bethought himself a moment, and inquired, "Where's Nicholas Vedder?"

There was a silence for a little while, when an old man replied, in a thin piping voice, "Nicholas Vedder! why, he is dead and gone these eighteen years! There was a wooden tombstone in the churchyard that used to tell all about him, but that's rotten and gone too."

"Where's Brom Dutcher?"

"Oh, he went off to the army in the beginning of the war; some say he was killed at the storming of Stony Point—others say he was drowned in a squall at the foot of Antony's Nose. I don't know—he never came back again."

"Where's Van Bummel, the schoolmaster?"

"He went off to the wars too, was a great militia general, and is now in congress."

Rip's heart died away at hearing of these sad changes in his home and friends, and finding himself thus alone in the world. Every answer puzzled him too, by treating of such enormous lapses of time, and of matters which he could not understand: war—congress—Stony Point—he had no courage to ask after any more friends, but cried out in despair, "Does nobody here know Rip Van Winkle?"

"Oh, Rip Van Winkle!" exclaimed two or three, "oh, to be sure! that's Rip Van Winkle yonder, leaning against the tree."

Rip looked, and he beheld a precise counterpart of himself, as he went up the mountain; apparently as lazy, and certainly as ragged. The poor fellow was now completely confounded. He doubted his own identity, and whether he was himself or another man. In the midst of his bewilderment, the man in the cocked hat demanded who he was, and what was his name.

"God knows," exclaimed he, at his wit's end; "I'm not myself—I'm somebody else—that's me yonder—no—that's somebody else got into my shoes—I was myself last night, but I fell asleep on the mountain, and they've changed my gun, and everything's changed, and I'm changed, and I can't tell what's my name, or who I am!"

The by-standers began now to look at each other, nod, wink significantly, and tap their fingers against their foreheads. There was a whisper, also, about securing the gun, and keeping the old fellow from doing mischief, at the very suggestion of which the self-important man in the cocked hat retired with some precipitation. At this critical moment a fresh, comely woman pressed through the throng to get a peep at the gray-bearded man. She had a chubby child in her arms, which, frightened at his looks, began to cry. "Hush, Rip," cried she, ~~"hush, you little fool;~~ the old man won't hurt you." The name of the child, the air of the mother, the tone of her voice, all awakened a train of recollections in his mind. "What is your name, my good woman?" asked he.

"Judith Gardenier."

"And your father's name?"

"Ah, poor man, Rip Van Winkle was his name, but it's twenty years since he went away from home with his gun, and never has been heard of since,—his dog came home without him; but whether he shot himself, or was carried away by the Indians, nobody can tell. I was then but a little girl."

Rip had but one question more to ask; but he put it with a faltering voice: "Where's your mother?"

"Oh, she too had died but a short time since; she broke a bloodvessel in a fit of passion at a New England pedler."

There was a drop of comfort, at least, in this intelligence. The honest man could contain himself no longer. He caught his daughter and her child in his arms. "I am your father!" cried he—"Young Rip Van Winkle once—old Rip Van Winkle now!—Does nobody know poor Rip Van Winkle?"

All stood amazed, until an old woman, tottering out from among the crowd, put her hand to her brow, and peering under it in his face for a moment, exclaimed, "Sure enough! it is Rip Van Winkle—it is himself! Welcome home again, old neighbor. Why, where have you been these twenty long years?"

Rip's story was soon told, for the whole twenty years had been to him but as one night. The neighbors stared when they heard it; some were seen to wink at each other, and put their tongues in their cheeks: and the self-important man in the cocked hat, who, when the alarm was over, had returned to the field, screwed down the corners of his mouth, and shook his head—upon which there was a general shaking of the head throughout the assemblage.

It was determined, however, to take the opinion of old Peter Vanderdonk, who was seen slowly advancing up the road. He was a descendant of the historian of that name, who wrote one of the earliest accounts of the province. Peter was the most ancient inhabitant of the village, and well versed in all the wonderful events and traditions of the neighborhood. He recollected Rip at once, and corroborated his story in the most satisfactory manner. He assured the company that it was a fact, handed down from his ancestor the historian, that the Kaatskill mountains had always been haunted by strange beings. That it was affirmed that the great Hendrick Hudson, the first discoverer of the river and country, kept a kind of vigil there every twenty years, with his crew of the *Half-moon;* being permitted in this way to revisit the scenes of his enterprise, and keep a guardian eye upon the river and the great city called by his name. That his father had once seen them in their old Dutch dresses playing at ninepins in a hollow of the mountain; and that he himself had heard, one summer afternoon, the sound of their balls, like distant peals of thunder.

To make a long story short, the company broke up and returned to the more important concerns of the election. Rip's daughter took him home to live with her; she had a snug, well-furnished house, and a stout, cheery farmer for a husband, whom Rip recollected for one of the urchins that used to climb upon his back. As to Rip's son and heir, who was the ditto of himself, seen leaning against the tree, he was employed to work on the farm; but evinced an hereditary disposition to attend to anything else but his business.

Rip now resumed his old walks and habits; he soon found many of his former cronies, though all rather the worse for the wear and tear of time; and preferred making friends among the rising generation, with whom he soon grew into great favor.

Having nothing to do at home, and being arrived at that happy age when a man can be idle with impunity, he took his place once more on the bench at the inn-door, and was reverenced as one of the patriarchs of the village, and a chronicle of the old times "before the war." It was some time before he could ~~get into the regular track of gossip, or could~~ be made to comprehend the strange events that had taken place during his torpor. How that there had been a revolutionary war, ~~—that the country had thrown off the yoke of old England,~~ and that, ~~instead of being a subject of his Majesty George the Third,~~ he was now a free citizen of the United States. Rip, in fact, was no politician; the changes of states and empires made but little impression on him; but there was one species of despotism under which he had long groaned, and that was—petticoat government. Happily that was at an end; he had got his neck out of the yoke of matrimony, and could go in and out whenever he pleased, without dreading the tyranny of Dame Van Winkle. Whenever her name was mentioned, however, he shook his head, shrugged his shoulders, and cast up his eyes; which might pass either for an expression of resignation to his fate, or joy at his deliverance.

He used to tell his story to every stranger that arrived at Mr. Doolittle's hotel. He was observed, at first, to vary on some points every time he told it, ~~which was, doubtless, owing to his having so recently awaked.~~ It at last settled down precisely to the tale I have related, and not a man, woman, or child in the neighborhood but knew it by heart. Some always pretended to doubt the reality of it, and insisted that Rip had been out of his head, and that this was one point on which he always remained flighty. The old Dutch inhabitants, however, almost universally gave it full credit. Even to this day they never hear a thunderstorm of a summer afternoon about the Kaatskill, but they say Hendrick Hudson, and his crew are at their game of ninepins; and it is a common wish of all hen-pecked husbands in the neighborhood, when life hangs heavy on their hands, that they might have a quieting draught out of Rip Van Winkle's flagon. ✗

NOTE.

The foregoing Tale, one would suspect, had been suggested to Mr. Knickerbocker by a little German superstition about the Emperor Frederick *der Rothbart,* and the Kypphäuser mountain: the subjoined note, however, which he had appended to the tale, shows that it is an absolute fact, narrated with his usual fidelity.

"The story of Rip Van Winkle may seem incredible to many, but nevertheless I give it my full belief, for I know the vicinity of our old Dutch settlements to have been very subject to marvellous events and appearances. Indeed, I have heard many stranger stories than this, in the villages along the Hudson; all of which were too well authenticated to admit of a doubt. I have even talked with Rip Van Winkle myself, who, when last I saw him, was a very venerable old man, and so perfectly rational and consistent on every other point, that I think no conscientious person could refuse to take this into the bargain; nay, I have seen a certificate on the subject taken before a country justice and signed with a cross, in the justice's own handwriting. The story, therefore, is beyond the possibiilty of doubt.

"D. K."

POSTSCRIPT.

The following are travelling notes from a memorandum-book of Mr. Knickerbocker.

The Kaatsberg, or Catskill Mountains, have always been a region full of fable. The Indians considered them the abode of spirits, who influenced the weather, spreading sunshine or clouds over the landscape, and sending good or bad hunting-seasons. They were ruled by an old squaw spirit, said to be their mother. She dwelt on the highest peak of the Catskills, and had charge of the doors of day and night to open and shut them at the proper hour. She hung up the new moons in the skies, and cut up the old ones into stars. In times of drought, if properly propitiated, she would spin light summer clouds out of cobwebs and morning dew, and send them off from the crest of the mountain, flake after flake, like flakes of carded cotton, to float in the air; until, dissolved by the heat of the sun, they would fall in gentle showers, causing the grass to spring, the fruits to ripen, and the corn to grow an inch an hour. If displeased, however, she would brew up clouds black as ink, sitting in the midst of them like a bottle-bellied spider in the midst of its web; and when these clouds broke, woe betide the valleys! ✗

In old times, say the Indian traditions, there was kind of Manitou or Spirit, who kept about the wildest recesses of the Catskill Mountains, and took a mischievous pleasure in wreaking all kinds of evils and vexations upon the red men. Sometimes he would assume the form of a bear, a panther, or a deer, lead the bewildered hunter a weary chase through tangled forests and among ragged rocks; and then spring off with a loud ho! ho! leaving him aghast on the brink of a beetling precipice or raging torrent.

The favorite abode of this Manitou is still shown. It is a great rock or cliff on the loneliest part of the mountains, and, from the flowering vines which clamber about it, and the wild flowers which abound in its neighborhood, is known by the name of the Garden Rock. Near the foot of it is a small lake, the haunt of the solitary bittern, with water-snakes basking in the sun on the leaves of the pond-lilies which lie on the surface. This place was held in great awe by the Indians, insomuch that the boldest hunter would not pursue his game within its precincts. Once upon a time, however, a hunter who had lost his way, penetrated to the Garden Rock, where he beheld a number of gourds placed in the crotches of trees. One of these he seized and made off with it, but in the hurry of his retreat he let it fall among the rocks, when a great stream gushed forth, which washed him away and swept him down precipices, where he was dashed to pieces, and the stream made its way to the Hudson, and continues to flow to the present day; being the identical stream known by the name of the Kaaterskill.

14. A Christmas Program

A program of Christmas selections requires selection from a profusion of literature. The readings must be chosen with attention to balance among old and new material, religious pieces, popular holiday anecdotes, songs of many traditions, the serious and the comic. The audience needs analysis and consideration, a special problem being the differing attention spans of children and adults.

Most audiences will accept gladly a traditional piece from one of Charles Dickens's Christmas books, perhaps the chapter from *The Pickwick Papers* that appears earlier in this book (Chapter 2); this lends itself well to readers'-theatre presentation. A more modern piece is Truman Capote's "A Christmas Memory," which can be effectively done by a single reader or by a group.

A CHRISTMAS MEMORY / Truman Capote [1]

Imagine a morning in late November. A coming of winter morning more than twenty years ago. Consider the kitchen of a spreading old house in a country town. A great black stove is its main feature; but there is also a big round table and a fireplace with two rocking chairs placed in front of it. Just today the fireplace commenced its seasonal roar.

A woman with shorn white hair is standing at the kitchen window. She is wearing tennis shoes and a shapeless gray sweater over a summery calico dress. She is small and sprightly, like a bantam hen; but, due to a long youthful illness, her shoulders are pitifully hunched. Her face is remarkable—not unlike Lincoln's, craggy like that, and tinted by sun and wind; but it is delicate too, finely boned, and her eyes are sherry-colored and timid. "Oh my," she exclaims, her breath smoking the windowpane, "it's fruitcake weather!"

The person to whom she is speaking is myself. I am seven; she is sixty-something. We are cousins, very distant ones, and we have lived together—well, as

---

long as I can remember. Other people inhabit the house, relatives; and though they have power over us, and frequently make us cry, we are not, on the whole, too much aware of them. We are each other's best friend. She calls me Buddy, in memory of a boy who was formerly her best friend. The other Buddy died in the 1880's, when she was still a child. She is still a child.

"I knew it before I got out of bed," she says, turning away from the window with a purposeful excitement in her eyes. "The courthouse bell sounded so cold and clear. And there were no birds singing; they've gone to warmer country, yes indeed. Oh, Buddy, stop stuffing biscuit and fetch our buggy. Help me find my hat. We've thirty cakes to bake."

It's always the same: a morning arrives in November, and my friend, as though officially inaugurating the Christmas time of year that exhilarates her imagination and fuels the blaze of her heart, announces: "It's fruitcake weather! Fetch our buggy. Help me find my hat."

The hat is found, a straw cartwheel corsaged with velvet roses out-of-doors has faded: it once belonged to a more fashionable relative. Together, we guide our buggy, a dilapidated baby carriage, out to the garden and into a grove of pecan trees. The buggy is mine; that is, it was bought for me when I was born. It is made of wicker, rather unraveled, and the wheels wobble like a drunkard's legs. But it is a faithful object; springtimes, we take it to the woods and fill it with flowers, herbs, wild fern for our porch pots; in the summer, we pile it with picnic para- phernalia and sugar-cane fishing poles and roll it down to the edge of a creek; it has its winter uses, too: as a truck for hauling firewood from the yard to the kitchen, as a warm bed for Queenie, our tough little orange and white rat terrier who has survived distemper and two rattlesnake bites. Queenie is trotting beside it now.

Three hours later we are back in the kitchen hulling a heaping buggyload of windfall pecans. Our backs hurt from gathering them: how hard they were to find (the main crop having been shaken off the trees and sold by the orchard's owners, who are not us) among the concealing leaves, the frosted, deceiving grass. Caarackle! A cherry crunch, scraps of miniature thunder sound as the shells collapse and the golden mound of sweet oily ivory meat mounts in the milk-glass bowl. Queenie begs to taste, and now and again my friend sneaks her a mite, though insisting we deprive ourselves. "We mustn't, Buddy. If we start, we won't stop. And there's scarcely enough as there is. For thirty cakes." The kitchen is growing dark. Dusk turns the window into a mirror: our reflections mingle with the rising moon as we work by the fireside in the firelight. At last, when the moon is quite high, we toss the final hull into the fire and, with joined sighs, watch it catch flame. The buggy is empty, the bowl is brimful.

We eat our supper (cold biscuits, bacon, blackberry jam) and discuss tomorrow. Tomorrow the kind of work I like best begins: buying. Cherries and citron, ginger and vanilla and canned Hawaiian pineapple, rinds and raisins and walnuts and whiskey and oh, so much flour, butter, so many eggs, spices, flavorings: why, we'll need a pony to pull the buggy home.

But before these purchases can be made, there is the question of money. Neither of us has any. Except for skinflint sums persons in the house occasionally provide (a dime is considered very big money); or what we earn ourselves from various activities: holding rummage sales, selling buckets of hand-picked blackberries, jars of homemade jam and apple jelly and peach preserves, rounding up flowers for funerals and weddings. Once we won seventy-ninth prize, five dollars, in a national football contest. Not that we know a fool thing about football. It's just that we enter any contest we hear about: at the moment our hopes are centered on the fifty-thousand-dollar Grand Prize being offered to name a new brand of coffee (we suggested "A.M."; and, after some hesitation, for my friend thought it perhaps sacrilegious, the slogan "A.M.! Amen!"). Te tell the truth, our only *really* profitable enterprise was the Fun and Freak Museum we conducted in a back-yard woodshed two summers ago. The Fun was a stereopticon with slide views of Washington and New York lent us by a relative who had been to those places (she was furious when she discovered why we'd borrowed it); the Freak was a three-legged biddy chicken hatched by one of our own hens. Everybody hereabouts wanted to see that biddy; we charged grownups a nickel, kids two cents. And took in a good twenty dollars before the museum shut down due to the decease of the main attraction.

But one way and another we do each year accumulate Christmas savings, a Fruitcake Fund. These moneys we keep hidden in an ancient bead purse under a loose board under the floor under a chamber pot under my friend's bed. The purse is seldom removed from this safe location except to make a deposit, or, as happens every Saturday, a withdrawal; for on Saturdays I am allowed ten cents to go to the picture show. My friend has never been to a picture show, nor does she intend to: "I'd rather hear you tell the story, Buddy. That way I can imagine it more. Besides, a person my age shouldn't squander their eyes. When the Lord comes, let me see him clear." In addition to never having seen a movie, she has never: eaten in a restaurant, traveled more than five miles from home, received or sent a telegram, read anything except funny papers and the Bible, worn cosmetics, cursed, wished someone harm, told a lie on purpose, let a hungry dog go hungry. Here are a few things she has done, does do: killed with a hoe the biggest rattle-snake ever seen in this country (sixteen rattles), dip snuff (secretly), tame hum-ming-birds (just try it) till they balance on her finger, tell ghost stories (we both believe in ghosts) so tingling they chill you in July, talk to herself, take walks in the rain, grow the prettiest japonicas in town, know the recipe for every sort of old-time Indian cure, including a magical wart-remover.

Now, with supper finished, we retire to the room in a faraway part of the house where my friend sleeps in a scrap-quilt-covered iron bed painted rose pink, her favorite color. Silently, wallowing in the pleasures of conspiracy, we take the bead purse from its secret place and spill its contents on the scrap quilt. Dollar bills, tightly rolled and green as May buds. Somber fifty-cent pieces, heavy enough to weight a dead man's eyes. Lovely dimes, the liveliest coin, the one that really jingles. Nickels and quarters, worn smooth as creek pebbles. But mostly a hateful heap of bitter-odored pennies. Last summer others in the house contracted to pay us a penny for every twenty-five flies we killed. Oh, the carnage of August: the flies that flew to heaven! Yet it was not work in which we took pride. And, as we sit counting pennies, it is as though we were back tabulating dead flies. Neither of us has a head for figures; we count slowly, lose track, start again. According to her calculations, we have $12.73. According to mine, exactly $13. "I do hope you're wrong, Buddy. We can't mess around with thirteen. The cakes will fall. Or put somebody in the cemetery. Why, I wouldn't dream of getting out of bed on the thirteenth." This is true: she always spends thirteenths in bed. So, to be on the safe side, we subtract a penny and toss it out the window.

Of the ingredients that go into our fruitcakes, whiskey is the most expensive, as well as the hardest to obtain: State laws forbid its sale. But everybody knows you can buy a bottle from Mr. Haha Jones. And the next day, having completed our more prosaic shopping, we set out for Mr. Haha's business address, a "sinful" (to quote public opinion) fish-fry and dancing café down by the river. We've been there before, and on the same errand; but in previous years our dealings have been with Haha's wife, an iodine-dark Indian woman with brassy peroxided hair and a dead-tired disposition. Actually, we've never laid eyes on her husband, though we've heard that he's an Indian too. A giant with razor scars across his cheeks. They call him Haha because he's so gloomy, a man who never laughs. As we approach his café (a large log cabin festooned inside and out with chains of garish-gray naked light bulbs and standing by the river's muddy edge under the shade of river trees where moss drifts through the branches like gray mist) our steps slow down. Even Queenie stops prancing and sticks close by. People have been murdered in Haha's café. Cut to pieces. Hit on the head. There's a case coming up in court next month. Naturally these goings-on happen at night when the colored lights cast crazy patterns and the victrola wails. In the daytime Haha's is shabby and deserted. I knock at the door, Queenie barks, my friend calls: "Mrs. Haha, ma'am? Anyone to home?"

Footsteps. The door opens. Our hearts overturn. It's Mr. Haha Jones himself! And he *is* a giant; he *does* have scars; he *doesn't* smile. No, he glowers at us through Satan-tilted eyes and demands to know: "What you want with Haha?"

For a moment we are too paralyzed to tell. Presently my friend half-finds her voice, a whispery voice at best: "If you please, Mr. Haha, we'd like a quart of your finest whiskey."

His eyes tilt more. Would you believe it? Haha is smiling! Laughing, too. "Which one of you is a drinkin' man?"

"It's for making fruitcakes, Mr. Haha. Cooking."

This sobers him. He frowns. "That's no way to waste good whiskey." Nevertheless, he retreats into the shadowed café and seconds later appears carrying a bottle of daisy yellow unlabeled liquor. He demonstrates its sparkle in the sunlight and says: "Two dollars."

We pay him with nickels and dimes and pennies. Suddenly, jangling the coins in his hand like a fistful of dice, his face softens. "Tell you what," he proposes, pouring the money back into our bead purse, "just send me one of them fruitcakes instead."

"Well," my friend remarks on our way home, "there's a lovely man. We'll put an extra cup of raisins in *his* cake."

The black stove, stoked with coal and firewood, glows like a lighted pumpkin.

Eggbeaters whirl, spoons spin round in bowls of butter and sugar, vanilla sweetens the air, ginger spices it; melting, nose-tingling odors saturate the kitchen, suffuse the house, drift out to the world on puffs of chimney smoke. In four days our work is done. Thirty-one cakes, dampened with whiskey, bask on window sills and shelves.

Who are they for?

Friends. Not necessarily neighbor friends: indeed, the larger share are intended for persons we've met maybe once, perhaps not at all. People who've struck our fancy. Like President Roosevelt. Like the Reverend and Mrs. J. C. Lucey, Baptist missionaries to Borneo who lectured here last winter. Or the little knife grinder who comes through town twice a year. Or Abner Packer, the driver of the six o'clock bus from Mobile, who exchanges waves with us every day as he passes in a dust-cloud whoosh. Or the young Wistons, a California couple whose car one afternoon broke down outside the house and who spent a pleasant hour chatting with us on the porch (young Mr. Wiston snapped our picture, the only one we've ever had taken). Is it because my friend is shy with everyone *except* strangers that these strangers, and merest acquaintances, seem to us our truest friends? I think yes. Also, the scrapbooks we keep of thank-you's on White House stationery, time-to-time communications from California and Borneo, the knife grinder's penny post cards, make us feel connected to eventful worlds beyond the kitchen with its view of a sky that stops.

Now a nude December fig branch grates against the window. The kitchen is empty, the cakes are gone; yesterday we carted the last of them to the post office, where the cost of stamps turned our purse inside out. We're broke. That rather depresses me, but my friend insists on celebrating—with two inches of whiskey left in Haha's bottle. Queenie has a spoonful in a bowl of coffee (she likes her coffee chicory-flavored and strong). The rest we divide between a pair of jelly glasses. We're both quite awed at the prospect of drinking straight whiskey; the taste of it brings screwed-up expressions and sour shudders. But by and by we begin to sing, the two of us singing different songs simultaneously. I don't know the words to mine, just: *Come on along, come on along, to the dark-town strutters' ball.* But I can dance: that's what I mean to be, a tap dancer in the movies. My dancing shadow rollicks on the walls; our voices rock the chinaware; we giggle: as if unseen hands were tickling us. Queenie rolls on her back, her paws plow the air, something like a grin stretches her black lips. Inside myself, I feel warm and sparky as those crumbling logs, carefree as the wind in the chimney. My friend waltzes round the stove, the hem of her poor calico skirt pinched between her fingers as though it were a party dress: *Show me the way to go home,* she sings, her tennis shoes squeaking on the floor. *Show me the way to go home.*

Enter: two relatives. Very angry. Potent with eyes that scold, tongues that scald. Listen to what they have to say, the words tumbling together into a wrathful tune: "A child of seven! whiskey on his breath! are you out of your mind? feeding a child of seven! must be loony! road to ruination! remember Cousin Kate? Uncle Charlie? Uncle Charlie's brother-in-law? shame! scandal! humiliation! kneel, pray, beg the Lord!"

Queenie sneaks under the stove. My friend gazes at her shoes, her chin quivers, she lifts her skirt and blows her nose and runs to her room. Long after the town had gone to sleep and the house is silent except for the chimings of clocks and the sputter of fading fires, she is weeping into a pillow already as wet as a widow's handkerchief.

"Don't cry," I say, sitting at the bottom of her bed and shivering despite my flannel nightgown that smells of last winter's cough syrup, "don't cry," I beg, teasing her toes, tickling her feet, "you're too old for that."

"It's because," she hiccups, "I *am* too old. Old and funny."

"Not funny. Fun. More fun than anybody. Listen. If you don't stop crying you'll be so tired tomorrow we can't go cut a tree."

She straightens up. Queenie jumps on the bed (where Queenie is not allowed) to lick her cheeks. "I know where we'll find real pretty trees, Buddy. And holly, too. With berries big as your eyes. It's way off in the woods. Farther than we've ever been. Papa used to bring us Christmas trees from there: carry them on his shoulder. That's fifty years ago. Well, now: I can't wait for morning."

Morning. Frozen rime lusters the grass; the sun, round as an orange and orange as hot-weather moons, balances on the horizon, burnishes the silvered winter woods. A wild turkey calls. A renegade hog grunts in the undergrowth. Soon, by the edge of knee-deep, rapid-running water, we have to abandon the buggy. Queenie wades the stream first, paddles across barking complaints at the swiftness of the current, the pneumonia-making coldness of it. We follow, holding our shoes and equipment (a hatchet, a burlap sack) above our heads. A mile more: of chastising thorns, burs and briers that catch at our clothes; of rusty pine needles brilliant with gaudy fungus and molted feathers. Here, there, a flash, a flutter, an ecstasy of shrillings remind us that not all the birds have flown south. Always, the path unwinds through lemony sun pools and pitch vine tunnels. Another creek to cross: a disturbed armada of speckled trout froths the water round us, and frogs the size of plates practice belly flops; beaver workmen are building a dam. On the farther shore, Queenie shakes herself and trembles. My friend shivers, too: not with cold but enthusiasm. One of her hat's ragged roses sheds a petal as she lifts her head and inhales the pine-heavy air. "We're almost there; can you smell it, Buddy?" she says, as though we were approaching an ocean.

And, indeed, it is a kind of ocean. Scented acres of holiday trees, prickly-leafed holly. Red berries shiny as Chinese bells: black crows swoop upon them screaming. Having stuffed our burlap sacks with enough greenery and crimson to garland a dozen windows, we set about choosing a tree. "It should be," muses my friend, "twice as tall as a boy. So a boy can't steal the star." The one we pick is twice as tall as me. A brave handsome brute that survives thirty hatchet strokes before it keels with a creaking rending cry. Lugging it like a kill, we commence the long trek out. Every few yards we abandon the struggle, sit down and pant. But we have the strength of triumphant huntsmen; that and the tree's virile, icy perfume revive us, goad us on. Many compliments accompany our sunset return along the red clay road to town; but my friend is sly and noncommittal when passers-by praise the treasure perched in our buggy: what a fine tree and where did it come from? "Yonderways," she murmurs vaguely. Once a car stops and the rich mill owner's lazy wife leans out and whines: "Giveya two-bits cash for that ol tree."

Ordinarily my friend is afraid of saying no; but on this occasion she promptly shakes her head: "We wouldn't take a dollar." The mill owner's wife persists. "A dollar, my foot! Fifty cents. That's my last offer. Goodness, woman, you can get another one." In answer, my friend gently reflects: "I doubt it. There's never two of anything."

Home: Queenie slumps by the fire and sleeps till tomorrow, snoring loud as a human.

A trunk in the attic contains: a shoebox of ermine tails (off the opera cape of a curious lady who once rented a room in the house), coils of frazzled tinsel gone gold with age, one silver star, a brief rope of dilapidated, undoubtedly dangerous candy-like light bulbs. Excellent decorations, as far as they go, which isn't far enough: my friend wants our tree to blaze "like a Baptist window," droop with weighty snows of ornament. But we can't afford the made-in-Japan splendors at the five-and-dime. So we do what we've always done: sit for days at the kitchen table with scissors and crayons and stacks of colored paper. I make sketches and my friend cuts them out: lots of cats, fish too (because they're easy to draw), some apples, some watermelons, a few winged angels devised from saved-up sheets of Hershey-bar tin foil. We use safety pins to attach these creations to the tree; as a final touch, we sprinkle the branches with shredded cotton (picked up in August for this purpose). My friend, surveying the effect, clasps her hands together. "Now honest, Buddy. Doesn't it look good enough to eat?" Queenie tries to eat an angel.

After weaving and ribboning holly wreaths for all the front windows, our next project is the fashioning of family gifts. Tie-dye scarves for the ladies, for the men a home-brewed lemon and licorice and aspirin syrup to be taken "at the first Symptoms of a Cold and after Hunting." But when it comes time for making each other's gift, my friend and I separate to work secretly. I would like to buy her a pearl-handled knife, a radio, a whole pound of chocolate-covered cherries (we tasted some once, and she always swears: "I could live on them, Buddy, Lord yes I could—and that's not taking His name in vain"). Instead, I am building her a kite. She would like to give me a bicycle (she's said so on several million occasions: "If only I could, Buddy. It's bad enough in life to do without something *you* want; but confound it, what gets my goat is not being able to give somebody something you want *them* to have. Only one of these days I will, Buddy. Locate you a bike. Don't ask how. Steal it, maybe"). Instead, I'm fairly certain that she is building me a kite—the same as last year, and the year before: the year before that we exchanged slingshots. All of which is fine by me. For we are champion kite-fliers who study the wind like sailors; my friend, more accomplished than I, can get a kite aloft when there isn't enough breeze to carry clouds.

Christmas Eve afternoon we scrape together a nickel and go to the butcher's to buy Queenie's traditional gift, a good gnawable beef bone. The bone, wrapped in funny paper, is placed high in the tree near the silver star. Queenie knows it's there. She squats at the foot of the tree staring up in a trance of greed: when bedtime arrives she refuses to budge. Her excitement is equaled by my own. I kick the covers and turn my pillow as though it were a scorching summer's night.

Somewhere a rooster crows: falsely, for the sun is still on the other side of the world.

"Buddy, are you awake?" It is my friend, calling from her room, which is next to mine; and an instant later she is sitting on my bed holding a candle. "Well, I can't sleep a hoot," she declares. "My mind's jumping like a jack rabbit. Buddy, do you think Mrs. Roosevelt will serve our cake at dinner?" We huddle in the bed, and she squeezes my hand I-love-you. "Seems like your hand used to be so much smaller. I guess I hate to see you grow up. When you're grown up, will we still be friends?" I say always. "But I feel so bad, Buddy. I wanted so bad to give you a bike. I tried to sell my cameo Papa gave me. Buddy—" she hesitates, as though embarrassed—"I made you another kite." Then I confess that I made her one, too; and we laugh. The candle burns too short to hold. Out it goes, exposing the starlight, the stars spinning at the window like a visible caroling that slowly, slowly daybreak silences. Possibly we doze; but the beginnings of dawn splash us like cold water: we're up, wide-eyed and wandering while we wait for others to waken. Quite deliberately my friend drops a kettle on the kitchen floor. I tap-dance in front of closed doors. One by one the household emerges, looking as though they'd like to kill us both; but its Christmas, so they can't. First, a gorgeous breakfast: just everything you can imagine—from flapjacks and fried squirrel to hominy grits and honey-in-the-comb. Which puts everyone in a good humor except my friend and I. Frankly, we're so impatient to get at the presents we can't eat a mouthful.

Well, I'm disappointed. Who wouldn't be? With socks, a Sunday school shirt, some handkerchiefs, a hand-me-down sweater and a year's subscription to a religious magazine for children. *The Little Shepherd*. It makes me boil. It really does.

My friend has a better haul. A sack of Satsumas, that's her best present. She is proudest, however, of a white wool shawl knitted by her married sister. But she *says* her favorite gift is the kite I built her. And it *is* very beautiful; though not as beautiful as the one she made me, which is blue and scattered with gold and green Good Conduct stars; moreover, my name is painted on it, "Buddy."

"Buddy, the wind is blowing."

The wind is blowing, and nothing will do till we've run to a pasture below the house where Queenie has scooted to bury her bone (and where, a winter hence, Queenie will be buried, too.) There, plunging through the healthy waist-high grass, we unreel our kites, feel them twitching at the string like sky fish as they swim into the wind. Satisfied, sun-warmed, we sprawl in the grass and peel Satsumas and watch our kites cavort. Soon I forget the socks and hand-me-down sweater. I'm as happy as if we'd already won the fifty-thousand-dollar Grand Prize in that coffee-naming contest.

"My, how foolish I am!" my friend cries, suddenly alert, like a woman remembering too late she has biscuits in the oven. "You know what I've always thought?" she asks in a tone of discovery, and not smiling at me but a point beyond. "I've always thought a body would have to be sick and dying before they saw the Lord. And I imagined that when He came it would be like looking at the Baptist window: pretty as colored glass with the sun pouring through, such a shine you don't know it's getting dark. And it's been a comfort: to think of that shine taking away all the spooky feeling. But I'll wager it never happens. I'll wager at the very end a body realizes the Lord has already shown Himself. That things as they are"— her hand circles in a gesture that gathers clouds and kites and grass and Queenie pawing earth over her bone—"just what they've always seen, was seeing Him. As for me, I could leave the world with today in my eyes."

This is our last Christmas together.

Life separates us. Those who Know Best decide that I belong in a military school. And so follows a miserable succession of bugle-blowing prisons, grim reveille-ridden summer camps. I have a new home too. But it doesn't count. Home is where my friend is, and there I never go.

And there she remains, puttering around the kitchen. Alone with Queenie. Then alone. ("Buddy dear," she writes in her wild hard-to-read script, "yesterday Jim Macy's horse kicked Queenie bad. Be thankful she didn't feel much. I wrapped her in a Fine Linen sheet and rode her in the buggy down to Simpson's pasture where she can be with all her Bones . . ."). For a few Novembers she continues to bake her fruitcakes single-handed; not as many, but some: and, of course, she always sends me "the best of the batch." Also, in every letter she encloses a dime wadded in toilet paper: "See a picture show and write me the story." But gradually in her letters she tends to confuse me with her other friend, the Buddy who died in the 1880's; more and more thirteenths are not the only days she stays in bed: a morning arrives in November when she cannot rouse herself to exclaim: "Oh my, it's fruitcake weather!"

And when that happens, I know it. A message saying so merely confirms a piece of news some secret vein had already received, severing from me an irreplaceable part of myself, lettting it loose like a kite on a broken string. That is why, walking across a school campus on this particular December morning, I keep searching the sky. As if I expected to see, rather like hearts, a lost pair of kites hurrying toward heaven.

15. The Climax of a Novel as Readers' Theatre

———•◦•———

This program presents the last four chapters of *Moby Dick* in dialog and narration, requiring about two hours for performance. The piece can represent an interesting study for students of oral interpretation who may not immediately perceive that some prose very nearly emerges as drama when marked for readers' theatre. Accordingly, the language is not modified; the only adjustment in the text of the novel is the indication of speakers' and Narrator's lines. The readers are encouraged to exercise discretion with respect to the "he said's." In some instances these may be omitted. In others, the Narrator may be delegated to read explanatory or descriptive phrases which Melville has used.

Four readers are needed:

NARRATOR

AHAB

STARBUCK (*this reader doubles for* DAGGOO, TASHTEGO, *and the* CARPENTER)

STUBB (*this reader doubles for the* OARSMEN *and with* STARBUCK *supplies voices for the* CREW.)

MOBY DICK: THE SYMPHONY; THE CHASE — FIRST DAY; SECOND DAY; THIRD DAY /
Herman Melville

[CHAPTER CXXXII. THE SYMPHONY]

NARRATOR   It was a clear steel-blue day. The firmaments of air and sea were hardly separable in that all-pervading azure; only, the pensive air was transparently pure and soft, with a woman's look, and the robust and man-like sea heaved with long, strong, lingering swells, as Samson's chest in his sleep.

Hither, and thither, on high, glided the snow-white wings of small, un-

NARRATOR *(continuing)*

speckled birds; these were the gentle thoughts of the feminine air; but to and fro in the deeps, far down in the bottomless blue, rushed mighty leviathans, sword-fish, and sharks; and these were the strong, troubled, murderous think-ings of the masculine sea.

But though thus contrasting within, the contrast was only in shades and shadows without; those two seemed one; it was only the sex, as it were, that distinguished them.

Aloft, like a royal czar and king, the sun seemed giving this gentle air to this bold and rolling sea; even as bride to groom. And at the girdling line of the horizon, a soft and tremulous motion—most seen here at the equator—denoted the fond, throbbing trust, the loving alarms, with which the poor bride gave her bosom away.

Tied up and twisted; gnarled and knotted with wrinkles; haggardly firm and unyielding; his eyes glowing like coals, that still glow in the ashes of ruin; un-tottering Ahab stood forth in the clearness of the morn; lifting his splintered helmet of a brow to the fair girl's forehead of heaven.

Oh, immortal infancy, and innocency of the azure! Invisible winged creatures that frolic all round us! Sweet childhood of air and sky! how oblivious were ye of old Ahab's close-coiled woe! But so have I seen little Miriam and Martha, laughing-eyed elves, heedlessly gambol round their old sire; sporting with the circle of singed locks which grew on the marge of that burnt-out crater of his brain.

Slowly crossing the deck from the scuttle, Ahab leaned over the side, and watched how his shadow in the water sank and sank to his gaze, the more and the more that he strove to pierce the profundity. But the lovely aromas in that enchanted air did at last seem to dispel, for a moment, the cankerous thing in his soul. That glad, happy air, that winsome sky, did at last stroke and caress him; the stepmother world, so long cruel—forbidding—now threw affectionate arms around his stubborn neck, and did seem to joyously sob over him, as if over one, that however wilful and erring, she could yet find it in her heart to save and to bless. From beneath his slouched hat Ahab dropped a tear into the sea; nor did all the Pacific contain such wealth as that one wee drop.

Starbuck saw the old man; saw him, how he heavily leaned over the side; and he seemed to hear in his own true heart the measureless sobbing that stole out of the centre of the serenity around. Careful not to touch him, or be noticed by him, he yet drew near to him, and stood there.

Ahab turned.

AHAB "Starbuck!"

STARBUCK "Sir."

AHAB "Oh, Starbuck! it is a mild, mild wind, and a mild looking sky. On such a day—very much such a sweetness as this—I struck my first whale—a boy-harpooner of eighteen! Forty—forty—forty years ago!—ago! Forty years of con-tinual whaling! forty years of privation, and peril, and storm-time! forty years on the pitiless sea! for forty years has Ahab forsaken the peaceful land, for

AHAB *(continuing)*

forty years to make war on the horrors of the deep! Aye and yes, Starbuck, out of those forty years I have not spent three ashore. When I think of this life I have led; the desolation of solitude it has been; the masoned, walled-town of a Captain's exclusiveness, which admits but small entrance to any sympathy from the green country without—oh, weariness! heaviness! Guinea-coast slavery of solitary command!—when I think of all this; only half-suspected, not so keenly known to me before—and how for forty years I have fed upon dry salted fare —fit emblem of the dry nourishment of my soul!—when the poorest landsman has had fresh fruit to his daily hand, and broken the world's fresh bread to my mouldy crusts—away, whole oceans away, from that young girl-wife I wedded past fifty, and sailed for Cape Horn the next day, leaving but one dent in my marriage pillow—wife? wife?—rather a widow with her husband alive! Aye, I widowed that poor girl when I married her, Starbuck; and then, the madness, the frenzy, the boiling blood and the smoking brow, with which, for a thousand lowerings old Ahab has furiously, foamingly chased his prey—more a demon than a man?—aye, aye! what a forty years' fool—fool—old fool, has old Ahab been! Why this strife of the chase? why weary, and palsy the arms at the oar, and the iron, and the lance? how the richer or better is Ahab now? Behold. Oh, Starbuck! is it not hard, that with this weary load I bear, one poor leg should have been snatched from under me? Here, brush this old hair aside; it blinds me, that I seem to weep. Locks so grey did never grow but from out some ashes! But do I look very old, so very, very old, Starbuck? I feel deadly faint, bowed, and humped, as though I were Adam, staggering beneath the piled centuries since Paradise. God! God! God!—crack my heart!—stave my brain!—mockery! mockery! bitter biting mockery of grey hairs, have I lived enough joy to wear ye; and seem and feel thus intolerably old? Close! stand close to me, Starbuck; let me look into a human eye; it is better than to gaze into sea or sky; better than to gaze upon God. By the green land; by the bright hearth-stone! this is the magic glass, man; I see my wife and my child in thine eye. No, no; stay on board, on board!—lower not when I do; when branded Ahab gives chase to Moby Dick. That hazard shall not be thine. No, no! not with the far away home I see in that eye!"

STARBUCK   "Oh, my Captain! my Captain! noble soul! grand old heart, after all! why should any one give chase to that hated fish! Away with me! let us fly these deadly waters! let us home! Wife and child, too, are Starbuck's—wife and child of his brotherly, sisterly, play-fellow youth; even as thine, sir, are the wife and child of thy loving, longing, paternal old age! Away! let us away!— this instant let me alter the course! How cheerily, how hilariously, O my Captain, would we bowl on our way to see old Nantucket again! I think, sir, they have some such mild blue days, even as this, in Nantucket."

AHAB   "They have, they have. I have seen them—some summer days in the morning. About this time—yes, it is his noon nap now—the boy vivaciously wakes; sits up in bed; and his mother tells him of me, of cannibal old me; how I am abroad upon the deep, but will yet come back to dance him again."

STARBUCK " 'Tis my Mary, my Mary herself! She promised that my boy, every morning, should be carried to the hill to catch the first glimpse of his father's sail! Yes, yes! no more! it is done! we head for Nantucket! Come, my Captain, study out the course, and let us away! See, see! the boy's face from the window! the boy's hand on the hill!"

NARRATOR But Ahab's glance was averted; like a blighted fruit tree he shook, and cast his last cindered apple to the soil.

AHAB "What is it, what nameless, inscrutable, unearthly thing is it; what cozening, hidden lord and master, and cruel, remorseless emperor commands me; that against all natural lovings and longings, I so keep pushing, and crowding, and jamming myself on all the time; recklessly making me ready to do what in my own proper, natural heart, I durst not so much as dare? Is Ahab, Ahab? Is it I, God, or who, that lifts this arm? But if the great sun move not of himself; but is an errand-boy in heaven; nor one single star can revolve, but by some invisible power; how then can this one small heart beat; this one small brain think thoughts; unless God does that beating, does that thinking, does that living, and not I. By heaven, man, we are turned round and round in this world, like yonder windlass, and Fate is the handspike. And all the time, lo! that smiling sky, and this unsounded sea! Look! see yon Albicore! who put it into him to chase and fang that flying-fish? Where do murderers go, man? Who's to doom, when the judge himself is dragged to the bar? But it is a mild, mild wind, and a mild looking sky; and the air smells now, as if it blew from a far-away meadow; they have been making hay somewhere under the slopes of the Andes, Starbuck, and the mowers are sleeping among the new-mown hay. Sleeping? Aye, toil we how we may, we all sleep at last on the field. Sleep? Aye, and rust amid greenness; as last years scythes flung down, and left in the half-cut swaths—Starbuck!"

NARRATOR But blanched to a corpse's hue with despair, the Mate had stolen away.

Ahab crossed the deck to gaze over on the other side; but started at two reflected, fixed eyes in the water there. Fedallah was motionlessly leaning over the same rail.

[CHAPTER CXXXIII. THE CHASE—FIRST DAY]

NARRATOR That night, in the mid-watch, when the old man—as his wont at intervals—stepped forth from the scuttle in which he leaned, and went to his pivot-hole, he suddenly thrust out his face fiercely, snuffing up the sea air as a sagacious ship's dog will, in drawing nigh to some barbarous isle. He declared that a whale must be near. Soon that peculiar odour, sometimes to a great distance given forth by the living sperm whale, was palpable to all the watch; nor was any mariner surprised when, after inspecting the compass, and then the dog-vane, and then ascertaining the precise bearing of the odour as nearly as possible, Ahab rapidly ordered the ship's course to be slightly altered, and the sail to be shortened.

The acute policy dictating these movements was sufficiently vindicated at daybreak, by the sight of a long sleek on the sea directly and lengthwise ahead, smooth as oil, and resembling in the pleated watery wrinkles bordering it, the polished metallic-like marks of some swift tide-rip, at the mouth of a deep, rapid stream.

AHAB   "Man the mast-heads! Call all hands!"

NARRATOR   Thundering with the butts of three clubbed handspikes on the fore-castle deck, Daggoo roused the sleepers with such judgment claps that they seemed to exhale from the scuttle, so instantaneously did they appear with their clothes in their hands.

AHAB   "What d'ye see?"

NARRATOR   —cried Ahab, flattening his face to the sky.

DAGGOO   "Nothing, nothing, sir!"

NARRATOR   —was the sound hailing down in reply.

AHAB   "T'gallant sails! stunsails alow and aloft, and on both sides!"

NARRATOR   All sail being set, he now cast loose the life-line, reserved for swaying him to the main royal-mast head; and in a few moments they were hoisting him thither, when, while but two-thirds of the way aloft, and while peering ahead through the horizontal vacancy betwen the main-top-sail and top-gallant-sail, he raised a gull-like cry in the air,

AHAB   "There she blows!—there she blows! A hump like a snow-hill! It is Moby Dick!"

NARRATOR   Fired by the cry which semed simultaneously taken up by the three look-outs, the men on deck rushed to the rigging to behold the famous whale they had so long been pursuing. Ahab had now gained his final perch, some feet above the other look-outs, Tashtego standing just beneath him on the cap of the top-gallant-mast, so that the Indian's head was almost on a level with Ahab's heel. From this height the whale was now seen some mile or so ahead, at every roll of the sea revealing his high sparkling hump, and regularly jetting his silent spout into the air. To the credulous mariners it seemed the same silent spout they had so long ago beheld in the moonlit Atlantic and Indian Oceans.

AHAB   "And did none of ye see it before?"

NARRATOR   —cried Ahab, hailing the perched men all around him.

TASHTEGO   "I saw him almost that same instant, sir, that Captain Ahab did, and I cried out," said Tashtego.

AHAB   "Not the same instant; not the same—no, the doubloon is mine, Fate reserved the doubloon for me. I only; none of ye could have raised the White Whale first. There she blows! there she blows!—there she blows! There again! —there again!"

NARRATOR   —he cried, in long-drawn, lingering, methodic tones, attuned to the gradual prolongings of the whale's visible jets.

AHAB   "He's going to sound! In stunsails! Down top-gallant-sails! Stand by three boats. Mr. Starbuck, remember, stay on board, and keep the ship. Helm there!

Luff, luff a point! So; steady, man, steady! There go flukes! No, no; only black water! All ready the boats there? Stand by, stand by! Lower me, Mr. Starbuck; lower, lower,—quick, quicker!"

NARRATOR   —and he slid through the air to the deck.

STUBB   "He is heading straight to leeward, sir," cried Stubb, "right away from us; cannot have seen the ship yet."

AHAB   "Be dumb, man! Stand by the braces! Hard down the helm!—brace up! Shiver her!—shiver her! So; well that! Boats, boats!"

NARRATOR   Soon all the boats but Starbuck's were dropped; all the boat-sails set —all the paddles plying; with rippling swiftness, shooting to leeward; and Ahab heading the onset. A pale, death-glimmer lit up Fedallah's sunken eyes; a hideous motion gnawed his mouth.

Like noiseless nautilus shells, their light prows sped through the sea; but only slowly they neared the foe. As they neared him, the ocean grew still more smooth; seemed drawing a carpet over its waves; seemed a noon-meadow, so serenely it spread. At length the breathless hunter came so nigh his seemingly unsuspecting prey, that his entire dazzling hump was distinctly visible, sliding along the sea as if an isolated thing, and continually set in a revolving ring of finest, fleecy, greenish foam. He saw the vast involved wrinkles of the slightly projecting head beyond. Before it, far out on the soft Turkish-rugged waters, went the glistening white shadow from his broad, milky forehead, a musical rippling playfully accompanying the shade; and behind, the blue waters interchangeably flowed over into the moving valley of his steady wake; and on either hand bright bubbles arose and danced by his side. But these were broken again by the light toes of hundreds of gay fowl softly feathering the sea, alternate with their fitful flight; and like to some flag-staff rising from the painted hull of an argosy, the tall but shattered pole of a recent lance projected from the white whale's back; and at intervals one of the cloud of soft-toed fowls hovering, and to and fro skimming like a canopy over the fish, silently perched and rocked on this pole, the long tail feathers streaming like pennons.

A gentle joyousness—a mighty mildness of repose in swiftness, invested the gliding whale. Not the white bull Jupiter swimming away with ravished Europa clinging to his graceful horns; his lovely, leering eyes sideways intent upon the maid; with smooth bewitching fleetness, rippling straight for the nuptial bower in Crete; not Jove, not that great majesty Supreme! did surpass the glorified White Whale as he so divinely swam.

On each soft side—coincident with the parted swell, that but once leaving him, then flowed so wide away—on each bright side, the whale shed off enticings. No wonder there had been some among the hunters who namelessly transported and allured by all this serenity, had ventured to assail it; but had fatally found that quietude but the vesture of tornadoes. Yet calm, enticing calm, oh, whale! thou glidest on, to all who for the first time eye thee, no matter how many in that same way thou may'st have bejuggled and destroyed before.

And thus, through the serene tranquillities of the tropical sea, among waves whose hand-clappings were suspended by exceeding rapture, Moby Dick moved

NARRATOR   (*continuing*)

on, still withholding from sight the full terrors of his submerged trunk, entirely hiding the wrenched hideousness of his jaw. But soon the fore part of him slowly rose from the water; for an instant his whole marbleized body formed a high arch, like Virginia's Natural Bridge, and warningly waving his bannered flukes in the air, the grand god revealed himself, sounded, and went out of sight. Hoveringly halting, and dipping on the wing, the white sea-fowls longingly lingered over the agitated pool that he left.

With oars apeak, and paddles down, the sheets of their sails adrift, the three boats now stilly floated, awaiting Moby Dick's reappearance.

AHAB   "An hour,"

NARRATOR   —said Ahab, standing rooted in his boat's stern; and he gazed beyond the whale's place, towards the dim blue spaces and wide wooing vacancies to leeward. It was only an instant; for again his eyes seemed whirling round in his head as he swept the watery circle. The breeze now freshened; the sea began to swell.

TASHTEGO   "The birds!—the birds!" cried Tashtego.

NARRATOR   In long Indian file, as when herons take wing, the white birds were now all flying towards Ahab's boat; and when within a few yards began fluttering over the water there, wheeling round and round, with joyous, expectant cries. Their vision was keener than man's; Ahab could discover no sign in the sea. But suddenly as he peered down and down into its depths, he profoundly saw a white living spot no bigger than a white weasel, with wonderful celerity uprising, and magnifying as it rose, till it turned, and then there were plainly revealed two long crooked rows of white, glistening teeth, floating up from the undiscoverable bottom. It was Moby Dick's open mouth and scrolled jaw; his vast, shadowed bulk still half blending with the blue of the sea. The glittering mouth yawned beneath the boat like an open-doored marble tomb; and giving one sidelong sweep with his steering oar, Ahab whirled the craft aside from this tremendous apparition. Then, calling upon Fedallah to change places with him, went forward to the bows, and seizing Perth's harpoon, commanded his crew to grasp their oars and stand by to stern.

Now, by reason of this timely spinning round the boat upon its axis, its bow, by anticipation, was made to face the whale's head while yet under water. But as if perceiving this stratagem, Moby Dick, with that malicious intelligence ascribed to him, sidelingly transplanted himself, as it were, in an instant, shooting his plated head lengthwise beneath the boat.

Through and through; through every plank and each rib, it thrilled for an instant, the whale obliquely lying on his back, in the manner of a biting shark, slowly and feelingly taking its bows full within his mouth, so that the long, narrow, scrolled lower jaw curled high up into the open air, and one of the teeth caught in a row-lock. The bluish pearl-white of the inside of the jaw was within six inches of Ahab's head, and reached higher than that. In this attitude the White Whale now shook the slight cedar as a mildly cruel cat her mouse.

NARRATOR (*continuing*)

With unastonished eyes Fedallah gazed, and crossed his arms; but the tiger-yellow crew were tumbling over each other's heads to gain the uttermost stern.

And now, while both elastic gunwales were springing in and out, as the whale dallied with the doomed craft in this devilish way; and from his body being submerged beneath the boat, he could not be darted at from the bows, for the bows were almost inside of him, as it were; and while the other boats involuntarily paused, as before a quick crisis impossible to withstand, then it was that monomaniac Ahab, furious with this tantalizing vicinity of his foe, which placed him all alive and helpless in the very jaws he hated; frenzied with all this, he seized the long bone with his naked hands, and wildly strove to wrench it from its gripe. As now he thus vainly strove, the jaw slipped from him; the frail gunwales bent in, collapsed, and snapped, as both jaws, like an enormous shears, sliding further aft, bit the craft completely in twain, and locked themselves fast again in the sea, midway between the two floating wrecks. These floated aside, the broken ends drooping, the crew at the stern-wreck clinging to the gunwales, and striving to hold fast to the oars to lash them across.

At that preluding moment, ere the boat was yet snapped, Ahab, the first to perceive the whale's intent, by the crafty upraising of his head, a movement that loosed his hold for the time; at that moment his hand had made one final effort to push the boat out of the bite. But only slipping further into the whale's mouth, and tilting over sideways as it slipped, the boat had shaken off his hold on the jaw; spilled him out of it, as he leaned to the push; and so he fell flat-faced upon the sea.

Ripplingly withdrawing from his prey, Moby Dick now lay at a little distance, vertically thrusting his oblong white head up and down in the billows; and at the same time slowly revolving his whole spindled body; so that when his vast wrinkled forehead rose—some twenty or more feet out of the water—the now rising swells, with all their confluent waves, dazzling broke against it; vindictively tossing their shivered spray still higher into the air. So, in a gale, the but half baffled Channel billows only recoil from the base of the Eddystone, triumphantly to overleap its summit with their scud.

But soon resuming his horizontal attitude, Moby Dick swam swiftly round and round the wrecked crew; sideways churning the water in his vengeful wake, as if lashing himself up to still another and more deadly assault. The sight of the splintered boat seemed to madden him, as the blood of grapes and mulberries cast before Antiochus's elephants in the book of Maccabees. Meanwhile Ahab half smothered in the foam of the whale's insolent tail, and too much of a cripple to swim,—though he could still keep afloat, even in the heart of such a whirlpool as that; helpless Ahab's head was seen, like a tossed bubble which the least chance shock might burst. From the boat's fragmentary stern, Fedallah incuriously and mildly eyed him; the clinging crew, at the other drifting end, could not succour him; more than enough was it for them to look to themselves. For so revolvingly appalling was the White Whale's aspect, and so planetarily swift the ever-contracting circles he made, that he seemed horizontally swooping upon them. And though the other boats, unharmed, still hovered hard by;

NARRATOR (*continuing*)

 still they dared not pull into the eddy to strike, lest that should be the signal
for the instant destruction of the jeopardised castaways, Ahab and all; nor in
that case could they themselves hope to escape. With straining eyes, then, they
remained on the outer edge of the direful zone, whose centre had now become
the old man's head.

 Meantime, from the beginning all this had been descried from the ship's
mast heads; and squaring her yards, she had borne down upon the scene; and
was now so nigh, that Ahab in the water hailed her;—

AHAB "Sail on the"—

NARRATOR But that moment a breaking sea dashed on him from Moby Dick, and
whelmed him for the time. But struggling out of it again, and chancing to rise
on a towering crest, he shouted,—

AHAB "Sail on the whale!—Drive him off!"

NARRATOR The Pequod's prows were pointed; and breaking up the charmed
circle, she effectually parted the white whale from his victim. As he sullenly
swam off, the boats flew to the rescue.

 Dragged into Stubb's boat with blood-shot, blinded eyes, the white brine
caking in his wrinkles; the long tension of Ahab's bodily strength did crack, and
helplessly he yielded to his body's doom: for a time, lying all crushed in the
bottom of Stubb's boat, like one trodden under foot of herds of elephants. Far
inland, nameless wails came from him, as desolate sounds from out ravines.

 But this intensity of his physical prostration did but so much the more ab-
breviate it. In an instant's compass, great hearts sometimes condense to one
deep pang, the sum total of those shallow pains kindly diffused through feebler
men's whole lives. And so, such hearts, though summary in each one suffering;
still, if the gods decree it, in their life-time aggregate a whole age of woe, wholly
made up of instantaneous intensities; for even in their pointless centres, those
noble natures contain the entire circumferences of inferior souls.

AHAB "The harpoon,"

NARRATOR —said Ahab, half-way rising, and draggingly leaning on one bended
arm

AHAB —"is it safe?"

STUBB "Aye, sir, for it was not darted; this is it," said Stubb, showing it.

AHAB "Lay it before me;—any missing men?"

STUBB "One, two, three, four, five;—there were five oars, sir, and here are five
men."

STUBB "That's good.—Help me, man; I wish to stand. So, so, I see him! there!
there! going to leeward still; what a leaping spout!—Hands off from me! The
eternal sap runs up in Ahab's bones again! Set the sail; out oars; the helm!"

NARRATOR It is often the case that when a boat is stove, its crew, being picked
up by another boat, help to work that second boat; and the chase is thus continued with what is called double-banked oars. It was thus now. But the added

NARRATOR   (*continuing*)

power of the boat did not equal the added power of the whale, for he seemed to have treble-banked his every fin; swimming with a velocity which plainly showed, that if now, under these circumstances, pushed on, the chase would prove an indefinitely prolonged, if not a hopeless one; nor could any crew endure for so long a period, such an unintermitted, intense straining at the oar; a thing barely tolerable only in some one brief vicissitude. The ship itself, then, as it sometimes happens, offered the most promising intermediate means of overtaking the chase. Accordingly, the boats now made for her, and were soon swayed up to their cranes—the two parts of the wrecked boat having been previously secured by her—and then hoisting everything to her side, and stacking her canvas high up, and sideways outstretching it with stun-sails, like the double-jointed wings of an albatross; the Pequod bore down in the leeward wake of Moby Dick. At the well known, methodic intervals, the whale's glittering spout was regularly announced from the manned mast-heads; and when he would be reported as just gone down, Ahab would take the time, and then pacing the deck, binnacle-watch in hand, so soon as the last second of the allotted hour expired, his voice was heard.—

AHAB   "Whose is the doubloon now? D'ye see him?"

NARRATOR   —and if the reply was

DAGGOO   "No, sir!"

NARRATOR   —straightway he commanded them to lift him to his perch. In this way the day wore on; Ahab, now aloft and motionless; anon, unrestingly pacing the planks.

As he was thus walking, uttering no sound, except to hail the men aloft, or to bid them hoist a sail still higher, or to spread one to a still greater breadth— thus to and fro pacing, beneath his slouched hat, at every turn he passed his own wrecked boat, which had been dropped upon the quarter-deck, and lay there reversed; broken bow to shattered stern. At last he paused before it; and as in an already over-clouded sky fresh troops of clouds will sometimes sail across, so over the old man's face there now stole some such added gloom as this.

Stubb saw him pause; and perhaps intending, not vainly, though, to evince his own unabated fortitude, and thus keep up a valiant place in his Captain's mind, he advanced, and eyeing the wreck exclaimed—

STUBB   "The thistle the ass refused; it pricked his mouth too keenly, sir; ha! ha!"

AHAB   "What soulless thing is this that laughs before a wreck? Man, man! did I not know thee brave as fearless fire (and as mechanical) I could swear thou wert a poltroon. Groan nor laugh should be heard before a wreck."

STARBUCK   "Aye, sir," said Starbuck drawing near, " 'tis a solemn sight; an omen, and an ill one."

AHAB   "Omen? omen?—the dictionary! If the gods think to speak outright to man, they will honourably speak outright; not shake their heads, and give an old wives' darkling hint.—Begone! Ye two are the opposite poles of one thing;

Starbuck is Stubb reversed, and Stubb is Starbuck; and ye two are all mankind; and Ahab stands alone among the millions of the peopled earth, nor gods nor men his neighbours! Cold, cold—I shiver!—How now? Aloft there! D'ye see him? Sing out for every spout, though he spout ten times a second!"

NARRATOR   The day was nearly done; only the hem of his golden robe was rustling. Soon, it was almost dark, but the lookout men still remained unset. Cried a voice from the air:

DAGGOO   "Can't see the spout now, sir;—too dark."

AHAB   "How heading when last seen?"

DAGGOO   "As before, sir,—straight to leeward."

AHAB   "Good! he will travel slower now 'tis night. Down royals and top-gallant stun-sails, Mr. Starbuck. We must not run over him before morning; he's making a passage now, and may heave-to a while. Helm there! keep her full before the wind!—Aloft! come down!—Mr. Stubb, send a fresh hand to the fore-mast head, and see it manned till morning."—

NARRATOR   Then advancing towards the doubloon in the mainmast—

AHAB   "Men, this gold is mine, for I earned it; but I shall let it abide here till the White Whale is dead; and then, whosoever of ye first raises him, upon the day he shall be killed, this gold is that man's; and if on that day I shall again raise him, then, ten times its sum shall be divided among all of ye! Away now!— the deck is thine, sir."

NARRATOR   And so saying, he placed himself half-way within the scuttle, and slouching his hat, stood there till dawn, except when at intervals rousing himself to see how the night wore on.

[CHAPTER CXXXIV. THE CHASE—SECOND DAY]

NARRATOR   At daybreak, the three mast-heads were punctually manned afresh. After allowing a little space for the light to spread:

AHAB   "D'ye see him?" cried Ahab.

DAGGOO   "See nothing, sir."

AHAB   "Turn up all hands and make sail! he travels faster than I thought for;— the top-gallant sails!—aye, they should have been kept on her all night. But no matter—'tis but resting for the rush."

NARRATOR   Here be it said, that this pertinacious pursuit of one particular whale, continued through day into night, and through night into day, is a thing by no means unprecedented in the South Sea fishery. For such is the wonderful skill, prescience of experience, and invincible confidence acquired by some great natural geniuses among the Nantucket commanders; that from the simple observation of a whale when last descried, they will, under certain given circumstances, pretty accurately foretell both the direction in which he will continue to swim for a time, while out of sight, as well as his probable rate of progression during that period. And, in these cases, somewhat as a pilot, when about losing

NARRATOR (*continuing*)

sight of a coast, whose general trending he well knows, and which he desires shortly to return to again, but at some further point; like as this pilot stands by his compass, and takes the precise bearing of the cape at present visible, in order the more certainly to hit aright the remote, unseen headland, eventually to be visited: so does the fisherman, at his compass, with the whale; for after being chased, and diligently marked, through several hours of daylight, then, when night obscures the fish, the creature's future wake through the darkness is almost as established to the sagacious mind of the hunter, as the pilot's coast is to him. So that to this hunter's wondrous skill, the proverbial evanescence of a thing writ in water, a wake, is to all desired purposes well-nigh as reliable as the steadfast land. And as the mighty iron Leviathan of the modern railway is so familiarly known in its every pace, that, with watches in their hands, men time his rate as doctors that of a baby's pulse; and lightly say of it, the up train or the down train will reach such or such a spot, at such or such an hour; even so, almost, there are occasions when these Nantucketers time that other Leviathan of the deep, according to the observed humour of his speed; and say to themselves, so many hours hence this whale will have gone two hundred miles, will have about reached this or that degree of latitude or longitude. But to render this acuteness at all successful in the end, the wind and the sea must be the whaleman's allies; for of what present avail to the becalmed or windbound mariner is the skill that assures him he is exactly ninety-three leagues and a quarter from his port? Inferable from these statements, are many collateral subtle matters touching the chase of whales.

The ship tore on; leaving such a furrow in the sea as when a cannon-ball, missent, becomes a ploughshare and turns up the level field.

STUBB "By salt and hemp!" cried Stubb, "but this swift motion of the deck creeps up one's legs and tingles at the heart. This ship and I are two brave fellows!—Ha! ha! Some one take me up, and launch me, spine-wise, on the sea, —for by live-oaks! my spine's a keel. Ha, ha! we go the gait that leaves no dust behind!"

DAGGOO "There she blows—she blows!—she blows!—right ahead!"

NARRATOR —was now the mast-head cry.

STUBB "Aye, aye!" cried Stubb, "I knew it—ye can't escape—blow on and split your spout, O whale! the mad fiend himself is after ye! blow your trump—blister your lungs!—Ahab will dam off your blood, as a miller shuts his watergate upon the stream!"

NARRATOR And Stubb did but speak out for well-nigh all that crew. The frenzies of the chase had by this time worked them bubblingly up, like old wine worked anew. Whatever pale fears and forebodings some of them might have felt before; these were not only now kept out of sight through the growing awe of Ahab, but they were broken up, and on all sides routed, as timid prairie hares that scatter before the bounding bison. The hand of Fate had snatched all their souls; and by the stirring perils of the previous day; the rack of the past night's

NARRATOR (*continuing*)

suspense; the fixed, unfearing, blind, reckless way in which their wild craft went plunging towards its flying mark; by all these things, their hearts were bowled along. The wind that made great bellies of their sails, and rushed the vessel on by arms invisible as irresistible; this seemed the symbol of that unseen agency which so enslaved them to the race.

They were one man, not thirty. For as the one ship that held them all; though it was put together of all contrasting things—oak, and maple, and pine wood; iron, and pitch, and hemp—yet all these ran into each other in the one concrete hull, which shot on its way, both balanced and directed by the long central keel; even so, all the individualities of the crew, this man's valour, that man's fear; guilt and guiltiness, all varieties were wedded into oneness, and were all directed to that fatal goal which Ahab their one lord and keel did point to.

The rigging lived. The mast-heads, like the tops of tall palms, were out-spreadingly tufted with arms and legs. Clinging to a spar with one hand, some reached forth the other with impatient wavings; others, shading their eyes from the vivid sunlight, sat far out on the rocking yards; all the spars in full bearing of mortals, ready and ripe for their fate. Ah! how they still strove through that infinite blueness to seek out the thing that might destroy them!

AHAB "Why sing ye not out for him, if ye see him?"

NARRATOR —cried Ahab, when, after the lapse of some minutes since the first cry, no more had been heard.

AHAB "Sway me up, men; ye have been deceived; not Moby Dick casts one odd jet that way, and then disappears."

NARRATOR It was even so; in their headlong eagerness, the men had mistaken some other thing for the whale-spout, as the event itself soon proved; for hardly had Ahab reached his perch; hardly was the rope belayed to its pin on deck, when he struck the key-note to an orchestra, that made the air vibrate as with the combined discharges of rifles. The triumphant halloo of thirty buckskin lungs was heard, as—much nearer to the ship than the place of the imaginary jet, less than a mile ahead—Moby Dick bodily burst into view! For not by any calm and indolent spoutings; not by the peaceable gush of that mystic fountain in his head, did the White Whale now reveal his vicinity; but by the far more wondrous phenomenon of breaching. Rising with his utmost velocity from the furthest depths, the Sperm Whale thus booms his entire bulk into the pure element of air, and piling up a mountain of dazzling foam, shows his place to the distance of seven miles and more. In those moments, the torn, enraged waves he shakes off, seem his mane; in some cases, this breaching is his act of defiance.

DAGGOO *and* TASHTEGO "There she breaches! there she breaches!"

NARRATOR —was the cry, as in his immeasurable bravadoes the White Whale tossed himself salmon-like to Heaven. So suddenly seen in the blue plain of the sea, anl relieved against the still bluer margin of the sky, the spray that he raised, for the moment, intolerably glittered and glared like a glacier; and stood there gradually fading and fading away from its first sparkling intensity, to the dim mistiness of an advancing shower in a vale.

AHAB   "Aye, breach your last to the sun, Moby Dick!" cried Ahab, "thy hour and thy harpoon are at hand!—Down! down all of ye, but one man at the fore. The boats!—stand by!"

NARRATOR   Unmindful of the tedious rope-ladders of the shrouds, the men, like shooting stars, slid to the deck, by the isolated backstays and halyards; while Ahab, less dartingly, but still rapidly, was dropped from his perch.

AHAB   "Lower away,"

NARRATOR   —he cried, so soon as he had reached his boat—a spare one, rigged the afternoon previous.

AHAB   "Mr. Starbuck, the ship is thine—keep away from the boats, but keep near them. Lower, all!"

NARRATOR   As if to strike a quick terror into them, by this time being the first assailant himself, Moby Dick had turned, and was now coming for the three crews. Ahab's boat was central; and cheering his men, he told them he would take the whale head-and-head,—that is, pull straight up to his forehead,—a not uncommon thing; for when within a certain limit, such a course excludes the coming onset from the whale's sidelong vision. But ere that close limit was gained, and while yet all three boats were plain as the ship's three masts to his eye; the White Whale churning himself into furious speed, almost in an instant as it were, rushing among the boats with open jaws, and a lashing tail, offered appalling battle on every side; and heedless of the irons darted at him from every boat, seemed only intent on annihilating each separate plank of which those boats were made. But skilfully manœuvred, incessantly wheeling like trained chargers in the field; the boats for a while eluded him; though, at times, but by a plank's breadth; while all the time, Ahab's unearthly slogan tore every other cry but his to shreds.

But at last in his untraceable evolutions, the White Whale so crossed and recrossed, and in a thousand ways entangled the slack of the three lines now fast to him, that they foreshortened, and, of themselves, warped the devoted boats towards the planted irons in him; though now for a moment the whale drew aside a little, as if to rally for a more tremendous charge. Seizing that opportunity, Ahab first paid out more line: and then was rapidly hauling and jerking in upon it again—hoping that way to disencumber it of some snarls—when lo! —a sight more savage than the embattled teeth of sharks!

Caught and twisted—corkscrewed in the mazes of the line, loose harpoons and lances, with all their bristling barbs and points, came flashing and dripping up to the chocks in the bows of Ahab's boat. Only one thing could be done. Seizing the boat-knife, he critically reached within—through—and then, without—the rays of steel; dragged in the line beyond, passed it, inboard, to the bowsman, and then, twice sundering the rope near the chocks—dropped the intercepted fagot of steel into the sea; and was all fast again. That instant, the White Whale made a sudden rush among the remaining tangles of the other

NARRATOR   (*continuing*)

lines; by so doing, irresistibly dragged the more involved boats of Stubb and Flask towards his flukes; dashed them together like two rolling husks on a surf-beaten beach, and then, diving down into the sea, disappeared in a boiling maelstrom, in which, for a space, the odorous cedar chips of the wrecks danced round and round, like the grated nutmeg in a swiftly stirred bowl of punch.

While the two crews were yet circling in the waters, reaching out after the revolving line-tubs, oars, and other floating furniture, while aslope little Flask bobbed up and down like an empty vial, twitching his legs upwards to escape the dreaded jaws of sharks; and Stubb was lustily singing out for some one to ladle him up; and while the old man's line—now parting—admitted of his pulling into the creamy pool to rescue whom he could;—in that wild simultaneousness of a thousand concreted perils,—Ahab's yet unstricken boat seemed drawn up towards Heaven by invisible wires,—as, arrow-like, shooting perpendicularly from the sea, the White Whale dashed his broad forehead against its bottom, and sent it, turning over and over, into the air; till it fell again—gunwale downwards—and Ahab and his men struggled out from under it, like seals from a sea-side cave.

The first uprising momentum of the whale—modifying its direction as he struck the surface—involuntarily launched him along it, to a little distance from the centre of the destruction he had made; and with his back to it, he now lay for a moment slowly feeling with his flukes from side to side; and whenever a stray oar, bit of plank, the least chip or crumb of the boats touched his skin, his tail swiftly drew back, and came sideways, smiting the sea. But soon, as if satisfied that his work for that time was done, he pushed his pleated forehead through the ocean, and trailing after him the intertangled lines, continued his leeward way at a traveller's methodic pace.

As before, the attentive ship having descried the whole fight, again came bearing down to the rescue, and dropping a boat, picked up the floating mariners, tubs, oars, and whatever else could be caught at, and safely landed them on her decks. Some sprained shoulders, wrists, and ankles; livid contusions; wrenched harpoons and lances: inextricable intricacies of rope; shattered oars and planks; all these were there; but no fatal or even serious ill seemed to have befallen any one. As with Fedallah the day before, so Ahab was now found grimly clinging to his boat's broken half, which afforded a comparatively easy float; nor did it so exhaust him as the previous day's mishap.

But when he was helped to the deck, all eyes were fastened upon him; as instead of standing by himself he still half-hung upon the shoulder of Starbuck, who had thus far been the foremost to assist him. His ivory leg had been snapped off, leaving but one short sharp splinter.

AHAB   "Aye aye, Starbuck, 'tis sweet to lean sometimes, be the leaner who he will; and would old Ahab had leaned oftener than he has."

CARPENTER   "The ferrule has not stood, sir,"

NARRATOR   —said the carpenter, now coming up;

CARPENTER   "I put good work into that leg."

STUBB   "But no bones broken, sir, I hope,"

NARRATOR   —said Stubb with true concern.

AHAB   "Aye! and all splintered to pieces, Stubb!—d'ye see it.—But even with a broken bone, old Ahab is untouched; and I account no living bone of mine one jot more me, than this dead one that's lost. Nor white whale, nor man, nor fiend, can so much as graze old Ahab in his own proper and inaccessible being. Can any lead touch yonder floor, any mast scrape yonder roof?—Aloft there! which way?"

DAGGOO   "Dead to leeward, sir."

AHAB   "Up helm, then; pile on the sail again, ship keepers! down the rest of the spare boats and rig them—Mr. Starbuck away, and muster the boat's crews."

STARBUCK   "Let me first help thee towards the bulwarks, sir."

AHAB   "Oh, oh, oh! how this splinter gores me now! Accursed fate! that the unconquerable captain in the soul should have such a craven mate!"

STARBUCK   "Sir?"

AHAB   "My body, man, not thee. Give me something for a cane—there, that shivered lance will do. Muster the men. Surely I have not seen him yet. By heaven it cannot be!—missing?—quick! call them all."

NARRATOR   The old man's hinted thought was true. Upon mustering the company, the Parsee was not there.

STUBB   "The Parsee!" cried Stubb—"he must have been caught in——"

AHAB   "The black vomit wrench thee!—run all of ye above, alow, cabin, fore-castle—find him—not gone—not gone!"

NARRATOR   But quickly they returned to him with the tidings that the Parsee was nowhere to be found.

STUBB   "Aye, sir," said Stubb—"caught among the tangles of your line—I thought I saw him dragging under."

AHAB   "*My* line! *my* line? Gone?—gone? What means that little word?—What death-knell rings in it, that old Ahab shakes as if he were the belfry. The harpoon, too!—toss over the litter there,—d'ye see it?—the forged iron, men, the white whale's—no, no, no,—blistered fool! this hand did dart it!—'tis in the fish! —Aloft there! Keep him nailed—Quick!—all hands to the rigging of the boats —collect the oars—harpooners! the irons, the irons!—hoist the royals higher— a pull on all the sheets!—helm there! steady, steady for your life! I'll ten times girdle the unmeasured globe; yea and dive straight though it, but I'll slay him yet!"

STARBUCK   "Great God! but for one single instant show thyself," cried Starbuck; "never never wilt thou capture him, old man.—In Jesus' name no more of this, that's worse than devil's madness. Two days chased; twice stove to splinters; thy very leg once more snatched from under thee; thy evil shadow gone—all

good angels mobbing thee with warnings:—what more wouldst thou have?—
Shall we keep chasing this murderous fish till he swamps the last man? Shall
we be dragged by him to the bottom of the sea? Shall we be towed by him to
the infernal world? Oh, oh,—Impiety and blasphemy to hunt him more!"

AHAB   "Starbuck, of late I've felt strangely moved to thee; ever since that hour
we both saw—thou know'st what, in one another's eyes. But in this matter of
the whale, be the front of thy face to me as the palm of this hand—a lipless,
unfeatured blank. Ahab is for ever Ahab, man. This whole act's immutably
decreed. 'Twas rehearsed by thee and me a billion years before this ocean rolled.
Fool! I am the Fates' lieutenant; I act under orders. Look thou, underling! that
thou obeyest mine.—Stand round me, men. Ye see an old man cut down to
the stump; leaning on a shivered lance; propped up on a lonely foot. 'Tis Ahab
—his body's part; but Ahab's soul's a centipede, that moves upon a hundred
legs. I feel strained, half stranded, as ropes that tow dismasted frigates in a gale;
and I may look so. But ere I break, ye'll hear me crack; and till ye hear *that,*
know that Ahab's hawser tows his purpose yet. Believe ye, men, in the things
called omens? Then laugh aloud, and cry encore! For ere they drown, drowning
things will twice rise to the surface; then rise again, to sink for evermore. So
with Moby Dick—two days he's floated—tomorrow will be the third. Aye, men,
he'll rise once more,—but only to spout his last! D'ye feel brave men, brave?"

STUBB   "As fearless fire," cried Stubb.

AHAB   "And as mechanical,"

NARRATOR   —muttered Ahab. Then as the men went forward, he muttered on:—

AHAB   "The things called omens! And yesterday I talked the same to Starbuck
there, concerning my broken boat. Oh! how valiantly I seek to drive out of
others' hearts what's clinched so fast in mine!—The Parsee—the Parsee!—gone,
gone? and he was to go before:—but still was to be seen again ere I could perish
—How's that?—There's a riddle now might baffle all the lawyers backed by the
ghosts of the whole line of judges:—like a hawk's beak it pecks my brain. *I'll,
I'll* solve it, though!"

NARRATOR   When dusk descended, the whale was still in sight to leeward.
So once more the sail was shortened, and everything passed nearly as on the
previous night; only, the sound of hammers, and the hum of the grindstone was
heard till nearly daylight, as the men toiled by lanterns in the complete and
careful rigging of the spare boats and sharpening their fresh weapons for the
morrow. Meantime, of the broken keel of Ahab's wrecked craft the carpenter
made him another leg; while still as on the night before, slouched Ahab stood
fixed within his scuttle; his hid heliotrope glance anticipatingly gone backward
on its dial; sat due eastward for the earliest sun.

[CHAPTER CXXXV. THE CHASE—THIRD DAY]

NARRATOR   The morning of the third day dawned fair and fresh, and once more
the solitary night-man at the fore-mast-head was relieved by crowds of the daylight look-outs, who dotted every mast and almost every spar.

AHAB   "D'ye see him?"

NARRATOR   —cried Ahab; but the whale was not yet in sight.

AHAB   "In his infallible wake, though; but follow that wake, that's all. Helm there; steady, as thou goest, and hast been going. What a lovely day again! were it a new-made world, and made for a summer-house to the angels, and this morning the first of its throwing open to them, a fairer day could not dawn upon that world. Here's food for thought, had Ahab time to think; but Ahab never thinks; he only feels, feels, feels, *that's* tingling enough for mortal man! to think's audacity. God only has that right and privilege. Thinking is, or ought to be, a coolness and a calmness; and our poor hearts throb, and our poor brains beat too much for that. And yet, I've sometimes thought my brain was very calm— frozen calm, this old skull cracks so, like a glass in which the contents turn to ice, and shiver it. And still this hair is growing now; this moment growing, and heat must breed it; but no, it's like that sort of common grass that will grow anywhere, between the earthly clefts of Greenland ice or in Vesuvius lava. How the wild winds blow it; they whip it about me as the torn shreds of split sails lash the tossed ship they cling to. A vile wind that has no doubt blown ere this through prison corridors and cells, and wards of hospitals, and ventilated them, and now comes blowing hither as innocent as fleeces. Out upon it!—it's tainted. Were I the wind, I'd blow no more on such a wicked, miserable world. I'd crawl somewhere to a cave, and slink there. And yet, 'tis a noble and heroic thing, the wind! who ever conquered it? In every fight it has the last and bitterest blow. Run tilting at it, and you but run through it. Ha! a coward wind that strikes stark naked men, but will not stand to receive a single blow. Even Ahab is a braver thing—a nobler thing than *that*. Would now the wind but had a body; but all the things that most exasperate and outrage mortal man all these things are bodiless, but only bodiless as objects, not as agents. There's a most special, a most cunning, oh, a most malicious difference! And yet, I say again, and swear it now, that there's something all glorious and gracious in the wind. These warm Trade Winds, at least, that in the clear heavens blow straight on, in strong and steadfast, vigorous mildness; and veer not from their mark, how- ever the baser currents of the sea may turn and tack, and mightiest Mississippi of the land swift and swerve about, uncertain where to go at last. And by the eternal Poles! these same Trades that so directly blow my good ship on; these Trades, or something like them—something so unchangeable, and full as strong, blow my keeled soul along! To it! Aloft there! What d'ye see?"

DAGGOO   "Nothing, sir."

AHAB   "Nothing! and noon at hand! The doubloon goes a begging! See the sun! Aye, aye, it must be so. I've oversailed him. How, got the start? Aye, he's chas- ing *me* now; not I, *him*—that's bad; I might have known it, too. Fool! the lines— the harpoons he's towing. Aye, aye, I have run him by last night. About! about! Come down, all of ye, but the regular look-outs! Man the braces!"

NARRATOR   Steering as she had done, the wind had been somewhat on the Pe- quod's quarter, so that now being pointed in the reverse direction, the braced ship sailed hard upon the breeze as she rechurned the cream in her own white wake.

STARBUCK "Against the wind he now steers for the open jaw,"

NARRATOR —murmured Starbuck to himself, as he coiled the new-hauled main-brace upon the rail.

STARBUCK "God keep us, but already my bones feel damp within me, and from the inside wet my flesh. I misdoubt me that I disobey my God in obeying him!"

AHAB "Stand by to sway me up!"

NARRATOR —cried Ahab, advancing to the hempen basket.

AHAB "We should meet him soon."

STARBUCK "Aye, aye, sir,"

NARRATOR —and straightway Starbuck did Ahab's bidding, and once more Ahab swung on high.

A whole hour now passed; gold-beaten out to ages. Time itself now held long breaths with keen suspense. But at last, some three points off the weather-bow, Ahab descried the spout again, and instantly from the three mast-heads three shrieks went up as if the tongues of fire had voiced it.

AHAB "Forehead to forehead I meet thee, this third time, Moby Dick! On deck there!—brace sharper up; crowd her into the wind's eye. He's too far off to lower yet, Mr. Starbuck. The sails shake! Stand over that helmsman with a top-maul! So, so; he travels fast, and I must down. But let me have one more good round look aloft here at the sea; there's time for that. An old, old sight, and yet somehow so young; aye, and not changed a wink since I first saw it, a boy, from the sand-hills of Nantucket! The same!—the same!—the same to Noah as to me. There's a soft shower to leeward. Such lovely leewardings! They must lead somewhere—to something else than common land, more palmy than the palms. Leeward! the white whale goes that way; look to windward, then; the better if the bitterer quarter. But good-bye, good-bye, old mast-head! What's this?—green? aye, tiny mosses in these warped cracks. No such green weather stains on Ahab's head! There's the difference now between man's old age and matter's. But aye, old mast, we both grow old together; sound in our hulls, though, are we not, my ship? Aye, minus a leg, that's all. By heaven this dead wood has the better of my live flesh every way. I can't compare with it; and I've known some ships made of dead trees outlast the lives of men made of the most vital stuff of vital fathers. What's that he said? he should still go before me, my pilot; and yet to be seen again? But where? Will I have eyes at the bottom of the sea, supposing I descend those endless stairs? and all night I've been sailing from him, wherever he did sink to. Aye, aye, like many more thou told'st direful truth as touching thyself, O Parsee; but, Ahab, there thy shot fell short. Good-bye, mast-head—keep a good eye upon the whale, the while I'm gone. We'll talk to-morrow, nay, to-night, when the white whale lies down there, tied by head and tail."

NARRATOR He gave the word; and still gazing round him, was steadily lowered through the cloven blue air to the deck.

In due time the boats were lowered; but as standing in his shallop's stern, Ahab just hovered upon the point of the descent, he waved to the mate,—who held one of the tackle-ropes on deck—and bade him pause.

AHAB "Starbuck!"

STARBUCK "Sir?"

AHAB "For the third time my soul's ship starts upon this voyage, Starbuck."

STARBUCK "Aye, sir, thou wilt have it so."

AHAB "Some ships sail from their ports, and ever afterwards are missing, Starbuck!"

STARBUCK "Truth, sir: saddest truth."

AHAB "Some men die at ebb tide; some at low water; some at the full of the flood;—and I feel now like a billow that's all one crested comb, Starbuck. I am old;—shake hands with me, man."

NARRATOR Their hands met; their eyes fastened; Starbuck's tears the glue.

STARBUCK "Oh, my captain, my captain!—noble heart—go not—go not!—see, it's a brave man that weeps; how great the agony of the persuasion then!"

AHAB "Lower away!"

NARRATOR —cried Ahab, tossing the mate's arm from him.

AHAB "Stand by the crew!"

NARRATOR In an instant the boat was pulling round close under the stern.

"The sharks! the sharks!" cried a voice from the low cabin-window there; "O master, my master, come back!"

But Ahab heard nothing; for his own voice was high-lifted then; and the boat leaped on.

Yet the voice spake true; for scarce had he pushed from the ship, when numbers of sharks, seemingly rising from out the dark waters beneath the hull, maliciously snapped at the blades of the oars, every time they dipped in the water; and in this way accompanied the boat with their bites. It is a thing not uncommonly happening to the whale-boats in those swarming seas; the sharks at times apparently following them in the same prescient way that vultures hover over the banners of marching regiments in the east. But these were the first sharks that had been observed by the Pequod since the White Whale had been first descried; and whether it was that Ahab's crew were all such tiger-yellow barbarians, and therefore their flesh more musky to the senses of the sharks—a matter sometimes well known to affect them,—however it was, they seemed to follow that one boat without molesting the others.

STARBUCK "Heart of wrought steel!"

NARRATOR —murmured Starbuck gazing over the side, and following with his eyes the receding boat

STARBUCK   —"canst thou yet ring boldly to that sight?—lowering thy keel among ravening sharks, and followed by them, open-mouthed to the chase; and this the critical third day?—For when three days flow together in one continuous intense pursuit; be sure the first is the morning, the second the noon, and the third the evening and the end of that thing—be that end what it may. Oh! my God! what is this that shoots through me, and leaves me so deadly calm, yet expectant,—fixed at the top of a shudder! Future things swim before me, as in empty outlines and skeletons; all the past is somehow grown dim. Mary, girl! thou fadest in pale glories behind me; boy! I seem to see but thy eyes grown wondrous blue. Strangest problems of life seem clearing; but clouds sweep between—Is my journey's end coming? My legs feel faint; like his who has footed it all day. Feel thy heart,—beats it yet?—Stir thyself, Starbuck!—stave it off—move, move! speak aloud!—Mast-head there! See ye my boy's hand on the hill?—Crazed;—aloft there!—keep thy keenest eye upon the boats:—mark well the whale!—Ho! again!—drive off that hawk! see! he pecks—he tears the vane"

NARRATOR   —pointing to the red flag flying at the main-truck—

STARBUCK   "Ha! he soars away with it!—Where's the old man now? sees't thou that sight, oh Ahab!—shudder, shudder!"

NARRATOR   The boats had not gone very far, when by a signal from the mast-heads—a downward pointed arm, Ahab knew that the whale had sounded; but intending to be near him at the next rising, he held on his way a little sideways from the vessel; the becharmed crew maintaining the profoundest silence, as the head-beat waves hammered and hammered against the opposing bow.

AHAB   "Drive, drive in your nails, oh ye waves! to their utter-most heads drive them in! ye but strike a thing without a lid; and no coffin and no hearse can be mine:—and hemp only can kill me! Ha! ha!"

NARRATOR   Suddenly the waters around them slowly swelled in broad circles; then quickly upheaved, as if sideways sliding from a submerged berg of ice, swiftly rising to the surface. A low rumbling sound was heard; a subterraneous hum; and then all held their breaths; as bedraggled with trailing ropes, and harpoons, and lances, a vast form shot lengthwise, but obliquely from the sea. Shrouded in a thin drooping veil of mist, it hovered for a moment in the rain-bowed air; and then fell swamping back into the deep. Crushed thirty feet upwards, the waters flashed for an instant like heaps of fountains, then brokenly sank in a shower of flakes, leaving the circling surface creamed like new milk round the marble trunk of the whale.

AHAB   "Give way!"

NARRATOR   —cried Ahab to the oarsmen, and the boats darted forward to the attack; but maddened by yesterday's fresh irons that corroded in him, Moby Dick seemed combinedly possessed by all the angels that fell from heaven. The wide tears of welded tendons overspreading his broad white forehead, beneath the transparent skin, looked knitted together; as head on, he came churning his tail among the boats; and once more flailed them apart; spilling

NARRATOR   (*continuing*)

out the irons and lances from the two mates' boats, and dashing in one side of the upper part of their bows, but leaving Ahab's almost without a scar.

While Daggoo and Queequeg were stopping the strained planks; and as the whale swimming out from them, turned, and showed one entire flank as he shot by them again; at that moment a quick cry went up. Lashed round and round to the fish's back; pinioned in the turns upon turns in which, during the past night, the whale had reeled the involutions of the lines around him, the half torn body of the Parsee was seen; his sable raiment frayed to shreds; his distended eyes turned full upon old Ahab.

The harpoon dropped from his hand.

AHAB   "Befooled, befooled!"

NARRATOR   —drawing in a long lean breath—

AHAB   "Aye, Parsee! I see thee again.—Aye, and thou goest before; and this, *this* then is the hearse that thou didst promise. But I hold thee to the last letter of thy word. Where is the second hearse? Away, mates, to the ship! those boats are useless now; repair them if ye can in time, and return to me; if not, Ahab is enough to die—Down, men! the first thing that but offers to jump from this boat I stand in, that thing I harpoon. Ye are not other men, but my arms and my legs; and so obey me.—Where's the whale? gone down again?"

NARRATOR   But he looked too nigh the boat; for as if bent upon escaping with the corpse he bore, and as if the particular place of the last encounter had been but a stage in his leeward voyage, Moby Dick was now again steadily swimming forward; and had almost passed the ship,—which thus far had been sailing in the contrary direction to him, though for the present her headway had been stopped. He seemed swimming with his utmost velocity, and now only intent upon pursuing his own straight path in the sea.

STARBUCK   "Oh! Ahab," cried Starbuck, "not too late is it, even now, the third day, to desist. See! Moby Dick seeks thee not. It is thou, thou, that madly seekest him!"

NARRATOR   Setting sail to the rising wind, the lonely boat was swiftly impelled to leeward, by both oars and canvas. And at last when Ahab was sliding by the vessel, so near as plainly to distinguish Starbuck's face as he leaned over the rail, he hailed him to turn the vessel about, and follow him, not too swiftly, at a judicious interval. Glancing upwards, he saw Tashtego, Queequeg, and Daggoo, eagerly mounting to the three mast-heads; while the oarsmen were rocking in the two staved boats which had but just been hoisted to the side, and were busily at work in repairing them. One after the other, through the port-holes, as he sped, he also caught flying glimpses of Stubb and Flask, busying themselves on deck among bundles of new irons and lances. As he saw all this; as he heard the hammers in the broken boats; far other hammers seemed driving a nail into his heart. But he rallied. And now marking that the vane or flag was gone from the main-mast-head, he shouted to Tashtego, who had just gained

NARRATOR *(continuing)*

that perch, to descend again for another flag, and a hammer and nails, and so nail it to the mast.

Whether fagged by the three days' running chase, and the resistance to his swimming in the knotted hamper he bore; or whether it was some latent deceitfulness and malice in him: whichever was true, the White Whale's way now began to abate, as it seemed, from the boat so rapidly nearing him once more; though indeed the whale's last start had not been so long a one as before. And still as Ahab glided over the waves the unpitying sharks accompanied him; and so pertinaciously stuck to the boat; and so continually bit at the plying oars, that the blades became jagged and crunched, and left small splinters in the sea, at almost every dip.

AHAB   "Heed them not! those teeth but give new rowlocks to your oars. Pull on! 'tis the better rest, the shark's jaw than the yielding water."

OARSMAN   "But at every bite, sir, the thin blades grow smaller and smaller!"

AHAB   "They will last long enough! pull on!—But who can tell"—he muttered —"whether these sharks swim to feast on the whale or on Ahab?—But pull on! Aye, all alive, now—we near him. The helm! take the helm; let me pass,"—

NARRATOR   —and so saying, two of the oarsmen helped him forward to the bows of the still flying boat.

At length as the craft was cast to one side, and ran ranging along with the White Whale's flank, he seemed strangely oblivious of its advance—as the whale sometimes will—and Ahab was fairly within the smoky mountain mist, which, thrown off from the whale's spout, curled round his great, Monadnock hump; he was even thus close to him; when, with body arched back, and both arms lengthwise high-lifted to the poise, he darted his fierce iron, and his far fiercer curse into the hated whale. As both steel and curse sank to the socket, as if sucked into a morass, Moby Dick sideways writhed; spasmodically rolled his nigh flank against the bow, and, without staving a hole in it, so suddenly canted the boat over, that had it not been for the elevated part of the gunwale to which he then clung, Ahab would once more have been tossed into the sea. As it was, three of the oarsmen—who foreknew not the precise instant of the dart, and were therefore unprepared for its effects—these were flung out; but so fell, that, in an instant two of them clutched the gunwale again, and rising to its level on a combing wave, hurled themselves bodily inboard again; the third man helplessly dropping astern, but still afloat and swimming.

Almost simultaneously, with a mighty volition of ungraduated, instantaneous swiftness, the White Whale darted through the weltering sea. But when Ahab cried out to the steersman to take new turns with the line, and hold it so; and commanded the crew to turn round on their seats, and tow the boat up to the mark; the moment the treacherous line felt that double strain and tug, it snapped in the empty air!

AHAB   "What breaks in me? Some sinew cracks!—'tis whole again; oars! oars! Burst in upon him!"

NARRATOR Hearing the tremendous rush of the sea-crashing boat, the whale wheeled round to present his blank forehead at bay; but in that evolution, catching sight of the nearing black hull of the ship; seemingly seeing in it the source of all his persecutions; bethinking it—it may be—a larger and nobler foe; of a sudden, he bore down upon its advancing prow, smiting his jaws amid fiery showers of foam.

Ahab staggered; his hand smote his forehead.

AHAB "I grow blind; hands! stretch out before me that I may yet grope my way. Is't night?"

OARSMEN "The whale! The ship!" cried the cringing oarsmen.

AHAB "Oars! oars! Slope downwards to thy depths, O sea, that ere it be for ever too late, Ahab may slide this last, last time upon his mark! I see: the ship! the ship! Dash on, my men! Will ye not save my ship?"

NARRATOR But as the oarsmen violently forced their boat through the sledge-hammering seas, the before whale-smitten bow-ends of two planks burst through, and in an instant almost, the temporarily disabled boat lay nearly level with the waves; its half-wading, splashing crew, trying hard to stop the gap and bale out the pouring water.

Meantime, for that one beholding instant, Tashtego's mast-head hammer remained suspended in his hand; and the red flag, half-wrapping him as with a plaid, then streamed itself straight out from him, as his own forward-flowing heart; while Starbuck and Stubb, standing upon the bowsprit beneath, caught sight of the down-coming monster just as soon as he.

STARBUCK "The whale, the whale! Up helm, up helm! Oh, all ye sweet powers of air, now hug me close! Let not Starbuck die, if die he must, in a woman's fainting fit. Up helm, I say—ye fools, the jaw! the jaw! Is this the end of all my bursting prayers? all my life-long fidelities? Oh, Ahab, Ahab, lo, thy work. Steady! helmsman, steady. Nay, nay! Up helm again! He turns to meet us! Oh, his unappeasable brow drives on towards one, whose duty tells him he cannot depart. My God, stand by me now!"

STUBB "Stand not by me, but stand under me, whoever you are that will now help Stubb; for Stubb, too, sticks here. I grin at thee, thou grinning whale! Who ever helped Stubb, or kept Stubb awake, but Stubb's own unwinking eye? And now poor Stubb goes to bed upon a mattress that is all too soft; would it were stuffed with brushwood! I grin at thee, thou grinning whale! Look ye, sun, moon and stars! I call ye assassins of as good a fellow as ever spouted up his ghost. For all that, I would yet ring glasses with ye, would ye but hand the cup! Oh, oh, oh, oh! thou grinning whale, but there'll be plenty of gulping soon! Why fly ye not, O Ahab? For me, off shoes and jacket to it; let Stubb die in his drawers! A most mouldy and over salted death, though;—cherries! cherries! cherries! Oh, Flask, for one red cherry ere we die!"

STARBUCK "Cherries? I only wish that we were where they grow. Oh, Stubb, I hope my poor mother's drawn my part-pay ere this; if not, few coppers will now come to her, for the voyage is up."

NARRATOR From the ship's bows, nearly all the seamen now hung inactive; hammers, bits of plank, lances, and harpoons, mechanically retained in their hands, just as they had darted from their various employments; all their enchanted eyes intent upon the whale, which from side to side strangely vibrating his predestinating head, sent a broad band of overspreading semicircular foam before him as he rushed. Retribution, swift vengeance, eternal malice were in his whole aspect, and spite of all that mortal man could do, the solid white buttress of his forehead smote the ship's starboard bow, till men and timbers reeled. Some fell flat upon their faces. Like dislodged trucks, the heads of the harpooners aloft shook on their bull-like necks. Through the breach, they heard the waters pour, as mountain torrents down a flume.

AHAB "The ship! The hearse!—the second hearse!" cried Ahab from the boat; "its wood could only be American!"

NARRATOR Diving beneath the settling ship, the whale ran quivering along its keel; but turning under water, swiftly shot to the surface again, far off the other bow, but within a few yards of Ahab's boat, where, for a time, he lay quiescent.

AHAB "I turn my body from the sun. What ho, Tashtego! let me hear thy hammer. Oh! ye three unsurrendered spires of mine; thou uncracked keel; and only god-bullied hull; thou firm deck, and haughty helm, and Pole-pointed prow, —death-glorious ship! must ye then perish, and without me? Am I cut off from the last fond pride of meanest shipwrecked captains? Oh, lonely death on lonely life! Oh, now I feel my topmost greatness lies in my topmost grief. Ho, ho! from all your furthest bounds, pour ye now in, ye bold billows of my whole foregone life, and top this one piled comber of my death! Towards thee I roll, thou all-destroying but unconquering whale; to the last I grapple with thee; from hell's heart I stab at thee; for hate's sake I spit my last breath at thee. Sink all coffins and all hearses to one common pool! and since neither can be mine let me then tow to pieces, while still chasing thee, though tied to thee, thou damned whale! *Thus,* I give up the spear!"

NARRATOR The harpoon was darted; the stricken whale flew forward; with igniting velocity the line ran through the groove;—ran foul. Ahab stooped to clear it; he did clear it; but the flying turn caught him round the neck, and voicelessly as Turkish mutes bowstring their victim, he was shot out of the boat, ere the crew knew he was gone. Next instant, the heavy eyesplice in the rope's final end flew out of the stark-empty tub, knocked down an oarsman, and smiting the sea, disappeared in its depths.

For an instant, the tranced boat's crew stood still; then turned.

CREW "The ship? Great God, where is the ship?"

NARRATOR Soon they through dim, bewildering mediums saw her side-long fading phantom, as in the gaseous Fata Morgana; only the uppermost masts out of water; while fixed by infatuation, or fidelity, or fate, to their once lofty perches, the pagan harpooners still maintained their sinking lookouts on the sea. And now, concentric circles seized the lone boat itself, and all its crew, and each floating oar, and every lance-pole, and spinning, animate and inanimate,

NARRATOR   (*concluding*)

all round and round in one vortex, carried the smallest chip of the Pequod out of sight.

But as the last whelmings intermixingly poured themselves over the sunken head of the Indian at the mainmast, leaving a few inches of the erect spar yet visible, together with long streaming yards of the flag, which calmly undulated, with ironical coincidings, over the destroying billows they almost touched;— at that instant, a red arm and a hammer hovered backwardly uplifted in the open air, in the act of nailing the flag faster and yet faster to the subsiding spar. A sky-hawk that tauntingly had followed the main-truck downwards from its natural home among the stars, pecking at the flag, and incommoding Tashtego there; this bird now chanced to intercept its broad fluttering wing between the hammer and the wood; and simultaneously feeling that etherial thrill, the sub-merged savage beneath, in his death-gasp, kept his hammer frozen there; and so the bird of heaven, with archangelic shrieks, and his imperial beak thrust upwards, and his whole captive form folded in the flag of Ahab, went down with his ship, which, like Satan, would not sink to hell till she had dragged a living part of heaven along with her, and helmeted herself with it.

Now small fowls flew screaming over the yet yawning gulf; a sullen white surf beat against its steep sides; then all collapsed, and the great shroud of the sea rolled on as it rolled five thousand years ago.

16. A Long Poem

———◆•◆———

Students of the humanities may take special interest in this program, which calls for nine readers and needs about fifty minutes. The readers can be held to six, with Ariel doubling as the Gnome Umbriel and as Thalestris and the Second Narrator doubling as Sir Plume. Anyone who does more than one voice must take care to distinguish each from the others.

The poem is intact; only the names of speakers are added. The speakers are, in order of first speaking:

First Narrator	Baron	Sir Plume
Ariel	Gnome	Belinda
Second Narrator	Thalestris	Clarissa

THE RAPE OF THE LOCK / Alexander Pope

[CANTO I]

First Narrator   What dire offence from am'rous causes springs,
  What mighty contests rise from trivial things,
  I sing—This verse to Caryll, Muse! is due:
  This, even Belinda, may vouchsafe to view:
  Slight is the subject, but not so the praise,   5
  If she inspire, and he approve my lays.
    Say what strange motive, goddess! could compel
  A well-bred lord t' assault a gentle belle?
  O say what stranger cause, yet unexplored,
  Could make a gentle belle reject a lord?   10
  In tasks so bold, can little men engage,
  And in soft bosoms dwells such mighty rage?
    Sol through white curtains shot a tim'rous ray,
  And oped those eyes that must eclipse the day:
  Now lap-dogs give themselves the rousing shake,   15
  And sleepless lovers, just at twelve, awake:
  Thrice rung the bell, the slipper knocked the ground,

250

FIRST NARRATOR   (*continuing*)
 And the pressed watch returned a silver sound.
 Belinda still her downy pillow prest,
 Her guardian sylph prolonged the balmy rest: 20
 'Twas he had summoned to her silent bed
 The morning-dream that hovered o'er her head;
 A youth more glitt'ring than a birth-night beau;
 (That even in slumber caused her cheek to glow)
 Seemed to her ear his winning lips to lay, 25
 And thus in whispers said, or seemed to say:—

ARIEL   "Fairest of mortals, thou distinguished care
 Of thousand bright inhabitants of air!
 If e'er one vision touched thy infant thought,
 Of all the nurse and all the priest have taught: 30
 Of airy elves by moonlight shadows seen,
 The silver token, and the circled green
 Or virgins visited by angel-pow'rs,
 With golden crowns and wreaths of heav'nly flow'rs;
 Hear and believe! thy own importance know, 35
 Nor bound thy narrow views to things below.
 Some secret truths, from learned pride concealed,
 To maids alone and children are revealed:
 What though no credit doubting wits may give?
 The fair and innocent shall still believe. 40
 Know then, unnumbered spirits round thee fly,
 The light militia of the lower sky:
 These, though unseen, are ever on the wing,
 Hang o'er the box, and hover round the Ring.
 Think what an equipage thou hast in air, 45
 And view with scorn two pages and a chair.
 As now your own, our beings were of old,
 And once enclosed in woman's beauteous mould;
 Thence, by a soft transition, we repair
 From earthly vehicles to these of air. 50
 Think not, when woman's transient breath is fled,
 That all her vanities at once are dead;
 Succeeding vanities she still regards,
 And though she plays no more, o'erlooks the cards.
 Her joy in gilded chariots, when alive, 55
 And love of ombre, after death survive.
 For when the fair in all their pride expire,
 To their first elements their souls retire:
 The sprites of fiery termagants in flame
 Mount up, and take a salamander's name. 60
 Soft yielding minds to water glide away,
 And sip, with nymphs, their elemental tea.

Ariel   (*continuing*)
The graver prude sinks downward to a gnome,
In search of mischief still on earth to roam.
The light coquettes in sylphs aloft repair,   65
And sport and flutter in the fields of air.
    "Know further yet; whoever fair and chaste
Rejects mankind, is by some sylph embraced:
For spirits, freed from mortal laws, with ease
Assume what sexes and what shapes they please.   70
What guards the purity of melting maids,
In courtly balls, and midnight masquerades,
Safe from the treach'rous friend, the daring spark,
The glance by day, the whisper in the dark,
When kind occasion prompts their warm desires,   75
When music softens, and when dancing fires?
'Tis but their sylph, the wise celestials know,
Though honour is the word with men below.
    "Some nymphs there are, too conscious of their face,
For life predestined to the gnomes' embrace.   80
These swell their prospects and exalt their pride,
When offers are disdained, and love denied:
Then gay ideas crowd the vacant brain,
While peers, and dukes, and all their sweeping train,
And garters, stars, and coronets appear,   85
And in soft sounds, 'Your Grace' salutes their ear.
'Tis these that early taint the female soul,
Instruct the eyes of young coquettes to roll,
Teach infant-cheeks a bidden blush to know,
And little hearts to flutter at a beau.   90
    "Oft, when the world imagine women stray,
The sylphs through mystic mazes guide their way,
Through all the giddy circle they pursue,
And old impertinence expel by new.
What tender maid but must a victim fall   95
To one man's treat, but for another's ball?
When Florio speaks what virgin could withstand,
If gentle Damon did not squeeze her hand?
With varying vanities, from ev'ry part,
They shift the moving toyshop of their heart;   100
Where wigs with wigs, with sword-knots sword-knots strive,
Beaux banish beaux, and coaches coaches drive.
This erring mortals levity may call;
Oh blind to truth! the sylphs contrive it all.
    "Of these am I, who thy protection claim,   105
A watchful sprite, and Ariel is my name.
Late, as I ranged the crystal wilds of air,

In the clear mirror of thy ruling star
I saw, alas! some dread event impend,
Ere to the main this morning sun descend. 110
But heaven reveals not what, or how, or where:
Warned by the sylph, O pious maid, beware!
This to disclose is all thy guardian can:
Beware of all, but most beware of man!"

FIRST NARRATOR   He said; when Shock, who thought she slept too long, 115
Leaped up, and waked his mistress with his tongue.
'Twas then, Belinda, if report say true,
Thy eyes first opened on a billet-doux;
Wounds, charms, and ardours were no sooner read,
But all the vision vanished from thy head. 120

SECOND NARRATOR   And now, unveiled, the toilet stands displayed,
Each silver vase in mystic order laid.
First, robed in white, the nymph intent adores,
With head uncovered, the cosmetic pow'rs.
A heav'nly image in the glass appears, 125
To that she bends, to that her eyes she rears;
Th' inferior priestess, at her altar's side,
Trembling begins the sacred rites of pride.
Unnumbered treasures ope at once, and here

The various off'rings of the world appear; 130
From each she nicely culls with curious toil,
And decks the goddess with the glitt'ring spoil.
This casket India's glowing gems unlocks,
And all Arabia breathes from yonder box.
The tortoise here and elephant unite, 135
Transformed to combs, the speckled, and the white.
Here files of pins extend their shining rows,
Puffs, powders, patches, Bibles, billet-doux.
Now awful beauty puts on all its arms;
The fair each moment rises in her charms, 140
Repairs her smiles, awakens every grace,
And calls forth all the wonders of her face;
Sees by degrees a purer blush arise,
And keener lightnings quicken in her eyes.
The busy sylphs surround their darling care, 145
These set the head, and those divide the hair,
Some fold the sleeve, whilst others plait the gown;
And Betty's praised for labours not her own.

[CANTO II]

FIRST NARRATOR   Not with more glories, in th' ethereal plain,

FIRST NARRATOR   (*continuing*)
   The sun first rises o'er the purpled main,
   Than, issuing forth, the rival of his beams
   Launched on the bosom of the silver Thames.
   Fair nymphs, and well-dressed youths around her shone,   5
   But ev'ry eye was fixed on her alone.
   On her white breast a sparkling cross she wore,
   Which Jews might kiss, and infidels adore.
   Her lively looks a sprightly mind disclose,
   Quick as her eyes, and as unfixed as those: 10
   Favours to none, to all she smiles extends;
   Oft she rejects, but never once offends.
   Bright as the sun, her eyes the gazers strike,
   And, like the sun, they shine on all alike.
   Yet graceful ease, and sweetness void of pride,   15
   Might hide her faults, if belles had faults to hide:
   If to her share some female errors fall,
   Look on her face, and you'll forget 'em all.

SECOND NARRATOR   This nymph to the destruction of mankind,
   Nourished two locks, which graceful hung behind,   20
   In equal curls, and well conspired to deck
   With shining ringlets the smooth iv'ry neck.
   Love in these labyrinths his slaves detains,
   And mighty hearts are held in slender chains.
   With hairy springes we the birds betray,   25
   Slight lines of hair surprise the finny prey,
   Fair tresses man's imperial race ensnare,
   And beauty draws us with a single hair.

FIRST NARRATOR   Th' advent'rous baron the bright locks admired;
   He saw, he wished, and to the prize aspired.   30
   Resolved to win, he meditates the way,
   By force to ravish, or by fraud betray;
   For when success a lover's toil attends,
   Few ask, if fraud or force attained his ends.

   For this, ere Phœbus rose, he had implored   35
   Propitious Heav'n, and ev'ry pow'er adored,
   But chiefly Love—to Love an altar built,
   Of twelve vast French romances, neatly gilt.
   There lay three garters, half a pair of gloves;
   And all the trophies of his former loves;   40
   With tender billet-doux he lights the pyre,
   And breathes three am'rous sighs to raise the fire.
   Then prostrate falls, and begs with ardent eyes
   Soon to obtain, and long possess the prize:
   The pow'rs gave ear, and granted half his pray'r,   45
   The rest, the winds dispersed in empty air.

SECOND NARRATOR   But now secure the painted vessel glides,
   The sunbeams trembling on the floating tides:
   While melting music steals upon the sky,
   And softened sounds along the waters die;   50
   Smooth flow the waves, the zephyrs gently play,
   Belinda smiled, and all the world was gay
   All but the sylph—with careful thoughts opprest,
   Th' impending woe sat heavy on his breast.
   He summons strait his denizens of air;   55
   The lucid squadrons round the sails repair:
   Soft o'er the shrouds aërial whispers breathe,
   That seemed but zephyrs to the train beneath.
   Some to the sun their insect wings unfold,
   Waft on the breeze, or sink in clouds of gold;   60
   Transparent forms, too fine for mortal sight,
   Their fluid bodies half dissolved in light.
   Loose to the wind their airy garments flew,
   Thin glitt'ring textures of the filmy dew,
   Dipped in the richest tincture of the skies,   65
   Where light disports in ever-mingled dyes,
   While ev'ry beam new transient colours flings,
   Colours that change whene'er they wave their wings.
   Amid the circle, on the gilded mast,
   Superior by the head, was Ariel placed;   70
   His purple pinions opening to the sun,
   He raised his azure wand, and thus begun:

ARIEL   "Ye sylphs and sylphids, to your chief give ear!
   Fays, fairies, genii, elves, and demons, hear!
   Ye know the spheres and various tasks assigned   75
   By laws eternal to th' aërial kind.
   Some in the fields of purest ether play,
   And bask and whiten in the blaze of day.
   Some guide the course of wand'ring orbs on high,
   Or roll the planets through the boundless sky.   80
   Some less refined, beneath the moon's pale light
   Pursue the stars that shoot athwart the night,
   Or suck the mists in grosser air below,
   Or dip their pinions in the painted bow,
   Or brew fierce tempests on the wintry main,   85
   Or o'er the glebe distil the kindly rain.
   Others on earth o'er human race preside,
   Watch all their ways, and all their actions guide:
   Of these the chief the care of nations own,
   And guard with arms divine the British throne.   90
     "Our humbler province is to tend the fair,
   Not a less pleasing, though less glorious care;

ARIEL   *(continuing)*
To save the powder from too rude a gale,
Nor let th' imprisoned essences exhale;
To draw fresh colours from the vernal flow'rs;   95
To steal from rainbows ere they drop in show'rs
A brighter wash; to curl their waving hairs,
Assist their blushes, and inspire their airs;
Nay oft, in dreams, invention we bestow,
To change a flounce, or add a furbelow.   100
   "This day, black omens threat the brightest fair
That e'er deserved a watchful spirit's care;
Some dire disaster, or by force, or slight;
But what, or where, the fates have wrapt in night.
Whether the nymph shall break Diana's law,   105
Or some frail china jar receive a flaw;
Or stain her honour or her new brocade;
Forget her pray'rs, or miss a masquerade;
Or lose her heart, or necklace, at a ball;
Or whether Heav'n has doomed that Shock must fall.   110
Haste, then, ye spirits! to your charge repair:
The flutt'ring fan be Zephyretta's care:
The drops to thee, Brillante, we consign;
And, Momentilla, let the watch be thine;
Do thou, Crispissa, tend her fav'rite lock;   115
Ariel himself shall be the guard of Shock.
   "To fifty chosen sylphs, of special note,
We trust th' important charge, the petticoat:
Oft have we known that seven-fold fence to fail,
Though stiff with hoops, and armed with ribs of whale;   120
Form a strong line about the silver bound,
And guard the wide circumference around.
   "Whatever spirit, careless of his charge,
His post neglects, or leaves the fair at large,
Shall feel sharp vengeance soon o'ertake his sins,   125
Be stopped in vials, or transfixed with pins;
Or plunged in lakes of bitter washes lie,
Or wedged, whole ages, in a bodkin's eye:
Gums and pomatums shall his flight restrain,
While clogged he beats his silken wings in vain;   130
Or alum styptics with contracting pow'r
Shrink his thin essence like a riveled flow'r:
Or, as Ixion fixed, the wretch shall feel
The giddy motion of the whirling mill,
In fumes of burning chocolate shall glow,   135
And tremble at the sea that froths below!"

SECOND NARRATOR   He spoke; the spirits from the sails descend;

Some, orb in orb, around the nymph extend;
Some thrid the mazy ringlets of her hair;
Some hang upon the pendants of her ear: 140
With beating hearts the dire event they wait,
Anxious, and trembling for the birth of fate.

[CANTO III]

FIRST NARRATOR   Close by those meads, for ever crowned with flowers,
  Where Thames with pride surveys his rising towers,
  There stands a structure of majestic frame,
  Which from the neighbouring Hampton takes its name.
  Here Britain's statesmen oft the fall foredoom   5
  Of foreign tyrants and of nymphs at home;
  Here thou, great Anna! whom three realms obey,
  Dost sometimes counsel take—and sometimes tea.
    Hither the heroes and the nymphs resort,
  To taste awhile the pleasures of a court;   10
  In various talk th' instructive hours they past,
  Who gave the ball, or paid the visit last:
  One speaks the glory of the British queen,
  And one describes a charming Indian screen,
  A third interprets motions, looks, and eyes;   15
  At ev'ry word a reputation dies.
  Snuff, or the fan, supply each pause of chat,
  With singing, laughing, ogling, and all that.

SECOND NARRATOR   Meanwhile, declining from the noon of day,
  The sun obliquely shoots his burning ray;   20
  The hungry judges soon the sentence sign,
  And wretches hang that jury-men may dine;
  The merchant from th' Exchange returns in peace,
  And the long labors of the toilet cease.
  Belinda now, whom thirst of fame invites,   25
  Burns to encounter two advent'rous knights,
  At Ombre singly to decide their doom;
  And swells her breast with conquests yet to come.
  Straight the three bands prepare in arms to join,
  Each band the number of the sacred nine.   30
  Soon as she spreads her hand, the aërial guard
  Descend, and sit on each important card:
  First Ariel perched upon a matadore,
  Then each, according to the rank they bore;
  For sylphs, yet mindful of their ancient race,   35
  Are, as when women, wondrous fond of place.

FIRST NARRATOR   Behold, four kings in majesty revered,
  With hoary whiskers and a forky beard;
  And four fair queens whose hands sustain a flow'r,

The expressive emblem of their softer pow'r;   40
Four knaves in garb succinct, a trusty band,
Caps on their heads and halberts in their hand;
And parti-colored troops, a shining train,
Draw forth to combat on the velvet plain.

SECOND NARRATOR   The skillful nymph reviews her troops with care   45

BELINDA   "Let spades be trumps!"

SECOND NARRATOR   she said, and trumps they were.

FIRST NARRATOR   Now move to war her sable matadores,
In show like leaders of the swarthy Moors.
Spadillio first, unconquerable lord!
Led off two captive trumps, and swept the board.   50
As many more Manillio forced to yield,
And marched a victor from the verdant field.
Him Basto followed, but his fate more hard
Gained but one trump and one plebeian card.
With his broad sabre next, a chief in years,   55
The hoary majesty of spades appears,
Puts forth one manly leg, to sight revealed,
The rest his many-colored robe concealed.
The rebel knave, who dares his prince engage,
Proves the just victim of his royal rage.   60
Even mighty Pam, that kings and queens o'erthrew,
And mowed down armies in the fights of Lu,
Sad chance of war! now destitute of aid,
Falls undistinguished by the victor spade!

SECOND NARRATOR   Thus far both armies to Belinda yield;   65
Now to the baron fate inclines the field.
His warlike amazon her host invades,
Th' imperial consort of the crown of spades.
The club's black tyrant first her victim died,
Spite of his haughty mien, and barb'rous pride: 70
What boots the regal circle on his head,
His giant limbs, in state unwieldly spread;
That long behind he trails his pompous robe,
And, of all monarchs, only grasps the globe?
    The baron now his diamonds pours apace;   75
The embroidered king who shows but half his face,
And his refulgent queen, with pow'rs combined
Of broken troops an easy conquest find.
Clubs, diamonds, hearts, in wild disorder seen,
With throngs promiscuous strew the level green.   80
Thus when dispersed a routed army runs,
Of Asia's troops, and Afric's sable sons,

With like confusion different nations fly,
Of various habit, and of various dye,
The pierced battalions disunited fall,   85
In heaps on heaps; one fate o'erwhelms them all.

FIRST NARRATOR   The knave of diamonds tries his wily arts,
And wins (O shameful chance!) the queen of hearts.
At this, the blood the virgin's cheek forsook,
A livid paleness spreads o'er all her look;   90
She sees, and trembles at th' approaching ill.
Just in the jaws of ruin, and codille.
And now (as oft in some distempered state)
On one nice trick depends the gen'ral fate.
An ace of hearts steps forth: the king unseen   95
Lurked in her hand, and mourned his captive queen:
He springs to vengeance with an eager pace,
And falls like thunder on the prostrate ace.
The nymph exulting fills with shouts the sky;
The walls, the woods, and long canals reply.   100

SECOND NARRATOR   O thoughtless mortals! ever blind to fate,
Too soon dejected, and too soon elate.
Sudden, these honours shall be snatched away,
And cursed for ever this victorious day.
    For lo! the board with cups and spoons is crowned, 105
The berries crackle, and the mill turns round;
On shining altars of Japan they raise
The silver lamp; the fiery spirits blaze:
From silver spouts the grateful liquors glide,
While China's earth receives the smoking tide: 110
At once they gratify their scent and taste,
And frequent cups prolong the rich repast.
Straight hover round the fair her airy band;
Some, as she sipped, the fuming liquor fanned,
Some o'er her lap their careful plumes displayed,   115
Trembling, and conscious of the rich brocade.

FIRST NARRATOR   Coffee (which makes the politician wise,
And see through all things with his half-shut eyes)
Sent up in vapours to the baron's brain
New stratagems, the radiant lock to gain.   120
Ah cease, rash youth! desist ere 'tis too late,
Fear the just Gods, and think of Scylla's fate!
Changed to a bird, and sent to flit in air,
She dearly pays for Nisus' injured hair!

SECOND NARRATOR   But when to mischief mortals bend their will 125
How soon they find fit instruments of ill!
Just then, Clarissa drew with tempting grace

SECOND NARRATOR *(continuing)*
> A two-edged weapon from her shining case:
> So ladies in romance assist their knight,
> Present the spear, and arm him for the fight.   130
> He takes the gift with rev'rence, and extends
> The little engine on his fingers' ends;
> This just behind Belinda's neck he spread,
> As o'er the fragrant steams she bends her head.
> Swift to the lock a thousand sprites repair,   135
> A thousand wings, by turns, blow back the hair;
> And thrice they twitched the diamond in her ear;
> Thrice she looked back, and thrice the foe drew near.
> Just in that instant anxious Ariel sought
> The close recesses of the virgin's thought;   140
> As on the nosegay in her breast reclined,
> He watched th' ideas rising in her mind,
> Sudden he viewed, in spite of all her art,
> An earthly lover lurking at her heart.
> Amazed, confused, he found his pow'r expired,   145
> Resigned to fate, and with a sigh retired.

FIRST NARRATOR   The peer now spreads the glittering forfex wide,
> T' inclose the lock; now joins it, to divide,
> Ev'n then, before the fatal engine closed,
> A wretched sylph too fondy interposed;   150
> Fate urged the shears, and cut the sylph in twain,
> (But airy substance soon unites again.)
> The meeting points the sacred hair dissever
> From the fair head, for ever, and for ever!

SECOND NARRATOR   Then flashed the living lightning from her eyes,   155
> And screams of horror rend th' affrighted skies.
> Not louder shrieks to pitying Heav'n are cast,
> When husbands or when lap-dogs breathe their last;
> Or when rich china vessels fall'n from high,
> In glitt'ring dust and painted fragments lie!   160

BARON   "Let wreaths of triumph now my temples twine,
> (The victor cried) the glorious prize is mine!
> While fish in streams, or birds delight in air,
> Or in a coach and six the British fair,
> As long as Atalantis shall be read,   165
> Or the small pillow grace a lady's bed,
> While visits shall be paid on solemn days,
> When num'rous wax-lights in bright order blaze,
> While nymphs take treats, or assignations give,
> So long my honour, name, and praise shall live!"   170

SECOND NARRATOR   What time would spare, from steel receives its date,

And monuments, like men, submit to fate!
Steel could the labour of the gods destroy,
And strike to dust th' imperial tow'rs of Troy;
Steel could the works of mortal pride confound,   175
And new triumphal arches to the ground.
What wonder then, fair nymph! thy hairs should feel
The conquering force of unresisted steel?

[CANTO IV]

FIRST NARRATOR   But anxious cares the pensive nymph oppressed,
And secret passions laboured in her breast.
Not youthful kings in battle seized alive,
Not scornful virgins who their charms survive,
Not ardent lovers robbed of all their bliss,   5
Not ancient ladies when refused a kiss,
Not tyrants fierce that unrepenting die,
Not Cynthia when her manteau's pinned awry,
E'er felt such rage, resentment, and despair,
As thou, sad virgin! for thy ravished hair.   10
    For, that sad moment, when the sylphs withdrew,
And Ariel weeping from Belinda flew,
Umbriel, a dusky, melancholy sprite,
As ever sullied the fair face of light,
Down to the central earth, his proper scene,   15
Repaired to search the gloomy cave of Spleen.
    Swift on his sooty pinions flits the gnome,
And in a vapour reached the dismal dome.
No cheerful breeze this sullen region knows,
The dreaded east is all the wind that blows.   20
Here in a grotto, sheltered close from air,
And screened in shades from day's detested glare,
She sighs for ever on her pensive bed,
Pain at her side, and Megrim at her head.
    Two handmaids wait the throne: alike in place,   25
But diff'ring far in figure and in face.
Here stood Ill-nature like an ancient maid,
Her wrinkled form in black and white arrayed;
With store of pray'rs for mornings, nights, and noons,
Her hand is filled; her bosom with lampoons.   30
    There Affectation, with a sickly mien,
Shows in her cheek the roses of eighteen,
Practised to lisp, and hang the head aside,
Faints into airs, and languishes with pride,
On the rich quilt sinks with becoming woe,   35
Wrapped in a gown, for sickness, and for show.
The fair ones feel such maladies as these,

When each new night-dress gives a new disease.

SECOND NARRATOR   A constant vapour o'er the palace flies;
   Strange phantoms rising as the mists arise;   40
   Dreadful, as hermits' dreams in haunted shades,
   Or bright, as visions of expiring maids.
   Now glaring fiends, and snakes on rolling spires,
   Pale spectres, gaping tombs, and purple fires:
   Now lakes of liquid gold, Elysian scenes,   45
   And crystal domes, and angels in machines.
      Unnumbered throngs on ev'ry side are seen,
   Of bodies changed to various forms by Spleen.
   Here living teapots stand, one arm held out,
   One bent; the handle this, and that the spout: 50
   A pipkin there, like Homer's tripod walks;
   Here sighs a jar, and there a goose-pie talks.
      Safe past the gnome through this fantastic band,
   A branch of healing spleenwort in his hand.
   Then thus addressed the pow'r:

GNOME   "Hail, wayward queen!   55
   Who rule the sex to fifty from fifteen:
   Parents of vapours and of female wit,
   Who give th' hysteric, or poetic fit,
   On various tempers act by various ways,
   Make some take physic, others scribble plays;   60
   Who cause the proud their visits to delay,
   And send the godly in a pet to pray.
   A nymph there is, that all thy pow'r disdains,
   And thousands more in equal mirth maintains.
   But oh! if e'er thy gnome could spoil a grace,   65
   Or raise a pimple on a beauteous face,
   Like citron-waters matrons' cheeks inflame,
   Or change complexions at a losing game;
   If e'er with airy horns I planted heads,
   Or rumpled petticoats, or tumbled beds,   70
   Or caused suspicion when no soul was rude,
   Or discomposed the head-dress of a prude,
   Or e'er to costive lap-dog gave disease,
   Which not the tears of brightest eyes could ease:
   Hear me, and touch Belinda with chagrin,   75
   That single act gives half the world the spleen."

FIRST NARRATOR   The goddess with a discontented air
   Seems to reject him, though she grants his pray'r.
   A wondrous bag with both her hands she binds,
   Like that where once Ulysses held the winds;   80
   There she collects the force of female lungs,

FIRST NARRATOR *(continuing)*
  Sighs, sobs, and passions, and the war of tongues.
  A vial next she fills with fainting fears,
  Soft sorrows, melting griefs, and flowing tears.
  The gnome rejoicing bears her gifts away,   85
  Spreads his black wings, and slowly mounts to day.
    Sunk in Thalestris' arms the nymph he found,
  Her eyes dejected and her hair unbound.
  Full o'er their heads the swelling bag he rent,
  And all the furies issued at the vent.   90
  Belinda burns with more than mortal ire,
  And fierce Thalestris fans the rising fire.

THALESTRIS   "O wretched maid!"

FIRST NARRATOR   she spread her hands, and cried,
  (While Hampton's echoes, "Wretched maid!" replied)

THALESTRIS   "Was it for this you took such constant care   95
  The bodkin, comb, and essence to prepare?
  For this your lócks in paper durance bound,
  For this with torturing irons wreathed around?
  For this with fillets strained your tender head,
  And bravely bore the double loads of lead?   100
  Gods! shall the ravisher display your hair,
  While the fops envy, and the ladies stare?
  Honour forbid! at whose unrivalled shrine
  Ease, pleasure, virtue, all our sex resign.
  Methinks already I your tears survey,   105
  Already hear the horrid things they say,
  Already see you a degraded toast,
  And all your honour in a whisper lost!
  How shall I, then, your helpless fame defend?
  'Twill then be infamy to seem your friend!   110
  And shall this prize, th' inestimable prize,
  Exposed through crystal to the gazing eyes,
  And heightened by the diamond's circling rays,
  On that rapacious hand for ever blaze?
  Sooner shall grass in Hyde Park Circus grow,   115
  And wits take lodgings in the sound of Bow;
  Sooner let earth, air, sea, to chaos fall,
  Men, monkeys, lap-dogs, parrots, perish all!"

FIRST NARRATOR   She said; then raging to Sir Plume repairs,
  And bids her beau demand the precious hairs: 120
  (Sir Plume of amber snuff-box justly vain,
  And the nice conduct of a clouded cane)
  With earnest eyes, and round unthinking face,

He first the snuff-box opened, then the case,
And thus broke out—

SIR PLUME   "My lord, why, what the devil?   125
Zounds! damn the lock! 'fore Gad, you must be civil!
Plague on't! 'tis past a jest—nay, prithee, pox!
Give her the hair"

FIRST NARRATOR   —he spoke, and rapped his box.

BARON   "It grieves me much"

FIRST NARRATOR   (replied the peer again)

BARON   "Who speaks so well should ever speak in vain,   130
But by this lock, this sacred lock I swear,
(Which never more shall join its parted hair;
Which never more its honours shall renew,
Clipped from the lovely head where late it grew)
That while my nostrils draw the vital air,   135
This hand, which won it, shall for ever wear."

FIRST NARRATOR   He spoke, and speaking, in proud triumph spread
The long-contended honours of her head.
    But Umbriel, hateful gnome! forbears not so;
He breaks the vial whence the sorrows flow.   140
Then see! the nymph in beauteous grief appears,
Her eyes half-languishing, half-drowned in tears;
On her heaved bosom hung her drooping head,
Which, with a sigh, she raised; and thus she said:

BELINDA   "For ever cursed be this detested day,   145
Which snatched my best, my favourite curl away!
Happy! ah, ten times happy had I been,
If Hampton Court these eyes had never seen!
Yet am I not the first mistaken maid,
By love of courts to numerous ills betrayed.   150
Oh, had I rather unadmired remained
In some lone isle, or distant northern land;
Where the gilt chariot never marks the way,
Where none learn ombre, none e'er taste Bohea!
There kept my charms concealed from mortal eye,   155
Like roses, that in deserts bloom and die.
What moved my mind with youthful lords to roam?
Oh, had I stayed, and said my pray'rs at home!
'Twas this, the morning omens seemed to tell,
Thrice from my trembling hand the patch-box fell,   160
The tott'ring china shook without a wind,
Nay, Poll sat mute, and Shock was most unkind!
A sylph, too, warned me of the threats of fate,
In mystic visions, now believed too late!

BELINDA *(continuing)*
  See the poor remnants of these slighted hairs! 165
  My hands shall rend what ev'n thy rapine spares:
  These in two sable ringlets taught to break,
  Once gave new beauties to the snowy neck;
  The sister-lock now sits uncouth, alone,
  And in its fellow's fate foresees its own; 170
  Uncurled it hangs, the fatal shears demands,
  And tempts, once more, thy sacrilegious hands.
  Oh, hadst thou, cruel! been content to seize
  Hairs less in sight, or any hairs but these!"

[CANTO V]

FIRST NARRATOR   She said: the pitying audience melt in tears,
  But fate and Jove had stopped the baron's ears.
  In vain Thalestris with reproach assails,
  For who can move when fair Belinda fails?
  Not half so fixed the Trojan could remain, 5
  While Anna begged and Dido raged in vain.
  Then gave Clarissa graceful waved her fan;
  Silence ensued, and thus the nymph began:

CLARISSA   "Say, why are beauties praised and honoured most,
  The wise man's passion and the vain man's toast? 10
  Why decked with all that land and sea afford,
  Why angels called, and angel-like adored?
  Why round our coaches crowd the white-gloved beaux?
  Why bows the side-box from its inmost rows?
  How vain are all these glories, all our pains, 15
  Unless good sense preserve what beauty gains:
  That men may say, when we the front-box grace:
  'Behold the first in virtue as in face!'
  Oh! if to dance all night, and dress all day,
  Charmed the small-pox, or chased old age away; 20
  Who would not scorn what housewife's cares produce,
  Or who would learn one earthly thing of use?
  To patch, nay ogle, might become a saint,
  Nor could it sure be such a sin to paint.
  But since, alas! frail beauty must decay, 25
  Curled or uncurled, since locks will turn to grey;
  Since painted, or not painted, all shall fade,
  And she who scorns a man, must die a maid;
  What then remains but well our pow'r to use,
  And keep good-humour still, whate'er we lose? 30
  And trust me, dear! good-humour can prevail,
  When airs, and flights, and screams, and scolding fail.
  Beauties in vain their pretty eyes may roll;

Charms strike the sight, but merit wins the soul."

FIRST NARRATOR   So spoke the dame, but no applause ensued;   35
Belinda frowned, Thalestris called her prude.

THALESTRIS   "To arms, to arms!"

FIRST NARRATOR   the fierce virago cries,
And swift as lightning to the combat flies.
All side in parties, and begin th' attack;
Fans clap, silks rustle, and tough whalebones crack;   40
Heroes' and heroines' shouts confusedly rise,
And bass and treble voices strike the skies.
No common weapons in their hands are found,
Like gods they fight, nor dread a mortal wound.

SECOND NARRATOR   So when bold Homer makes the gods engage,   45
And heavenly breasts with human passions rage;
'Gainst Pallas, Mars; Latona, Hermes arms;
And all Olympus rings with loud alarms:
Jove's thunder roars, heav'n trembles all around,
Blue Neptune storms, the bellowing deeps resound: 50
Earth shakes her nodding tow'rs, the ground gives way,
And the pale ghosts start at the flash of day!

FIRST NARRATOR   Triumphant Umbriel on a sconce's height
Clapped his glad wings, and sate to view the fight:
Propped on their bodkin spears, the sprites survey   55
The growing combat, or assist the fray.
   While through the press enraged Thalestris flies,
And scatters death around from both her eyes,
A beau and witling perished in the throng,
One died in metaphor, and one in song.   60
"O cruel nymph! a living death I bear,"
Cried Dapperwit, and sunk beside his chair.
A mournful glance Sir Fopling upwards cast,
"Those eyes are made so killing"—was his last.
Thus on Mænder's flowery margin lies   65
Th' expiring swan, and as he sings he dies.

SECOND NARRATOR   When bold Sir Plume had drawn Clarissa down,
Chloe stepped in, and killed him with a frown;
She smiled to see the doughty hero slain,
But, at her smile, the beau revived again.   70
   Now Jove suspends his golden scales in air,
Weighs the men's wits against the lady's hair;
The doubtful beam long nods from side to side;
At length the wits mount up, the hairs subside.

FIRST NARRATOR   See fierce Belinda on the baron flies,   75
With more than usual lightning in her eyes:

FIRST NARRATOR *(continuing)*
    Nor feared the chief th' unequal fight to try,
    Who sought no more than on his foe to die.
    But this bold lord, with manly strength endued,
    She with one finger and a thumb subdued: 80
    Just where the breath of life has nostrils drew,
    A charge of snuff the wily virgin threw.
    The gnomes direct, to ev'ry atom just,
    The pungent grains of titillating dust.
    Sudden, with starting tears each eye o'erflows,   85
    And the high dome re-echoes to his nose.

BELINDA   "Now meet thy fate,"

SECOND NARRATOR   incensed Belinda cried,
    And drew a deadly bodkin from her side.
    (The same, his ancient personage to deck,
    Her great-great-grandsire wore about his neck,   90
    In three seal-rings; which after, melted down,
    Formed a vast buckle for his widow's gown:
    Her infant grandame's whistle next it grew,
    The bells she jingled, and the whistle blew;
    Then in a bodkin graced her mother's hairs,   95
    Which long she wore, and now Belinda wears.)

BARON   "Boast not my fall" (he cried) "insulting foe!
    Thou by some other shalt be laid as low:
    Nor think, to die dejects my lofty mind:
    All that I dread is leaving you behind!   100
    Rather than so, ah let me still survive,
    And burn in Cupid's flames—but burn alive."

BELINDA   "Restore the lock!"

FIRST NARRATOR   she cries; and all around
    "Restore the lock!" the vaulted roofs rebound.
    Not fierce Othello in so loud a strain   105
    Roared for the handkerchief that caused his pain.
    But see how oft ambitious aims are crossed,
    And chiefs contend till all the prize is lost!
    The lock, obtained with guilt, and kept with pain,
    In ev'ry place is sought, but sought in vain: 110
    With such a prize no mortal must be blest,
    So Heav'n decrees; with Heav'n who can contest?

SECOND NARRATOR   Some thought it mounted to the lunar sphere,
    Since all things lost on earth are treasured there.
    There heroes' wits are kept in pond'rous vases,   115
    And beaux' in snuff-boxes and tweezer-cases.
    There broken vows and death-bed alms are found,

And lovers' hearts with ends of riband bound,
The courtier's promises, and sick man's pray'rs,
The smiles of harlots, and the tears of heirs,   120
Cages for gnats, and chains to yoke a flea,
Dried butterflies, and tomes of casuistry.

FIRST NARRATOR   But trust the Muse—she saw it upward rise,
Though marked by none but quick, poetic eyes:
(So Rome's great founder to the heav'ns withdrew,   125
To Proculus alone confessed in view)
A sudden star, it shot through liquid air,
And drew behind a radiant trail of hair.
Not Berenice's locks first rose so bright,
The heav'ns bespangling with dishevelled light.   130
The sylphs behold it kindling as it flies,
And pleased pursue its progress through the skies.

SECOND NARRATOR   This the beau monde shall from the Mall survey,
And hail with music its propitious ray;
This the blest lover shall for Venus take,   135
And send up vows from Rosamonda's lake.
This Partridge soon shall view in cloudless skies,
When next he looks through Galileo's eyes;
And hence the egregious wizard shall foredoom
The fate of Louis, and the fall of Rome.   140

FIRST NARRATOR   Then cease, bright nymph! to mourn thy ravished hair,
Which adds new glory to the shining sphere!
Not all the tresses that fair head can boast,
Shall draw such envy as the lock you lost.
For after all the murders of your eye,   145
When, after millions slain, yourself shall die:
When those fair suns shall set, as set they must,
And all those tresses shall be laid in dust,
This lock the Muse shall consecrate to fame,
And 'midst the stars inscribe Belinda's name.   150

Index of Quoted Selections

Index: Subject, Author, and Title